Crime and Corruption at the Yard

CRIME AND CORRUPTION AT THE YARD

David Woodland

PEN & SWORD
TRUE CRIME

First published in Great Britain in 2015 by
Pen & Sword True Crime
an imprint of
Pen & Sword Books Ltd
47 Church Street
Barnsley
South Yorkshire
S70 2AS

ISBN 978 1 47383 385 2

A CIP catalogue record for this book is available from the British Library

Typeset in Plantin by
Mac Style Ltd, Bridlington, East Yorkshire
Printed and bound in the UK by CPI Group (UK) Ltd, Croydon, CR0 4YY

Pen & Sword Books Ltd incorporates the imprints of Pen & Sword Archaeology, Atlas, Aviation, Battleground, Discovery, Family History, History, Maritime, Military, Naval, Politics, Railways, Select, Transport, True Crime, and Fiction, Frontline Books, Leo Cooper, Praetorian Press, Seaforth Publishing and Wharncliffe.

For a complete list of Pen & Sword titles please contact
PEN & SWORD BOOKS LIMITED
47 Church Street, Barnsley, South Yorkshire, S70 2AS, England
E-mail: enquiries@pen-and-sword.co.uk
Website: www.pen-and-sword.co.uk

Contents

Acknowlegements

My thanks are due firstly to Brigadier Henry Wilson, Barnaby Blacker, Matt Jones, Jon Wilkinson and the staff at Pen and Sword Publishers who had the courage to take on an unknown author and the patience to guide him through the intricacies of book publishing. Thanks also to the help received from many sources and in particular to my old chum Dick Kirby, author, a great 'hands on' copper of the old school, ex Flying and Serious Crime Squads, who has been a source of inspiration and help throughout the process; to my three sons David, Tony and Richard for their support and in particular to Tony for his help on the computer with picture collation and transmissions and help with copyright approvals; to Richard who took pity on his dad and undertook the laborious task of indexing the final manuscript; to the friends and ex colleagues, at least most of them, with whom I had the privilege to serve; to all serving Police Officers who despite the overwhelming restraints imposed by political correctness and the loony, liberal left, still place their lives at risk daily to protect the public for little or no thanks; also to their wives and partners who loyally support and stand by them.

Thanks to Linda Rhodes, Local Studies Librarian, Barking and Dagenham and to Lee Shelden – authors of *The Dagenham Murder* published by London Borough of Dagenham and Barking for the photograph of the restored memorial to PC George Clark, murdered in 1846. Thanks to Jimmy Smith, photographer and author of *Undaunted*, my old colleague from C11 days for the help and photographs he kindly allowed me to reproduce; to Adam Shand author, *The Kangaroo Gang*, the team of Full Box Production and some of the Aussies we met up with again in London in 2010 whilst shooting the BBC TV series. Also to Getty Images for pictures of Lord Moynihan of

Leeds and Rex Agency for the picture of John Du Rose, Nude Murder Squad.

Every effort has been made to trace and contact copyright holders for pictures used in the plate section and I offer my apologies for any inadvertent omissions which will be corrected in future print runs.

All net proceeds of sale will be distributed in full by way of donations to the following charities: Metropolitan and City Police Orphans Fund, Ex-CID Officers Association Welfare Fund, Rotary International, Orbis Flying Eye Hospital UK and Cancer Research UK.

Prologue

A good police force is one that catches
more criminals than it employs
Sir Robert Mark 1917–2010

In May, 1972, Sir Robert Mark, newly appointed Commissioner of Police marched into the Conference Room at New Scotland Yard, London. Assembled before him were the whole of the senior CID Officers responsible for containing crime within the seven hundred and fifty square mile area of operation of London's Metropolitan Police (The Met). A buzz of nervous anticipation swept throughout the room. New brooms usually have a habit of sweeping clean and this man like so many before, would certainly wish to place his own imprimatur upon this new command.

Mark had long held pre-conceived ideas concerning the probity of the Metropolitan CID and would certainly lose no opportunity to put these into effect. Mark glanced, almost scornfully around the room and the tension was clearly discernible and rising. What he said then was to change long established methods of policing throughout London, all major cities and indeed the whole country forever.

"You men represent what has long been the most routinely corrupt organisation in London. Nothing and nobody will prevent me from putting an end to this corruption and if necessary I will put the whole of the CID back into uniform and start again." Gasps of astonishment swept throughout the room as the totally uncompromising import of his words swept home. There was to be no mere tinkering around the edges, this was a declaration of full blooded war and the assembled senior officers and the whole of London CID were the avowed targets.

One of the most influential members at that select gathering was David Clarence Dilley, Commander, Criminal Intelligence

Department, (C.11) charged with investigation into organised crime and criminals within the Metropolis. Tremendous power lay within this man's hands, through the vast network of detectives, contacts and assets at his disposal including sophisticated surveillance and electronic equipment that his Department possessed. Perhaps the most potent was the means and ability to officially eavesdrop upon any telephone conversation made within the United Kingdom. This alone was sufficient to make Dilley the repository of more secrets than perhaps it was safe for any one man to possess.

Sir Robert Mark would have been astonished when at the end of his short but forceful peroration, Dilley strode purposefully back to his office on the fourth floor and called a meeting of his whole command. He told the assembled group of the meeting and of Mark's determination to wipe out any vestiges of corruption. The vast majority of his subordinates were honest, hard working cops and to their astonishment, in what can only be described as a momentous Freudian slip from his usual bland inscrutability, he made this extraordinary comment. "The good times are over, there's no longer any chance of 'doing the business'. If any of you have got anything going, get out of it now."

As Mark makes clear in his autobiography, *In the Office of Constable*, over the following months the impact of the internal complaints department (A.10), formed to investigate allegations of corruption within the Force, was considerable. Suspensions from duty averaged about fifty a month and very few suspended officers ever resumed duty. Along with the crooked cops against which Mark's crusade was directed, a number of honest officers decided to call it a day and retired on pension. What led to this extraordinary state of affairs where the once world famous Scotland Yard had fallen so far from grace? In no small part their credibility as a body was deliberately shattered by their leader.

At the time of Mark's declaration of war, for that is precisely what it was, I was a Detective Inspector (D.I.) serving under Commander Dilley in C.11 Department. This book covers my journey through this turbulent period of police history and the profound effects it had upon myself and upon the vast majority of honest, dedicated detectives with whom I was privileged to work. It also touches upon the more seamy side and illustrates the difficulties faced by honest coppers betrayed or sabotaged by the minority.

Did detectives always play by the rules in the 1970s and before? – I think not, but I believe that if they had, the vicious razor gangs that dominated horse racing tracks in the twenties and thirties, the mobsters like Jack Spot and Billy Hill who terrorised the West End, the Kray twins, the Richardson gangs, the armed robbers, may never have been brought to justice. Defects in the criminal law led to the phenomenon, 'noble cause corruption' which caused many an honest detective to bend the rules. The public needed reassurance and the belief it was safe to walk the streets and go about their business unmolested. All participants in the criminal justice system had a vested interest in maintaining that belief and all who partook, turned a blind eye or acquiesced in the practice of 'noble cause corruption' were equally culpable.

This book does not share the view of the politically correct who have managed to swing the balance from protecting the victim to protecting the 'socially disadvantaged' perpetrators of crime. The chances of being caught, convicted and imprisoned have declined dramatically over the past fifty years.

I make no apology for the way things were done but wish to tell it as it was, warts and all and to pay tribute to the overwhelming majority of honest coppers of that era who did their best to keep the streets of London safe. I have nothing to say to the handful of rogue cops – you have to live with yourselves.

One final word; I hope at least a few of the people I arrested may now be living honest lives and I have no wish to cause them or their families the embarrassment of naming them so where I consider it appropriate I have changed their names as I have with some, but not all, Police Officers. Also, Anno Domini catches up with us all and whilst I have done my best to maintain accuracy, it is inevitable that with the passing of time my memory may have let me down so if and where it has, I apologise in advance.

Chapter One

The Law is the true embodiment of everything that's excellent,
It has no kind of fault or flaw, and I my Lords embody the Law.
'The Gondoliers' Sir William Gilbert, 1836–1911

What makes a young man join the Police? Idealism? The desire to serve? A less altruistic motive? Who knows? I had a more personal reason. In July 1952, I completed my schooling at John Ruskin Grammar School, Croydon. I had a clutch of 'O' levels passes but absolutely no desire to stay on into the sixth form, gain my 'A' levels then possibly secure a steady job in a Bank or Insurance Company.

That year, the shooting of Police Constable (PC) Miles, by Christopher Craig and Derek Bentley on the roof of Barlow and Parkers, confectioners, Tamworth Road, Croydon decided matters for me. I was sixteen years old and in March 1953 joined the newly formed Metropolitan Police Cadet Force – my ambition, to become a detective in Scotland Yard.

That was the dream and I came close to achieving it but on the road I had chosen to tread there were many pitfalls for the unwary, perhaps the greatest of which was the loss of innocence and realisation that life was far different from the romantic ideal.

After passing out, I was posted to Croydon, "Z" Division and finished up in the quiet suburb of Norbury. The Cadet scheme was in its embryonic stages and nobody seemed to know quite what to do with us when we reached Division where our working week was split into a series of attachments covering the Station or front office, patrolling in the area radio car and attending Court.

Thursday was the day of the week I really looked forward to when I was allowed into that holy of holies, the CID Office. The senior officer was Detective Sergeant (DS) (1st Class) Bert Read. Actually there was a Detective Inspector also but I was never quite sure what he did as his office was strictly out of bounds to young sprogs like myself where, canteen rumour had it, copious amounts of scotch were consumed on a regular basis over never ending card games. That is of course if he wasn't at the local betting shop having a flutter or drinking with his cronies at the local boozer.

I found out much later in my career this rather stereotypical conception was not confined to the canteen but extended much higher up the uniform chain of command.

Norbury nick (police station) was still reeling from the aftermath of the Craig and Bentley saga when the unarmed PC Miles was savagely gunned down. Much discussion took place at the time and since of the fatal words that intimated to the jury that Bentley was aware his accomplice was armed when he was reported as shouting across the rooftops whilst in police custody, 'Let him have it Chris'.

At the trial, defence counsel tried vainly to convince the jury that Bentley was urging Craig to surrender his weapon when he uttered these fateful words. The prosecution placed a different, interpretation upon them contending that Bentley, at that time under arrest, was urging his confederate to fire upon the officers. The jury accepted the latter interpretation and despite appeals to the Home Secretary, Bentley was hanged for his part in the murder.

Had this happened twenty years later, defence counsel would have vigorously attacked the Police evidence and put forward the defence of a Police fit-up that would in all probability have been accepted by the jury.

Those were happy, carefree days and I looked forward to completing my Army National Service and returning to the job as a fully-fledged copper. When the time came to register, I wasn't short of advice from old pre war coppers who had re-joined the job at the end of hostilities and were close to drawing their pensions. Like many others returning from the war, they were tough guys and didn't give a damn for anyone.

"Go for the cushiest number going lad," recommended one, "I served in the RAOC (Royal Army Ordnance Corps) and spent my time dishing out the equipment in the stores".

"No, no," counselled another, "get yourself into the Royal Army Service Corps, at least they will teach you to drive."

I presented myself to the Army recruiting office in West Croydon and sat in a room with a bunch of lads all registering for their National Service. I think I was probably the first and last to actually volunteer for the Royal Army Ordnance Corps and not surprisingly was granted my wish. I remembered another stricture passed to me by one laconic, copper. "Just remember laddy, never volunteer for anything".

Before being called up, one final parting shot in the police canteen was, "Never forget my old son, don't volunteer for anything. They can make you do anything in the Army except put you in the family way."

Chapter Two

Shillin' a day, blooming good pay,
Lucky to touch it, a shillin' a day
Rudyard Kipling

My initial basic training was spent in RAOC, Hilsea Barracks, Portsmouth. Passing out parade over, I was preparing myself for a quiet posting to enjoy a two year skive before my demob when I was summoned before the Personnel Selection Officer. "I see from your records you were a Police Cadet before joining up, get your bags packed, you're posted to the RMP (Royal Military Police) Training Depot at Woking." Inkerman Barracks, Woking, was one long slog of drilling, marching, physical exercise, self defence, weapon training and learning the Military manual of dos and don'ts. I had no idea that so many 'don'ts existed. Before call up I heard these ridiculous, far- fetched stories of cutting grass with scissors, polishing coke stoves until it was possible to shave in their reflection etc.

I didn't believe them then – I do now! My squad was designated for postings to the Far East upon passing out and Hong Kong was the prize we all hoped for. I wonder why? Any way that dream was not to be and we all received Home postings! Happily, with logic only the Army could fathom, my Home posting was to 103 Provost Company, RMP stationed in Dusseldorf, Germany.

In 1954, we were still the occupying forces there. Scenes of bomb damage were everywhere although large parts of the city, unlike Dresden and Berlin were relatively untouched. Our duties were pretty routine, Town patrols in open jeeps, showing the flag and dealing with calls to rowdy squaddies, full of lager that seemed unaware that the Second World War had finished some nine years earlier.

As the occupying power at the time we took precedence over the civil Police with complete autonomy over crimes and incidents involving military personnel, vehicles and equipment. Another task which wasn't likely to endear oneself to the Army of Occupation was to routinely raid black-listed brothels and send any military personnel packing,

Black market was another area in which we were expected to be active with N.A.A.F.I. fags (cigarettes) being the usual token of trade. These were freely bartered for cameras, souvenirs and other goodies such as street ladies' favours. It didn't take me too long to realise why as a non-smoker, I quickly made new friends keen to acquire my weekly allowance of two hundred fags for a modest sum.

For the first eighteen months of service, we received the princely sum of thirty bob (shillings) per week, which was doubled up for the last six months in an overt but usually vain attempt to induce us National Servicemen to sign on for another year.

There wasn't much love lost in those days between the troops and the vanquished and who could expect any different? In the aftermath of the war, with illicit firearms still in circulation, petty crime and black marketeering combined with the remnants of a defeated, humiliated Army meant there was still an element of risk to squaddies caught in the wrong circumstances.

I spent much time attending and investigating road traffic accidents with the assistance of the splendidly efficient and well equipped German Police. I also spent much of my time formulating accident reports detailing as favourably as possible upon the driving competence of military personnel.

At a time when an accident was the precursor to disciplinary proceedings and could lead to drastic loss of pay, I found myself in great demand and acquired something of a reputation as a contemporary Hans Christian Andersen. Some of my later contemporaries may feel this skill remained with me later in my life, but of course they would be wrong.

The Army was certainly an experience of life I wouldn't want to have missed. In fact, many times since I would gladly have inflicted it upon some of the mindless hooligans I was to meet up with in later life to straighten them out.

Upon demob, I left with a happy heart to rejoin the Met. One chapter in life closed and another of my own choosing now beckoned. Unlike my old man who served during the war, I didn't get issued with a demob suit.

Chapter Three

"Taking one consideration with another,
When Constabulary's duty's to be done,
a policeman's lot is not a happy one."
Sir William Gilbert

After the formal discipline of the military, I soon settled into the training routine at Police Training School located at the old wartime aerodrome at Hendon. I was particularly fortunate in allocation of Class Instructor. Jock Hood was a kindly old Scot's Inspector who survived more operational sorties in Bomber Command than he cared to remember.

"So, why do you want to be a policeman? It doesn't run in the family. I see you've got a fairly good educational record, are you interested in promotion?"

"Not really sir, I would like to try CID when I've done my two years probation".

"You could do worse," Hood counselled, "just remember there are plenty of senior officers who don't approve of the Department, so my advice is to keep your head down, get stuck into the I.B. (Instruction Book), get as many crime arrests as you can and above all keep out of bother, the job doesn't like people who make waves".

We were taught the rudiments of criminal law, a plethora of legislation dealing with everything from actions to be taken under every conceivable emergency and unlikely situation such as dealing with outbreaks of sheep's scabies or, an old examiner's favourite, epizootic lymphangitis.

Just the sort of thing you would need to know about pounding the beat in Inner London. Nobody seemed bothered to question the reason for such esotericism, it was in the good book and that was enough. It carried such literary gems as 'how to catch a runaway horse' which started with the classic instruction, 'run in the same direction as the horse'. Provided candidates covered sheets of paper with extracts of the IB they were almost assured of a pass in the final examination.

Jock Hood recounted an amusing anecdote of how, as a young police constable (PC) he appeared before a well known lady magistrate, Dame Sybil Campbell, at Tower Bridge Magistrates court. Police had effected their routine swoop upon the prostitutes who frequented the area and it was their usual wont to plead guilty, pay their £2 fine then hurry back to the patch to ply their trade. One such 'tom', as they were referred to by one and all, actually had the temerity to plead 'not guilty' which required Jock to go into the witness box to give evidence under oath as to how he had seen the lady indulging in sexual intercourse with a foreign seaman while standing in a shop doorway.

Dame Sybil threw down her pen and glanced up sharply from the Bench, "What's that you say officer? Having intercourse standing up, that's nonsense, a physical impossibility, case dismissed."

The next evening a police patrol car took Dame Sybil on a conducted tour of docklands where she was able to witness at first hand one of the little known facts of life which had obviously eluded her until then. Jock had a quick succession of similar cases, who all, true to form, pleaded 'guilty'. When called to give brief evidence of the facts of the case, he responded with a straight face, "The facts are the same as that in the last case, your worship."

Chapter Four

"I'll sing you a song; it won't take very long,
All coppers are bastards"
Old Music Hall ditty.

Having passed out of Training School I was posted to "C" Division which covered Soho and the West End of London. The initial euphoria was somewhat dissipated later when, having reported to Divisional Office I was assigned to Tottenham Court Road, a Sub Division on the north east boundary which although busy, didn't quite have the same cachet as the much coveted West End Central posting, where reputations were made and quite frequently broken.

Soho was the centre of criminal activity in London including drugs, unlicensed drinking clubs, brothels and the pornographic film and book industry. Inevitably, a small number of policemen succumbed to temptation and in the fullness of time most suffered the consequences.

(It was my misfortune, much later in my career, to meet one such officer, a close associate of Bernie Silver who, in the 1960s was one of London's leading crime bosses, responsible for corrupting several senior Police Officers at New Scotland Yard.)

I was taken to see the Inspector in charge of the relief and the next day was put 'learning beats' with an experienced old PC, Paddy Starling, who had worked the Canadian Railroads and was as tough as nails. Paddy was a man of few words, "Just remember this, you've only got one friend out here, and that's Johnny Wood"

"Johnny Wood, who's he?" I asked innocently.

Paddy tapped his truncheon pocket knowingly, "Let me introduce you to Johnny Wood, the best friend you'll ever have and don't ever forget it."

In the days before personal radios the only way to summons assistance was by giving three short sharp blasts upon the Police issue whistle and hope that somebody would be close enough to respond. After a couple of weeks, Inspector Browning, relief Inspector, sent for me.

"Paddy thinks you're ready to launch upon the poor, unsuspecting public, I'll put you out on a month's nights to get you used to being on your own." At last I had a chance to prove myself, not only to the Inspector and the rest of the relief but more importantly to myself.

Before being let out amongst the 'poor unsuspecting public', we were paraded and lined up for inspection by the patrolling Sgt (sergeant) and the Duty Inspector. After the briefing we were brought to attention and had to produce our truncheon, pocket book and whistle. On night duty we also had to produce a torch and marking materials, such as matchsticks wedged into door frames and lengths of cotton tied over ladder rungs, to ensure that shops, houses and other premises if not broken into were at least detected.

My first solo night was quite eventful, patrolling Great Portland St. I saw a man sneaking furtively along a row of parked cars, checking to ensure he wasn't being watched, tugging at car door handles, obviously looking for an unlocked door. In true Training School fashion I followed behind, notebook in hand, faithfully recording the index number of every car approached and dutifully noted those which contained visible property. I just couldn't believe my luck, a 'sus' charge upon my first solo patrol.

Section 4, Vagrancy Act, 1824, was perhaps one of the most controversial pieces of legislation to survive from the Napoleonic Wars. Marauding bands of disaffected soldiery, many deformed or crippled, returning from the wars with no jobs, prospects or pensions from an ungrateful Nation wrought havoc throughout Britain, begging and stealing to survive. This particular Act, referred to irrelevantly by future generations of Bobbies as 'the breathing act' or simply the 'sus law' was designed to deter thieves by the simple expedient of creating a criminal offence of 'loitering with intent to commit a felony.' It was widely used, or, as many defence lawyers would claim abused, especially by Aids to CID, uniform officers patrolling in plain clothes that aspired to the detective branch and were judged purely upon results. Well abused or not, statistics don't lie and the numbers of cars broken into or driven away by thieves or joy riders manifestly demonstrated the prevalence of motor crime and much effort was put into containing the menace.

As the man looked behind him, he saw me and ran. I chased and caught him, "I am arresting you", I announced to the astonished villain, "for being a suspected person loitering with intent to steal from cars, you do not need to say anything but whatever you do say will be taken down in writing and may be given in evidence."

In theory, this caution must be given to everybody being arrested for crime but the man stared at me as if I had two heads. It was probably the first time in what later proved to have been an active life of villainy that anybody had actually told him his rights and it obviously displayed my lack of experience. I don't think I am betraying too many confidences when disclosing the shortened version of the caution was usually a more informal "You're nicked".

At the Station I outlined the facts to the Duty Sergeant who called the night duty CID officer. Detective Constable (DC) Peter Walton was a man destined eventually to become a distinguished Assistant Commissioner and awarded the Queens Police Medal. Walton listened patiently as I outlined the facts. As a long list of car numbers were recited, Walton shook his head in disbelief. "Hold on, hold on, there's no need to overdo it," he counselled in a cynical way which spoke volumes, "two or three cars will be enough."

"But that is precisely what I saw" I protested, "He went down a long line of cars, obviously looking for something to nick."

"Doing it by the book are we?" OK, release him, there's not enough evidence".

I couldn't believe my ears and Walton, realising I was inexperienced explained, not unkindly, "Look old son, you saw a continuous series of acts, in law, that only constitutes one act, all that does is turn your man into a 'suspected person'. You must see a totally separate act to justify his arrest for 'loitering with intent to steal.'"

I felt quite bewildered, surely it wasn't right to let a villain go upon a technicality, after all it was clear as the nose on my face exactly what he had been up to. Walton spelled it out, "Now, if you had lost sight of the man when he turned a corner and then saw him trying door handles again, that would be a completely different kettle of fish, that constitutes two separate acts. Have you checked CRO? "(Criminal Record Office, Scotland Yard)

"Not yet" I replied and went upstairs to the canteen for a well-earned cup of tea to write my notes. I sat at a table with an experienced aid to CID who soon put me right. "It's time to learn the facts of life, not the crap they teach you at Training School, just remember this, the criminal law and justice are two quite separate things, the legal system is one big charade invented by lawyers for their own benefit with very little regard for either justice or the truth."

Twenty minutes later, Peter Walton had my prisoner's history at his fingertips having phoned CRO, manned twenty-four hours of the day.

"You've picked a good one here" he said, approvingly, "he's got form as long as your arm, only just released this morning from a five stretch for robbery with violence. Now it's make up your mind time, did you lose sight of him or not, it's as simple as that?"

There was not the slightest doubt in my mind what the man had been doing. "Well I did actually lose sight of him momentarily, but only for a minute or so when he turned the corner" I replied.

Walton smiled to himself, obviously thinking perhaps there was chance he could make something of this rookie yet. "In future don't ever bring in a 'sus' until you check CRO first, I don't want you locking up the whole West End population single handed".

From the very beginning of my service all my actions and sympathies were directed towards the innocent victims of crime and not to the perpetrators. After all, they had a choice, the victim didn't. I am old fashioned enough to still subscribe to this outmoded way of thinking. Perhaps it would be a safer, better world if all the 'do gooders' and bleeding heart brigades of today were to adopt a similar approach.

The rest of that month's tour of night duty was a blinder for me. The next night I disturbed two men armed with a crowbar breaking into the basement area of a fashion shop in Margaret Street. I caught one after a chase. My prisoner was a Guardsman stationed at Knightsbridge Barracks and at an impromptu confrontation in the barracks, I recognised the second man. At the nick I could see D.C. Walton was impressed. "You've got bloody good eyesight" he said "that Margaret Street is pretty dim at nights particularly at the distance you say you gave chase." Guess that's what comes from eating carrots! Both men were convicted at County of London Sessions of shop-breaking and I received my first of several Commissioners' commendations.

I was posted to night duty for a month walking around the British Museum beat. This was considered a punishment posting and was a virtual graveyard at night time. My sin was failing to slip the duty PS a tin of cat food for his moggy, a heinous crime in his eyes only expurgated by a spell upon the dreaded ten beat. One night, I slipped into the back of the Dominion Cinema, in Tottenham Court Road to watch the legendary Bill Haley and his Comets bringing rock and roll to London.

It was a great show and as I left and stepped into a side street, I almost literally fell over two men breaking a car's quarter light window to get access to the parcels strewn invitingly on the back seat.

At the nick, enjoying a quick cuppa, an anxious PS collared me. "Where the hell have you been, the Duty Officer is doing his nut, he's walked round and round ten beat and you're in for the high jump so get out of this canteen right now before you're put on the dab."

I laughed, "Sorry skip, guilty to abandoning the beat but what could I do? I was called to two men loitering outside the Dominion Theatre; they're in the charge room now for attempted theft."

The Sergeant grinned approvingly, "You lucky sod, you'd fall into a sewer and come out smelling of roses".

I was developing a nose for crime, this was helped in no small way by my disconcerting habit of emerging at the right time from places nobody would ever expect a copper should be.

I spent as much time as I could in Court, watching, observing, and learning. My admiration grew for the CID and especially the Flying Squad (C.8.Branch) that undoubtedly became my role model. Once, a DS from the Squad was aggressively cross-examined by Defence Counsel.

"I put it to you officer that you verballed my client."

"No sir".

"No sir" mimicked Counsel, "so at least officer you know what I mean by 'verballed'? Perhaps you can explain precisely to this Court just exactly what a verbal is?"

The DS didn't hesitate, "Certainly sir, a verbal is an incriminating admission made by the accused at the time or shortly after his arrest that on the advice of his Counsel he later denies."

The 'verbal'(statement) was one of the most contentious but effective weapons in the armoury of the detective. I am now of course talking in those far off days before PACE, (Police and Criminal Evidence Act, 1984) CCTV cameras and sophisticated forensic investigations that could place a suspect at the seat of a crime.

In the absence of a reliable witness prepared to undergo the ordeal of sometimes hostile cross examination by Defence Counsel at Court, quite often the only evidence that could be presented by the prosecution was a verbal admission to the arresting officer. Did professional villains, well versed in criminal procedure ever make incriminating admissions in the heat of capture or whilst being interrogated? Of course they did. Were they sometimes verballed? Of course they were, or so it is often alleged.

Judge Lord Justice Devlin once said, *"The very high degree of proof the English law requires often could not be achieved by the prosecution without the assistance of the accused's own statement."*

A barrister, later to become an eminent High Court judge elaborated, *"If suspects, when questioned by police, only answered questions put to them in writing through their solicitors, there would be very few police convictions indeed. Between the police and the public there is a tacit understanding that as long as convictions remain high, few questions will be asked as to the methods of obtaining them. A high number of convictions are as necessary for the public as it is to the police force for its existence. This licence is the price the public have agreed to pay for the maintenance of law and order. They trust the police not to abuse it and on the whole their trust is justified."*

For many years and certainly during the early part of my service, there was undoubtedly an unspoken tacit agreement between lawyers, trial judges, police and the Press. There seemed no other obvious way to keep a fair balance between the public interest and the rights of wrongdoers.

Regrettably, through a series of highly documented episodes like The Challenor enquiry, the *Times* enquiry, which is mentioned later, the Guildford four and Birmingham six affairs, this trust has now been eroded. The result meant that equal balance has been destroyed resulting in the scandal of wrongful acquittals linked to a handful of wrongful convictions, both two sides of the same coin, also destroyed the confidence of the British people in the Police and administration of justice.

Life at Tottenham Court Road was not all grim; I quickly learned that policemen, like nurses, doctors and others whose daily work brought them into contact with sudden and often violent death, developed a somewhat macabre sense of humour hard to understand by outsiders. Without the ability to laugh and to laugh at oneself, the casualty rate of stress related illness would have been higher.

Anyway, back to work. 'Stops in the street' under Section 66 Metropolitan Police Act, 1839, were another useful measure widely used in active crime prevention and provided one could justify the reason for the stop, proved an effective way of nicking shop breakers, joy riders and others who, at some stage in their activities by necessity have to take to the streets with their ill gotten gains. With the high prevalence of crime in the West End and the support that would be given in those far off days to diligent conscientious coppers, it wasn't too difficult to show 'just cause' for stops, statistics clearly showed that ten per cent of stops led to crime arrests. This was a small price to pay for the inconvenience caused to the other ninety per cent, some of whom would be the victims of crime and would justifiably want to know what the Police were doing to protect them.

One night duty, I stood on the corner of Oxford Street and Tottenham Court Road waiting to take 'one o'clock grub' in the nearby Trenchard Police Section House when a black guy walked past me carrying a large holdall. Take it from me; the colour of his skin made no difference whatsoever, anybody walking through the West End at that time of night carrying a holdall had to be good for a stop.

"What's in the bag guv?" I asked genially – this was all part of a day's work. The man tossed the bag down on the pavement in front of me and said quite brusquely, "Look for yourself man".

If anybody had accused me of intending to turn the contents of the bag out onto the pavement and leave him to pick it up I would of course have denied it, nothing was further from my mind. The thought of any such action was quickly forgotten as a large python, disturbed from its rest, curled around my arm. I dropped the bag quickly, withdrew the arm smartly and automatically reached for my stick. The man was doubled up with laughter, howls of mirth rending the quiet of the night, tears rolling down his cheeks. "Man, you should have seen your face" he hollered, "I swear I should have had a camera".

For one brief second I hesitated then joined the laughter, perhaps with just the slightest tinge of a hysterical ring. The man was a cabaret performer innocently making his way home after a gig and over the past weeks had become accustomed to coppers sticking their noses into his affairs. He was a regular visitor after that and always passed with a friendly, reciprocated wave as he made his way home. It did strike me that having established his bona fides, that presented the perfect cover for carrying stolen goods through the street but then, you can't win them all.

We had a wonderful old Divisional surgeon covering Tottenham Court Road called 'Doc' Kennedy who lived in Maida Vale. I think it would be fair to say he enjoyed a tipple. By the nature of their irregular hours and shift work, quite a few coppers suffered from haemorrhoids or 'Farmer Giles' as they were universally known. The Doc had a theory that most complaints from which we all tended to suffer from time to time were related to irregular bowel movements and the best cure was to squat, knees raised into a more natural position. "Stands to reason," he would argue to any bemused listener, "just like an Arab in the desert, have you even known an Arab suffering from piles?"

Doc Kennedy was collected from home one night to check out a drunken driver. The man was paralytic and sprawled across the charge room floor. The Doc looked at the recumbent figure and pronounced him fit to drive. We couldn't believe our ears as the Doc, having collected a handsome night call out fee, asked the Station Officer for a lift home. "Sorry Sir, all the cars are out on shouts, it will be a couple of hours before we can take you back, still this gentleman lives at Maida Vale, perhaps he could give you a lift." The Doctor looked aghast as the man, still sprawled across the floor, continued to shout abuse. "What? Drive with that maniac, you must be mad! Give me the Surgeons Report Book, he's not capable of standing on his own two feet let alone drive me home."

After certifying the man drunk in charge, surprisingly enough a patrol car arrived shortly after and took the good Doc Kennedy home. This just goes to prove the old adage, 'justice must not only be done but must be manifestly seen to be done.'

Within the two-year target I had set myself, my probationary period safely behind me and with glowing reports from my supervising officers, I was posted to Croydon as a budding "aid to CID".

Chapter Five

To know all is to understand all
1st Corinthians

Any initial exuberance at being selected as aid to CID was somewhat blunted when I found I was posted back to Norbury. Although greeted warmly enough by my old mentor DS Bert Read and the other aids it didn't augur too well for my chances of getting into the Department. Norbury, a relatively quiet backwater suburb of Croydon, was known to one and all as the aids' cemetery. Not one had been selected for the Department for twenty five years and inevitably, after two to three years of aiding, they were returned to uniform duty, not necessarily for lack of ability but through lack of arrests. One of the aids, Harry Nicol explained the facts of life to his crestfallen listener. "As far as the guv'nors are concerned there is plenty of crime being committed and unless you get enough red ink in the back of your book you can forget the Department in a couple of years, so just sit back and enjoy it."

The 'book' to which he alluded, was the CID officers' diary, in which we had to scrupulously record every person we saw and every allegation investigated.

An exhortation in the front of the diary instructed the writer to make, 'full accurate and near contemporaneous entries as the first line of defence and means of protecting an officer from false allegations of misconduct.' What a joke! Far from being 'a means of protection' a very hastily inscribed entry in the diary very often terminated in discipline proceedings being taken for 'making false entries in an official document'. A record of all crime arrests were made in red ink in the back of the diary and that was the yardstick by which everybody was judged when it came to selection boards.

Aids to CID invariably patrolled in twos and I was unfortunate enough to be paired up with PC Barnett, a particularly thick wooden top. Even in plain clothes, he looked a copper through and through. His major ambition was to clock off at 5pm and get home to his wife and kids. Month after month went by, with nothing more exciting then nicking juveniles for stealing cycles, a pretty lucrative first step into a life of crime but hardly earth shattering stuff and certainly not the stuff that led to promotion. Life was becoming a boring routine and I scoured the daily sitrep (situation report) only to read with envy and mounting frustration the results my fellow aids were achieving in neighbouring Croydon and Streatham. I took to leaving Barnett to his own devices and patrolling alone.

Bert Read was not unaware of the tension and one day, cigarette firmly between two fingers and trilby on his head he collared me in the Station yard. "David, there have been a few housebreakings in the Streatham Hill area; I suggest you and your mate try a few stops around the Common, you may just get lucky."

Barnett wasn't too enthusiastic at the prospect of putting in too much leg work and I was quite happy to wend my own way up the north side of the Common to see if any local villains were about but was totally unprepared for what did happen.

Under the cover of a grove of trees in a clearing a man was indecently assaulting a small six year old boy who was crying and trying without success to break away. I had two young sons of my own at that time and my reaction was intuitive, not of a trained policeman but an outraged parent. Lord Justice Devlin once described the "*honest indignation which led police to be less fair or dispassionate than they ought to be when brought into contact with some pestilential crime in which an innocent child is maltreated or poor man defrauded*".

That appropriately summed up my reaction to catching a man 'in flagrante delicto' with an innocent child. Fortunately for me, it was not a fair contest; the man was on his knees as I forcibly intervened between him and his young victim. The Marquis of Queensbury rules were not strictly adhered to.

There was one important lesson I learned from that encounter, however it may appear on film screens it is a true maxim that invariably, 'He who strikes first, strikes last'. In a fair fight the man would have eaten me for breakfast. Later at the nick I found he was a successful amateur boxer with a string of previous convictions for serious sexual assaults on kids, several of them involving violence. On one occasion he broke a woman's jaw when she found him assaulting her son in a public lavatory. That actually made me feel much better for what had been a somewhat unorthodox and certainly out of character arrest. The next morning the man appeared at Croydon Magistrates' Court, his face looking the worse for wear. He was not without means and the case was adjourned for two weeks for him to brief counsel.

At the trial he looked a little better but his brief, not without a degree of justification I must confess, was obviously going to play the police brutality card. I gave my evidence in a truthful and factual way but was conscious of the Police shorthand writer taking notes for the complaint that had been made. Defence Counsel rose to his feet, a sarcastic sneer on his face. "I suppose officer; you are going to tell the Court that my client received his injuries when he stumbled up the Police Station steps after his arrest?"

It was hardly unexpected. "No sir," I replied truthfully, "Your client was a strong violent man and ordinary means of restraint would have failed, I took such action as I deemed necessary at the time to prevent his escape."

He was convicted and I felt the punishment of three months was hardly adequate but then after all, that was not my business. Perhaps the Magistrate took the view that some degree of summary justice had already been administered. I gained some satisfaction when the boy's parents came up to me afterwards and thanked me for the action I had taken.

My mentor, Bert Read, was at the back of the Court, performing a pastoral role, taking care of his fledglings. He was obviously pleased with the outcome but as was his wont, somewhat stinting in his praise. He looked me straight in the eye, an unlit cigarette clasped between fingers. "Don't you ever go into Court and commit perjury" he said sternly and walked away. After several steps he turned, "unless by doing so you get closer to the truth."

Later in my career I managed to grasp what Bert was trying to convey. It meant little at the time; I was still in a state of grace where I believed in the nobility of justice and quite erroneously thought that criminal law in all its majesty invariably existed to dispense that justice. How gratifying it would have been to go through my service without being disillusioned.

In making that arrest alone, I left myself particularly vulnerable to a complaint, through my so called partner's indolent ways and lack of backup certainly contributed to my over reaction that day. It didn't escape Bert's notice although nothing was said. Barnett was beginning to get to me and shortly after we had a monumental bust up. He complained to the DI of my alleged aggressive demeanour. The DI, a nice enough chap, had only a couple of years to go for his pension and certainly didn't want anybody making waves.

"Martin has complained you threatened to thump him" he said, in a not too unfriendly way. We can't have this sort of behaviour; I'm putting you back to uniform."

That night, with a heavy heart I wrote out my letter of resignation. The next day I was surprised to be summonsed to Croydon to see Albert Denton, the Detective Chief Superintendent and his deputy, Supt. ''Daddy' Marshall.

I was not a snitch and put no reason in my letter but Denton had obviously been well briefed. "I hear you don't get on too well with PC Barnett,"

I shrugged my shoulders, I had nothing to lose. "I'm sorry guv, but the man is a tosser, a waste of space, he'll do better on a school crossing patrol." The two men exchanged knowing glances, Denton smiled sympathetically, looking down at Barnett's official complaint. "Well, I can't say I think much of an officer who makes a formal complaint against his partner and I tend to agree, he is hardly a bundle of energy. I see you have been quite busy, three arrests in the last month, tell me, would you reconsider if I were to post you to Croydon?"

Reconsider? I could hardly believe my good luck. There was nothing to think about, but full of the arrogance of youth I played hard to get. "I don't know guv; I think I should sleep on it."

"Be here at 9am tomorrow and let me know your decision, but if you do decide to stay, I will split you from your present partner and post you to Croydon just as soon as a vacancy arises". True to his word, several weeks later I found myself at Croydon where any aid worth his salt could prove his worth.

There was always a close camaradie in those days no doubt because many officers had been through the war years where their survival depended upon it. There was also a fair sprinkling of 'skivers' who knew all the tricks in the book. One particular PC, when posted to night duty, developed the habit of slipping into the railway sidings at East Croydon Railway Station, finding an empty carriage, setting his alarm clock and settling down for the night. That worked well for him until one morning his alarm failed to go off causing consternation at the nick. Night duty and early turn were deployed looking for the lost PC who could have been attacked and lying somewhere on the patch, injured or even dead. Meanwhile the bold PC woke up, looked out of the window, found he was in Eastbourne and took careful assessment of the predicament in which he found himself. Obviously he had committed numerous disciplinary offences which could lead to either hefty fines or even dismissal. He buttoned up his tunic, walked out of the Railway Station to the seafront where he calmly started directing traffic. Instead of a discipline hearing he was deemed to be under stress, placed sick and spent two weeks convalescence recovering at Brighton Convalescent Home.

It was at Croydon I first served with DC Harry Challenor, Military Medal, a tough ex S.A.S. NCO who brought the same energy into putting away villains as he had fighting the Germans behind lines in occupied France. What can I say about Harry that hasn't already been said or written about? All that needs to be added is the impact his later arrest for planting a half brick during a demonstration against the King and Queen of Greece was the first in a series of incidents that marked the end of an era. Three aids involved in that arrest with Harry went to prison but he was deemed unfit to plea and committed to a mental hospital.

We are all too some degree a product of our own upbringing and that is particularly true in this case. Nobody would disagree that Harry was unorthodox in his approach to Police duties. Nor could even his adversaries and detractors deny he was highly successful in breaking up dangerous Soho gangs and in helping to bring some semblance of order to the streets of post war London in the grip of dangerous gangsters like Billy Hill, and Jack 'Spot' Comer.

What happened with Harry was tragic but those who know what he went through during the war should think twice before saying a word against him. He was a brave man and his wartime experiences undoubtedly contributed to the breakdown in his mental health. Harry was dropped far behind enemy lines in Normandy tasked with creating the maximum mayhem and carnage. Indeed so successful were the regiment that Hitler gave orders that any members captured should be shot on sight as saboteurs and assassins. Harry was a relic of a bygone age, as, later on and in a far different context was I. One ex detective recalled Harry as being a successful prosecutor of 'tasty' people. The villains feared him and many complaints were made about his unorthodox approach to Police duties. On one occasion Harry nicked a three handed team for conspiracy to commit burglary and they appeared before Reggie Seaton, Q.C, Chairman at County of London Sessions. When the jury returned a verdict of guilty upon two of the offenders but acquitted the third, Seaton was furious. He let the jury know in no uncertain terms exactly what he thought of this perverse verdict when calling Harry back into the witness box. "Who do you consider the ringleader in this gang officer?"

Harry wasn't slow to get Reggie's drift and replied to the amusement of onlookers in the Court, "The one the jury let off Sir."

On another occasion outside Marlborough St Court Harry arrested two men for attempting to pervert the course of justice. Harry's evidence was simply he saw them approach witnesses in a threatening manner, point aggressively towards them and draw their thumbs sharply across their throats. Nobody could mistake the threat behind the gestures. That must go down in the annals of crime as the only time that deaf and dumb prisoners complained of being 'verballed'. In a more enlightened age Harry's subsequent behaviour and ultimate disgrace would have been recognised for what it was, namely post traumatic stress disorder.

One Sunday morning Police were called to a shop-breaking at Woolworths, North End, Croydon where building work was being undertaken. Whitgift Middle Grammar School playing fields gave direct access to some inviting scaffolding at the rear of the premises.

The thieves gained access through the roof dropping straight into the high value storeroom. More than ten grand's (ten thousand pound) worth of razor blades and other compact goodies were stored under tarpaulins on the flat room obviously waiting collection that weekend; not a bad little tickle. This had all the hallmarks of a professional team, the perpetrators skilfully bypassing a fairly sophisticated burglar alarm system. Had it not been for a store manager making an unexpected call on Sunday morning to do some paper work and spotting some Mars bar wrappings on the floor of the main shop there is a fair chance this would have been yet another undetected crime statistic.

DS Fred Fairfax, GC, was on duty that Sunday morning. Fred was decorated for his courage when, despite being shot and wounded, he arrested Christopher Craig and Derek Bentley, the cold-blooded murderers of PC Miles at Barlow and Parkers, Croydon. Fred detailed me, my partner Lofty Hudson, a tall, powerful ex matelot and PS Richardson, a uniform dog handler to keep observation at the back of the shop. We found an old school van in the playing fields that afforded some degree of shelter from the cold March winds and presented a good vantage point overlooking the scaffolding.

After nearly four hours, we were getting rather cramped and cold when in the falling dusk, I saw two shadowy figures climb over a high fence in Wellesley Road into the playing fields and run silently to the back of a cricket sight screen. I waited with bated breath and whispered to the PS to keep his bloody dog quiet. Lofty was outside stretching his legs, having a strain off, totally unaware of the drama unfolding less than twenty yards away.

It was at least five minutes before three other figures, satisfied no alarm had been raised, jumped the fence and joined their compatriots and I began to wonder what the hell had happened to Lofty. Wouldn't it have been lovely if we had personal radios in those far off days?

Without a word being spoken, the men mounted the scaffolding onto the flat roof. Then I heard the sound of muffled voices as the villains realised their prize had disappeared back into the secured building. I needed to warn Lofty otherwise we risked showing out and slipped quietly from the van, cursing the dog who was yawning and growling in boredom. By now the adrenaline was running and as I reached the edge of the building I saw Lofty in what was rapidly turning into pure farce. There he stood, thermos flask in one hand and a half eaten sandwich in the other. He stared through the gloom and in a voice that would have wakened the dead said, "Here, is that you Dave?"

Well, as you can imagine, it was all off. Bodies came tumbling and sliding down the scaffolding, hightailing it across the sports field leaving behind a tasty collection of jemmies and other implements showing they obviously intended to have another dip into the lucky jackpot. It's easy in a situation like that to get confused and there were five very confused villains being chased by two confused aids to CID and a dog. I fixed upon one and Lofty chased after the others shouting rather unnecessarily as I thought at the time, "Stop, Police". As for the dog, he chased Lofty and caught him by the trouser leg bringing him to the ground. I brought my man crashing down and soon had him secured.

Looking up I saw Lofty with a superhuman effort kick the bloody dog clear, continue the chase and collar one of the others just as he was climbing the wire fence. Under the circumstances Lofty did well to effect the arrest.

By the time we got back to the nick, fingerprinted, booked the suspects and recovered their tools from the scene, the night duty CID officer had arrived from another Station to handle the ongoing investigations. I was rather concerned when, without asking either of us arresting officers to accompany him, this particular DS (Detective sergeant) took the prisoners into the Detention room for what appeared to be a cosy chat.

I was even more concerned when one of the prisoners was allowed to make a phone call, an unheard of concession when there were still three suspects at large. It didn't help put my mind at ease when I learned the DS had recently been transferred from Wandsworth where the two prisoners, both with long criminal records, came from.

By now it was past midnight and I couldn't believe my ears when the DS told the Station Officer to charge the men with the comparatively minor offence of possessing housebreaking implements (hbi) by night and bail them to Court next morning. This was just not on. I confronted the DS indignantly. "Just what is going on skip, these blokes are up for the screwing last night."

The man wasn't used to being spoken to by a rooky aid like that. This came across loud and clear from the look he flashed at me and the menacing tone in his voice. "You haven't got a jot of evidence to connect them with the screwing; all you have them for is possession of hbi".

He turned away dismissively, but there was no way I was swallowing that. "Excuse me sergeant but I heard those men talking up on the roof and you should have spoken to us before reaching your decision."

The man turned in amazement, a look of hesitancy and disbelief on his face, "Oh yes, and what precisely did you hear?"

Seeing very clearly the way the wind was blowing, I ignored the DS and directed my remarks to the Station Officer, by now joined by the Duty Officer. Pointing to my prisoner I said, "I distinctly heard that man saying to the other, 'I told you we should have had the gear away last night".

The Duty Officer who obviously had his own thoughts as to how this little scenario was being acted out said, not unkindly, "Write up your pocket book officer" which I did in double quick time.

The out ranked night duty DS, muttering under his breath, stalked off in high dudgeon. Lofty obviously hadn't heard those incriminating words as he had been round the corner. I was in the canteen writing up my notes, when he came over, "Here Dave, did you really hear them say that?"

"Course I did Lofty, you know how sound travels at night."

The men eventually received a three year sentence, which their actions and previous records richly merited and in due course both Lofty and I received a Commissioners commendation. There was a lot of protestation from the rear of the Court together with a little 'dock asthma' as I gave my evidence.

As I walked out carrying the exhibits, a woman with heavily peroxide hair turned to her mate and said in a loud voice, "Get out of his bleeding way Gladys or he'll have that lot on you."

These weren't bad guys, they were merely doing their job and I was doing mine, no hard feelings on either side and that's the way it was in those days. As for the DS who knows? Was he hoping for an 'earner' and prepared to sabotage an arrest or was there perhaps another less dishonourable reason for his actions? Could be, but I somehow doubt it.

It wasn't unknown to do deals in return for favours such as information about other bigger fish but I soon learned you didn't do that with other peoples' arrests and you certainly didn't do it without clearing it first with a senior officer and never with somebody else's arrest. I was learning and learning fast and in this case it was a lesson I would rather not have had to learn. The age of innocence was fast disappearing.

At Croydon nick I was introduced to the Friday evening conference. It was not unusual to work eighty hour weeks but Friday night was designated 'debriefing' night. Once the business formalities were over, the bottles of Scotch would appear from lockers and the serious business of the evening would begin. Daddy Marshall was an excellent Detective Superintendent who should have been destined for the higher echelons at the Yard. He had an impressive record of solved murders and unfortunately it was one of those that proved his undoing.

There was a particularly newsworthy murder on his old patch at Twickenham when two girls were bound, raped and butchered with an axe on the towpath in what was inevitably to be known and widely reported in the National Press as 'The towpath murders'. Local CID had a suspect who was lifted and taken to the nick 'to assist enquiries'. Unfortunately the man managed to secrete the murder weapon behind the rear seat of the CID car. He was subsequently released through lack of evidence and the axe lay undetected for nearly a week until a PC posted to yard duties was detailed to wash down the CID car and found it.

Being totally unaware of its significance, the PC took the murder weapon home and happily used it to chop firewood in his back yard until canteen talk disclosed to the hapless officer the significance of his find.

Knowing the possible consequences, it was to his credit he returned the axe to the nick and reported the facts. Forensic scientists were still able to discover blood and traces of bone on the axe and the culprit was eventually arrested, tried and hanged for murder.

By that time, the enquiry was taken over by Supt. Hannam of the Yard who submitted a scathing report upon the shortcomings in the investigation.

Of course the press had a field day and somebody's head had to fall. Poor old 'Daddy' Marshall, the officer in the case who, incidentally was on holiday in the United States at the time the axe was discovered, took the rap. His career nose-dived and he was posted to Croydon to while away the last few years of his service.

There was another vital lesson to be learned from this namely, the job was a hard task master and did not allow for errors, even honest ones, nobody was allowed to make a mistake and one incident could end an otherwise spotless career. This blind, inhuman and rigid disciplinary system had the opposite effect to that intended. Was it little wonder in the light of such harsh measures that police officers would tend to stick together, close ranks and cover up minor transgressions knowing the possible consequences? Was there no room for the honest mistake? Mr Marshall never allowed the injustice meted out to him to affect his work or his attitude and he eventually went into honourable retirement. I often wondered whether it was the strain of living with the after effects of this injustice or the fact he lived with a wife and six daughters that brought about his ulcer.

The ulcer didn't effect Friday evening 'de-briefings', he would take two glasses from his locker, fill one with milk, the other with scotch. With a grimace he would down the former proclaiming, "That's for my ulcer". He then downed the scotch, licked his lips and said, "and that's for me!"

I spent literally weeks mentally preparing for the final CID Selection board, knew almost every villain on the patch and could recognise most photographs of wanted persons in *Police Gazette* before being summoned to the Yard. The President of the Board was Commander George Hatherill. He was a big mover on the International scene and had represented UK at Interpol conferences. Reputed to speak eight foreign languages, he successfully conducted many famous murder investigations. The great man slouched back in his chair, looking slightly untidy, a cigarette in hand, ash dropping onto his woollen waistcoat. He looked down, reading the dossier in front of him. "I see you were in the Army in Germany" he said and I nodded in acquiescence. So far so good. "Well now, what do you think of the German economic threat to English industry?"

I swallowed hard; here was the catch question that nobody could have prepared for. He wasn't interested in my views upon the German economic threat but what he did want to do was judge my reaction to the unexpected question that occasionally faces every experienced detective when giving evidence from the witness box. My mind flashed back to 1954, the scenes of devastation I had witnessed in Düsseldorf, of builders working through the night under arc lights restoring the shattered city. "Well sir, I think the difficulty we face is the Germans live for work while we work to live".

That seemed to go down well, the rest of the interview was a breeze and I felt sure even as I walked through the door I had passed the Board. I could now look forward to being a permanent member of the proud and at that time still considered honourable brotherhood of CID officers.

Chapter Six

Them what can, do, them what can't, teach
George Bernard Shaw 1856–1950

It was as a fledgling detective I returned to Hendon Training School on the junior Detective Course. My class instructor was D.I. Ian Forbes, a powerfully built Scotsman who earned his promotion the hard way on Division and the Flying Squad (C8). He was first and foremost a hands on, practical copper who was to eventually rise to Detective Chief Superintendent on the Yard's Murder Squad. It must have been with tongue in cheek or perhaps a wry sense of humour that somebody determined that Jock Forbes should lecture the trainees on 'Judges' Rules' and interrogation. He invariably finished his lectures with a gripping yarn of his exploits on the Squad and the explicit instruction, "Right, laddies, now go out there and nick them". And that my friends was how he became known to one and all as 'Nickem Forbes'.

It was 1960, and I was to make a close friend who has remained such to this day. Most intakes to Detective Training School contained one or two police officers from one of our rapidly diminishing colonies. I speak Spanish so to my mind it was quite natural that I should seek out DC Luis Ghio, from Gibraltar and offer whatever assistance I could. Luis was a larger than life character, dark haired with a disarming smile and physique that had a devastating effect upon the ladies. He was a man of many parts and lived a varied and exciting life. Born in La Linea, Spain, at the time of the Spanish Civil war his father, a high-ranking Mason, was tipped off that Franco's forces were about to enter La Linea and kill all freemasons. A few days later the Falangists entered the Ghio household after shooting through the door with machine guns, stole everything of value, destroyed the rest and threw the debris into the street.

Fortunately the family had been evacuated in time to Gibraltar, thence to Casablanca and after the French capitulation to Crystal Palace in London.

At the age of sixteen, Luis added a few years to his age and volunteered to join the R.A.F. for training in Canada. His father got wind of this and thwarted the move that with hindsight probably saved his life. After the war, Luis returned to Gibraltar and served as a detective in the local Police Force. He was something of a keep fit fanatic and in 1965 he won the first 'Mr Gibraltar' competition.

The intricacies of the Vagrancy Act, 1824, or the Metropolitan Police Act 1839, served no place in policing Gibraltar and merely kept him, albeit temporarily, from the more enjoyable things of life. When it came to our final written examination it was the moment of truth. As I scribbled happily away I couldn't help but notice that poor Luis sat staring at the paper as if it were written in a foreign language, making no attempt to put pencil to paper.

This didn't escape the attention of Ian Forbes, the eagle eyed invigilator and as the clock ticked by it was clear that nothing short of a miracle would rescue Luis from his predicament. Of course, miracles sometimes do happen in this particular instance it was in the shape of the large figure of Mr Forbes who loomed over the hapless Luis. "Ghio, you look ill, get yourself into the toilet".

Luis, looking somewhat puzzled did as instructed and Jock Forbes turned to me. "You Woodland, get in there and make sure that Ghio is OK, he doesn't look at all well".

As they say, a nod is as good as a wink to a blind man and I did the great man's bidding whilst from outside the toilet in a rich Scot's accent came the enjoinder, "And I'll stand outside here to ensure there's no bloody cheating!"

Luis passed his final examination comfortably but I wasn't particularly surprised when several years later he threw in the job and finished up as a Director of the Casino in Gibraltar. We have enjoyed many a friendly drink since those far off days, chuckling over our exploits at Hendon. Luis was a formidable detective in his day and ran many informants. Many years later one of my little party pieces whenever I met anybody from the Rock was to ask him or her whether they knew Detective Luis Ghio and I was rarely disappointed with the response.

After Detective Training School we all went our separate ways and I was disappointed to find myself posted to Criminal Record Office (CRO) New Scotland Yard, the central record office for the whole of U.K. It wasn't what I had hoped for but in hindsight I realise this was a useful training ground for anybody aspiring to higher ranks within the Department. CRO was divided into various sections, the Nominal and Wanted indices, Method Index, Photo Albums and *Police Gazette* Office. I was going to be there for at least eighteen months and decided to make the most of it.

The Department was made up of us transient officers, some who had reached the highest echelons and a nucleus of permanent staff. The majority of the latter, having fallen foul of some senior officer, or somehow or other blotted their copy book were sent to CRO as a punishment posting to see out their time away from the trials and pitfalls of Divisional CID life.

Nominal Index was manned 24 hours a day and received calls from all over the British Isles often from solitary policemen in remote country areas, far from assistance so of necessity these calls were given absolute priority

I spent a useful attachment in Method Index which operated on the principle the majority of villains were sufficiently lacking in imagination and tended to stick to their preferred modus operandi throughout their working lives. The index also recorded character peculiarities, physical deformities, tattoos, all of which could occasionally throw out a suspect for the lucky fellows on Division who were busy 'nicking them'.

A Los Angeles detective, Hugh McDonald developed a system called 'Identikit' a useful investigative tool that created photographic facial composite sketches based upon descriptions given by victims and witnesses to crime. Using the basis of what I learned in Method Index I enhanced the system by adding the other non altering features to the system: approximate year of birth, height, method and the facial scars and tattoos, deformities and other character peculiarities to build up a more rounded picture of a suspect which I called 'Identicode'.

The object was to produce a manageable number of potential suspects. I submitted my paper to the Research and Planning Department and received a commendation for initiative. Needless to say, nothing ever happened with it and I was informed the idea whilst good on paper would need a dedicated computer to put into practice. It probably didn't help that for a start that in those days the Force possessed no such computer and secondly I had the temerity to preface my paper with a quotation from that much maligned 15th century political thinker Niccolo Machiavelli.

"There is nothing more difficult to achieve than attempt to impose a new order of things. It will make enemies of all who benefit from the old order and lukewarm defenders from those who may benefit from the new." That must have gone down like a ton of bricks with the hierarchy.

I couldn't let these memoirs pass without reference to DI Albert Abrams, one of many characters at CRO. Albert blotted his copy book by the simple expedient of moving outside the Met area to Haywards Heath without consent. He was promptly threatened with discipline proceedings unless he moved back. Albert produced a letter from his friendly family doctor showing his wife suffered from respiratory problems that were considerably eased by his move to the country and in the face of such convincing medical evidence nothing could be done. In a fit of pure spite, the authorities moved Albert to CRO and told him in no uncertain terms he had ruined his chances of promotion.

In those days there was one other disciplinary offence that was almost an automatic sacking for bringing the job into disrepute. I refer to the heinous crime of adultery, or to be more precise, the crime of being caught. Albert compounded his previous crimes by forming an association with a charming lady from General Registry, despite repeated warnings as to his conduct. No doubt their relationship was perfectly proper but he would insist upon coming to work each morning with bowler hat and rolled umbrella and the charming lady on his arm. As if that by itself wasn't enough, he rubbed salt into the wound by insisting upon arriving through the main steps of the Commissioner's entrance in full view of the world at large. Two senior officers decided this upstart must be taught a lesson and ordered a detailed investigation into his behaviour.

We often wondered what Albert got up to in his office for long periods of the day, bent over books and taking copious notes and eventually we learned. Well, at least we like to think we did but nobody was telling, certainly not Albert. Rumour had it that Albert had discovered that overtime cards had been incorrectly calculated for many years and a legion of CRO officers deprived of their rightful compensation. Strictly speaking, every week when four hours was put onto the time off cards it should have accrued overtime rates at time and a quarter before the four hours for which payment was made were deducted. Hence hundreds of officers over many years were deprived of one and quarter hours pay every week. Albert painstakingly calculated that the amount improperly withheld came to a staggering sum well in excess of ten thousand pounds.

Had this been pursued, heads would certainly have rolled and they would have been at the top of the Department, curiously those very heads who had been so determined to topple dear old Albert.

Well, all is well that ends well so they say. Albert was quite unexpectedly given the next rank and until such time as Detective Chief Inspector Abrams retired from the Metropolitan Police Force he continue to arrive up the Commissioner's stairs at New Scotland Yard wearing his bowler hat, rolled umbrella and charming lady upon his arm.

Eighteen months was the minimum, two years maximum for we pressed men to remain at CRO. Police Orders, containing details of promotions and postings were published every Tuesday and Friday and every Tuesday and Friday I would knock on a very patient Chief Superintendent's door and demand when my release would come.

Eventually the poor man's patience wore thin. "Get out of my bloody office, I promise you will get the next vacancy on Division that comes up." Lord bless him, he was true to his word and I found myself posted to Dagenham, "K" Division twenty one miles from where I was living at Croydon and had to negotiate the Blackwall Tunnel twice daily to and from home. To add to the misery, in those days there was a single tunnel with two way traffic which didn't exactly enhance the experience.

There were lots of open spaces at Dagenham and it soon became clear one of the most prevalent crimes was 'flashing' a rather unsocial form of behaviour that the law in its infinite wisdom outlawed by the name of indecent exposure. I suppose it was the fact that Dagenham had more than its fair share of parks and commons but flashing appeared to be a rather regular pastime and it was not just confined to the stereotyped dirty raincoat brigade. One particularly tough looking guy, the complete opposite to what one would suspect, was nicked and brought into the charge room. Curiosity led to my posing the question, "What on earth makes a guy like you flash at women in the park?"

The man looked at me sheepishly. "To tell the truth mate, I'm no good at the chat up stakes so I just flashes. It's not bad actually, for every five or six birds I flash to I get the occasional complaint but at least one who takes up the offer."

What can you say to that except please don't try it? Cheaper than calling cards I suppose but chances are you will end up with the one who makes a complaint and gets you nicked.

One of the first ports of call for every copper posted to Dagenham was a visit to the local churchyard to a tombstone commemorating one PC George Clark who according to the inscription *'was inhumanly and barbarously murdered whilst on duty on the morning of 30th June, 1846, aged 20 years'*. PC Clark was described as being religious and non-drinking – quite a unique combination for in those days, it has been whispered, members of the constabulary were notorious for their alcoholic intake. The tombstone inscription testifies *'his uniform good conduct gained him the respect of all who knew him and his melancholy end was universally deplored.'*

Local history books attribute various theories as to how he met his untimely death. What was beyond any dispute is that he was beaten, stabbed and slashed with his own cutlass and it was equally clear that robbery was not the motive. Among the theories put forward were that he was murdered by a band of passing gypsies, by a local man with a grudge against the police or that he came across, or was involved in corn smuggling, a serious crime in those days. Indeed two men were arrested some time later and tried for his murder but acquitted through lack of evidence. Perhaps it is worthy of mention the two men arrested were serving Police officers, one being his supervising Sergeant, William Parsons. Police canteens are notorious for gossip and the story passed down through generations of Police Officers to this present day is that our virtuous PC Clark was having an affair with Maria, his Relief Sergeant's wife. Sergeant Parsons, recorded as being missing from his beat on that night, got wind of the rumours, met PC Clark by arrangement and put him to death with his own cutlass. Parsons was charged with murder and stood trial at the Old Bailey. Although acquitted through lack of evidence, the disgraced Sgt Parsons, together with his new wife, left England to start a fresh life in British Columbia, Canada.

It didn't come too much amiss when I was posted to East Ham nick, a stage closer to home via the old one-way Blackwall tunnel. We had an old, disillusioned and cynical DS at East Ham. One of his many supervisory jobs was to ensure all applications for search warrants were properly recorded before being executed. On occasions I turned over local villains known to be at the game and was surprised at the lack of positive results these produced. Then one day I chanced upon this particular Sgt drinking in a local pub with a known receiver I had recently turned over with no success. From that day onwards, quite contrary to standing orders, I never entered details of any search warrants I applied for until after they were executed and was not overly surprised when I found my success rate rose quite dramatically. Of course, it could all have been coincidental, but on the other hand....

Life although busy was by no means a round of unmitigated successes. We notched up our fair share of failures, long, tedious observations, abortive early morning turnovers, lost cases in Courts, often against the weight of evidence. The one thing I learned was: never look back, yesterday is gone there is only today and tomorrow.

During the bad December fogs of 1962, after pretty painstaking enquiries I arrested Robert Withers known locally as 'Dodgy Bob' and recovered a van load of car accessories from a shed at the bottom of his garden. He appeared at Court and was granted bail (as a reward for having offered up spurious information about a well-known East End villain who had commissioned a set of keys for the local Barclays Bank.)

But the wicked man jumped bail and I circulated him as 'wanted'.

Two years later whilst I was serving on a Murder Squad in West London, Bob was nicked and remanded in custody for trial. Before the hearing Prosecuting Counsel approached me. "I understand he's going to run a Challenor defence". This was a foretaste of what many a CID officer has had to undergo ever since DS Harry Challenor was convicted of planting bricks upon a suspect.

Allegations of planting became commonplace and more to the point, jury after jury were swallowing it. Bob offered to plead guilty to receiving if the breaking charge was dropped and in the absence of witnesses this was reluctantly accepted. He received three years so all in all that wasn't a bad result although it signalled a clear sign of change in public perceptions and a taste of things to come.

It goes to show that things often don't go as smoothly as one would wish which was very much the case of an escaped convict Billy Holmes. A nosy neighbour tipped the wink that Billy was visiting his young lady a few doors down the road and they heard he was over the side from Dartmoor. After prompting, they remembered he had 'love' and 'hate' tattooed on his fingers. A quick call to Method Index at the Yard revealed Billy's identity and we kept a close watch on Molly, the girl friend who was heavily pregnant. Escaped convicts have little choice but to resort to crime and I stepped up the observations but in an covert manner that gave Molly no opportunity of meeting up with Billy. It was a long shot but it paid off. Within two weeks Molly was at the nick asking for me. "Look Mr. Woodland, we know you're following me and you'll never get Billy that way, he's got a deal for you. My kid's due soon and we want to get married at the Registry Office next Saturday. Let us do that and Billy promises to give himself up to you immediately after."

I'm really a bit of a softie at heart, how could I resist such an offer? As Les Troman my D.I. said later with a grin, "It's good to see the age of chivalry is still alive".

Well the deed was done, we stayed away from the Registry Office, the happy couple were spliced and the babe eventually born in wedlock. As for Billy, he surrendered as promised at his new in-law's house and we all enjoyed a piece of cake and a glass of champagne. God alone knows what the nosy neighbour must have been thinking.

"O.K. Billy, it's time to go" I said.

"Thanks Mr Woodland, can I just pop upstairs with the missus for five minutes then I'm all yours."

Well, it was their wedding day after all. Five minutes passed, then another and then another. By no means could this be considered a 'quickie' and I thought it was time to interrupt the happy couples nuptials. I knocked discreetly on the bedroom door, "Right Billy, let's go".

As I opened the door I saw the open first floor bedroom window where Billy had jumped and taken it upon his toes across the open fields.

I said some rather ungracious things to poor Molly and she spiritedly responded, "Well, Mr Woodland, Billy kept his word, he surrendered to you as promised but that never stopped him escaping once he'd done so."

It was a couple of weeks before Billy telephoned and quietly gave himself up. I often wonder what happened to them both, in fact I was quite surprised I wasn't asked to be godfather.

After a few months I was suddenly moved to North Woolwich nick in the East End Docklands to take the place of D.C. Roy Eyles. Detective Supt. 'Doughy' Baker was looking for somewhere locally to launch his boat and Roy introduced him to John Gold, a local wharfinger of German Jewish extraction who conveniently had a ramp on his wharf. John was a most pleasant man, highly intelligent and good company, that is, when he was sober. Unfortunately he had suffered a most unpleasant war and was a child survivor of one of Hitler's extermination camps where he suffered unspeakable deprivations. He was lucky to survive but when in drink John occasionally underwent a remarkable transformation where he became aggressive, highly abusive and prone to violence. It just happened it was Roy's bad luck that he effected the introduction to his guv 'nor when John was on one of his benders and 'Doughy' had to be rescued by an embarrassed Roy. Doughy was livid, quite certain this was deliberate and poor Roy found himself at Plaistow for his sins and I moved to the Docks which were then a flourishing, vibrant community where numerous shipping companies including the Blue Star Line, P & O Lines and many others brought cargo and passengers from all over the Globe. The only other CID Officer at the nick was Det. Sgt Sidney Simcox, a great man who became a close personal friend until he died following his retirement. Sid joined the paratroopers during the war, was dropped on the ill fated Arnhem raid and taken prisoner after being shot through the face and leg. Contrary to the Geneva Convention, Sid, with other prisoners, was force worked at the Herman Goering Steelworks in Germany until the end of hostilities when he re-joined the job.

The Metropolitan Police policed outside the Docks, the Port of London Authority Police (PLA) being responsible for everything within its walls. The Met had jurisdiction for any crimes committed on the high seas such as murder and piracy.

I never did get to see a real live pirate but was called out one Saturday morning to deal with a fatal stabbing of a ship's cook. The perpetrator, a Chinese seaman, was locked in irons by the Captain until handed over to the civil authorities – me! The poor prisoner was brought up manacled from the hold and it soon transpired he spoke not one word of English. My Chinese extended no further than 'one portion of 24 and one of 42'.

"Does anybody here speak Chinese?" I shouted over the melee of Port Police, Customs and Immigration officials crowded around the poor man. Eventually a PLA PS remembered there was a Dock PC on the interpreter's list who actually spoke the language. The man lived at Romford and a police car was dispatched to fetch him.

Eventually the man arrived and I took him to one side to explain his duties. An expectant hush fell over the throng as the

PC addressed the trembling figure seated before him. "Why for you stabbee cookie in belly with knifee?"

There was a stunned silence – that was it, the sum total of his Chinese vocabulary! For goodness knows how many years, the intrepid linguist had been drawing an interpreter's allowance of five shillings a week and of course nobody had sussed it up till that moment.

I don't know how Peter Gannon, Chief Officer PLA Police dealt with that one but I would bet a day's pay the PC was placed straight on a fizzer; indeed he would be lucky not to be nicked for obtaining money by false pretences. Fortunately, we were still inside the Dock gates and that placed him outside my jurisdiction. I'm not sure whether, had the choice been mine, I would have nicked him or bought him a pint for his cheek, on reflection probably the latter.

We all recognize the expression, 'work hard – play hard' well that was just the way it went at North Woolwich. Most of the locals worked in the Docks and with the great ocean liners docking in King George V and Royal Albert Docks, there were seamen of all races drinking, fighting and whoring either at the end of or at the beginning of voyages all over the world. It was a fascinating time, I was privileged to witness that, it only lasted a few years more before all the Docks closed; I wouldn't have missed it for the world.

The nick was strategically placed on a corner, with pubs on the other three. One pub was in East Ham licensing area, one in West Ham and one in (South) Woolwich areas, the former two having 10.30pm closing whilst the latter being within London County Council area closed at 11pm.

There was always a mad rush at closing time to the other pub to get in the last half hour's drinking and of course that's where the trouble would invariably break out nice and convenient for the nick just across the road. This strange territorial anomaly also extended to the Magistrate's Courts. I frequently found myself back at East Ham or West Ham Magistrate's Court dealing with cases before the beak or committing prisoners for trial.

West Ham Quarter Sessions (Q.S.) was something quite different, unique in fact. The permanent Recorder, Wally

Raeburn, Q.C. was a devote Buddhist who, we convinced ourselves, found it against his principles to put anybody inside, however heinous the crime. In fact it is fair to say that nobody, with the exception of child molesters, was ever convicted at West Ham Q.S. for anything! Well, practically nobody.

The National Dock union members would meet before each session and as the majority of jurors and defendants were dockers, one could see how the system operated. I have taken open and closed cases before Wally and seen jurors, complete with cloth caps and scarves, openly giving the thumbs up sign to their mates in the Dock before acquitting them completely against the weight of evidence.

As mindless, drink induced violence was one of the regular types of cases dealt with, we eventually adapted our own strategies to overcome this handicap or one could argue, effrontery to justice.

Boundary anomalies could and did arise and when framing a charge it was not unknown to miscalculate precisely where some street fracas had taken place. This guaranteed a trial at East Ham QS and at least the fair chance that some semblance of justice would be done. After all, isn't that what the criminal law system is supposed to achieve?

Similarly, grievous bodily harm (gbh) or actual bodily harm (abh) could be dealt with at Sessions. When circumstances made it difficult to stretch the boundary jurisdiction, it became common practice to charge offenders with the more serious offence of 'gbh with intent to cause gbh' under Section 18, Offences Against the Person Act, 1861 which, punishable by life, could only be dealt with at the Old Bailey. Having thus successfully bypassed West Ham QS, unless the gravity of the assault justified, it was possible at the Old Bailey to accept a plea to the lesser offence of gbh (Section 20) thus ensuring that justice of sorts was done.

The powers that be eventually decided that West Ham Quarter Sessions had to go and it disappeared, along with dear old Wally, in the boundary changes that came about with the formation of Greater London Council. Some may say it really didn't achieve much as most cases then finished up at Snaresbrook Crown Court that wasn't any better!

We had more than a fair share of true East End characters at North Woolwich, one of the outstanding being a local licensee, Danny Cousins.

Danny and his wife, Rene, both served as stewards on passenger liners before saving enough to buy The Royal Oak, a small lock up pub in Woodman Street. Danny soon attracted the sea going fraternity by exchanging seaman's advance notes at a lower discount rate than the official moneychangers in the Docks. After all, he could afford to as invariably a large portion of the advances, designed to allow a seaman to equip himself for the forthcoming voyage, found its way into the tills at 'The Royal Oak'. This made Danny very wealthy and he soon bought another pub further along the road.

One Friday night some Dutch seamen nicked a cat from the Royal Oak. That cat was the pride and joy of Rene's life and Danny swore to kill every Dutchman in the Docks unless it was retrieved. By one of those peculiar quirks in English law, while it was a crime to steal a dog there was no corresponding offence for theft of a cat, they were considered to be feral animals and as such were unprotected.

Unprotected or not, I was not happy to see open warfare break out on my patch, one didn't play around with Danny Cousins. Happily for a change, it was a fairly quiet Saturday morning and I visited the only two Dutch boats in the Port of London overnight and was obliged purely in the line of duty to quaff moderate quantities of Dutch gin and brandy with two understanding skippers while diplomatically explaining my mission. I struck lucky at the second boat.

Upon the promise of no Court proceedings (for a non existing crime I stress) one of the seamen admitted taking the cat from the pub but was ordered to return it to the dockside by the ship's bos'n.

It happened to be at Spillers Wharf where, in order to keep rats away from the flour stored in the warehouses, the Company employed an armed rat catcher at night to shoot rats. Very effective he was, in this particular case unfortunately too effective. I searched the area and found moggy, soaked through and stiff as a board, obviously shot by mistake. At least, the Dutchmen were exonerated from the heinous crime of 'cat napping' and open warfare averted. I phoned Danny but he insisted upon attending the scene of the crime. He went down on his knees, ear to the dead cat's heart.

"Dave, it's still breathing, let's get it to a vet."

Eventually we found a vet who of course pronounced life extinct. We decided to give it a Christian burial via John Gold's slipway on the Thames. "Dave, you must promise me, don't ever let Rene know the cat is dead, it will break her heart."

How to account for my time? Much later that afternoon and somewhat the worse for wear, I returned to the nick, diligently recorded the alleged theft of a cat's collar in the Crime Book then immediately scrubbed it, writing up quite truthfully that the property had been traced and restored to its rightful owner.

Please do not assume that policing the East End of London in those days was all beer and skittles. Hardly a Bank holiday went by without a shooting, affray or serious wounding mostly between rival gang members fighting for control of their patch or settling old scores. In the East End of London it was considered a cardinal offence, virtually akin to grassing, to make an official complaint or to give evidence in court which goes to show how notorious gangsters like the Kray twins managed to operate with seeming impunity for so long. That is until that superb detective, Detective Superintendent Nipper Read and his team of 'untouchables' broke through that wall of silence using unorthodox but totally correct methods.

During the summing up at the Old Bailey in 1969, the trial judge Melford Stevenson QC made the following sagacious observation. "The needs of justice sometimes require that truth be dredged from very muddy waters." And so say all of us.

Chapter Seven

East is east and West is west and ne'er
the twain shall meet
Rudyard Kipling 1865–1936

My introduction to Cannon Row was curious to say the least. The uniform Chief Superintendent left me in no doubt I was now serving in "Royal A" Division and I could forget the rough and ready ways of the East End of London, the all important thing to remember being we policed the seat of Government and we certainly did not make waves. I began to wonder whether or not I had joined the Diplomatic Corps and realised this was my reluctant introduction into the political elements of policing. Not a lot of serious crime happened at Cannon Row probably due in no small part due to the amount of fixed posts outside Embassies and the like but the Sub Division also took in Hyde Park where there was the occasional robbery, theft and of course a high level of still illegal homosexual activity that engendered more Police attention than it does today.

Most nights the uniform branch would arrest a motley collection of men in Hyde Park charged with varying acts of indecency and it fell to the Department to dispose of the cases at Court the following morning. One couldn't help but feel a degree of sympathy for some of these unfortunates, many otherwise respectable members of society who succumbed to their moment of madness.

Usually we managed to dispose of the minor cases under Park bye-laws without dragging the poor wretches through the humiliating process of being fingerprinted and branded with the indignity of being given a criminal record. Of course there was another side to the equation, particularly when acts between consenting adults in private were still subject to the criminal law and this situation wasn't rectified until the passing of The Sexual Offender Act, 1967 which decriminalised the practice whilst not totally removing the stigma that in the eyes of some people still exists to this day. As Oscar Wilde put it so succinctly nearly one hundred years earlier, *"No spectacle is so ridiculous as the British public in one of its periodical fits of morality."*

We occasionally had to deal with cases of blackmail and violence committed by homophobes who would prey upon these people well aware of the reluctance of their victims to report such crimes with the ensuing publicity this would bring.

Cannon Row Police Station was located immediately outside the imposing entrance to the old Scotland Yard building. It was intriguing to watch the attitudes of people in Derby Gate from the first floor CID office window overlooking those splendid, ornate gates. Some appeared to be drawn almost like a magnet to Scotland Yard before contemplating whether or not to surrender for some misdemeanour or crime and subject themselves to the due process of law. Naturally I was happy to oblige but with the blessing of hindsight what good did this really achieve? As the writer Daniel Defoe put it some two hundred years earlier. *"These are but cobweb laws in which small flies are catched and the great break through'*

Cannon Row was my first introduction to the much-vaunted forensic Crime Laboratory at C.7. Not having been long out of Detective Training School and brimming with knowledge, I was eager to put Professor Edmond Locard's exchange principle into practice. Boy, this was heady stuff. Locard was an early pioneer in forensic science and adduced that when two objects came into contact with each other, each would leave or transfer particles to the other. There was a pretty mundane robbery at Hyde Park one evening at dusk when a young tearaway threw pepper in a woman's face and made off with her handbag. I say mundane, but that didn't make it any less traumatic to the victim. After a hue and cry, the bandit, a Borstal escapee, was captured. He knew the score, refused to say a word so I decided to improve my education and put Professor Locard's Exchange Control principle to work.

I religiously took swabs from the victim's face, traces of powder from the suspect's pocket and pepper from the pot recovered from the scene. Eventually the result came back from a laboratory scientist with a string of qualifications after his name. "I have examined a substance found upon facial swabs and find – it contained pepper; I have examined a substance found in the left jacket pocket of the suspect and find – it contained pepper; I have examined the substance found in a pepper pot and find – it contained pepper."

That was yet another prime example where with hind sight, had I succeeded in obtaining a verbal or written admission from the accused, it may well have expedited justice, spared a nervous complainant from undergoing the ordeal of giving evidence at the subsequent trial and saved a considerable amount of time and money. After all, what did the suspect have to lose? He received free legal aid and a few days outing from the slammer which no doubt broke the monotony of stir and his daily diet of porridge.

Cannon Row was home to a transient population, very few actually living on the patch except of course the Queen, Prime Minister and half of the Cabinet, they had their own 'minders' and didn't make too many calls upon our services.

I did manage to cultivate one snout I shall call Keith, who set me up with a few little jobs including Mick, a shop breaker hailing from Liverpool, anxious to dispose of a load of stolen Parker pen and pencil sets. To say Keith was frightened of Mick would be an understatement, he was terrified and not without reason. Mick's last arrest was for gbh on two coppers in Liverpool and they certainly don't come small so I guessed he had to be a tasty handful.

I introduced myself as manager of the now defunct Serpentine Restaurant in Hyde Park. We drove to North London where Mick returned with two large, heavy suitcases full of expensive boxed Parker pen sets. We agreed upon a price and returned to Central London under the pretext of collecting the money from the restaurant safe.

At Shaftesbury Avenue we stopped at the traffic lights immediately outside the Princes Theatre. I had an uncomfortable few moments when Geordie Clarkson, a D.I. at Hendon Training School, emerged from the theatre with his good lady.

To add to my discomfort Geordie was sporting a distinctive CID tie and looked every inch what he was. He stood at the lights, looked straight into the car, recognised me and gave a cheery wave. I wished the ground could have opened up and swallowed me.

"That's an 'effing copper" Mick growled and things began to look rather ugly.

"Telling me" I said, "that's the bastard that nicked me the last time round". It wasn't all that clever as a one liner but was all I could think of on the spur of the moment and after all Mick hardly qualified as the brains of Britain. He relaxed slightly although I sensed a strange whiff emanating from the rear seat where Keith was anxiously perched.

At Trafalgar Square I stopped the car, opened my wallet and handed Keith a £5 note urging a reluctant Mick to do likewise. Keith grabbed the money and bolted like a rabbit down a hole.

We drove through Hyde Park, turning left just before reaching the Serpentine into a small service road that led straight into Hyde Park Nick.

"Here, just where do you think you are going" the man growled suspiciously. By now I had my cover story worked out in advance.

"Round the back of course" I said confidently, "the last thing I want to do is be seen with you".

"Why's that?" he demanded belligerently.

"Well, next weekend I'm going to walk out of that restaurant with the takings to bank at the night safe in Knightsbridge and you are going to give me a little tap on the head".

This little spontaneous ploy helped dispel the growing suspicion I sensed Mick was feeling and he sounded quite interested in the little scam I was proposing. "How much involved?"

"Oh, nearly two thousand quid, you take the night bag with the paying in book and you'll find £500 for yourself. Drop the bag and leave the paying in book inside then you and I will never meet again."

Mick thought this over. "But that means you'll get fifteen hundred, why don't we split fifty-fifty".

By this time I was driving through the archway into the yard at the rear of the nick and didn't have to play the game any longer. "Forget it, I'll find someone else" I said, and almost as an afterthought as the car came to a halt added, "oh, by the way, you're nicked."

Mick got six months for his pains and that lovely haul of expensive rolled gold Parker fountain pens finished up in Prisoners Property Office at Chalk Farm, the final resting home for all stolen property where Police failed to trace the owners.

It was much later that I discovered to my disgust, that after six months, all recovered property was auctioned off and the proceeds given to 'The Discharged Prisoners Aid Society.'

Whilst still serving at Cannon Row on paper, I was seconded to Shepherd's Bush Police Station where Det. Supt Bill Marchant was investigating the murder of a prostitute, Hannah Tailford. She was found strangled on the foreshore near Hammersmith Bridge, naked, her underwear stuffed into her mouth. Little was I to know at the time but this became one of a series that became infamous as the first British serial murders. Within two months, the body of a second prostitute, Eileen Lockwood was found on the Thames foreshore at Duke's Meadows, Chiswick, a place that due to forensic samples taken from the dead women, for obvious reasons will forever be known to officers on the ensuing murder hunt as 'gobbler's gulch'.

When a third naked victim, Helen Barthelemy, a strip tease dancer and prostitute was found in Brentford it would be no exaggeration to say the whole of London's' vice trade was thrown into a terrible panic. Little did we know it at the time but this was destined to become the largest police manhunt in the history of the Met.

George Hatherill made a personal appeal to the vice girls to set aside their traditional distrust of Police and to report in confidence any information about kinky clients.

We were assigned to individual toms (prostitutes) as 'protection officers' and literally, by arrangement with them, followed them from their beats around Queensway area as they were picked up by punters and driven to Gobblers Gulch or some other quiet venue. We kept a discreet watch until their business was concluded and the girls dropped off back on their beat to await the next client. It placed a heavy onus upon us as the girls, placed in very real danger, were effectively being used as 'live bait' and was a rather hit and miss affair.

Neither, incidentally did it go down too well with their pimps. I and my aid were assigned to Maggie, who worked out of Queensway and lived in Maida Vale. She was a cheerful soul and worked from about 9pm until midnight or one in the morning when we would take her for coffee, debrief her upon any potentially dangerous clients then drop her off home before going back to Shepherds Bush nick to complete the never ending paperwork that was building up, comparing notes and compiling a list of punters and of course their vehicle details.

One night Maggie was looking more tired than usual and out of politeness I asked if everything was OK. "No it's bloody not; I didn't get a wink of sleep last night thanks to you lot"

"What have we done now?" I asked wearily.

"Well" Maggie explained, "when you dropped me off last night my feller saw you and he's quite paranoiac you're going to fit him up. He's got more than fifteen suits at home and he made me stitch up every bleeding single pocket so you couldn't slip him a packet of weed and do him for possession".

The murder team was fully occupied from information emanating from local toms but when yet another dead body, this time Mary Fleming, was found in Chiswick, public alarm grew, press activity increased and we became more pro-active.

A team of WPCs were attached to the squad and paraded up and down the Queensway chatting up kerbside punters whilst we clocked their car numbers to allow follow up enquiries to be made the following day. One man tried to bodily drag my protégée WPC Purvis into his car, a large pink Vauxhall Cresta. Yes, it did have mock leopard skin seat covers and pink plastic flowers on the rear window shelf, all done in the best possible taste.

The consequences didn't bear thinking about and I bounded across the road and dragged her clear. The man, a large Jamaican came striding purposefully towards me but a swift punch to the solar plexus region sent him sprawling in the road. We both realised what a close shave he'd had. He jumped to his feet shouting out, "White ponce, white ponce, I'm reporting you to the Police" which I thought was rather rich. He loped off to his car and then drove off presumably in the direction of the nearest nick so I made a quick telephone call to the Station Officer at Paddington Green to inform him what happened.

Later that night, I phoned again. "Don't worry about him" the Sgt counselled, "he came in screaming and shouting, I told him to calm down and go away but he wouldn't so I arrested him for causing a disturbance in a Police Station." Poetic justice indeed.

The following February, after a brief spell back at Cannon Row, the sixth victim, Bridie O'Hara was found on a patch of waste land at Acton. By now, questions were being asked in high places as to why the suspect was still at large and it would be true to use that old hackneyed expression 'panic was stalking the streets'. Chief Superintendent John Du Rose, and Detective Inspector Ken Oxford, later to become Chief Constable of Merseyside Police, were brought in to head a fresh team.

As far as I was concerned it was back to long observations at 'Gobbler's Gulch' and altogether I did sixteen weeks night duty on the trot that did no good to my digestion or my marriage.

I had now been promoted Detective Sergeant in charge of a small team, all engaged on surveillance work. The atmosphere in the Murder Office was brilliant, we were working twelve hour shifts, seven days a week but there was an enthusiasm and determination to bring this fellow to book and it literally took over the whole of our lives.

One of my new team was an aid to CID, Taffy Roberts, deep from the Rhonda Valley. One night Taffy came into the office, more white faced and red rimmed than the rest of us. He was clutching a crumpled, tear stained telegram that revealed his fiancée Blodwyn had been killed in a car crash in Wales and was being buried later that week.

Taffy was obviously emotional and to his credit, Ken Oxford immediately granted him compassionate leave. He wanted to drive down to Wales but Ken wouldn't hear of it.

"You're too emotionally upset, Taf, he said kindly, "Leave your car in the Yard, one of the boys will drive you to Paddington Station."

We had an impromptu whip around and Taffy soon had fifty pounds to see him through. The squad had a good team spirit and the next day it was decided we should send a wreath. One of the office lads telephoned the local Constabulary to find out where the funeral was taking place. He put the phone down, a puzzled look on his face.

"What's the problem?" Ken Oxford asked.

"Dunno, guv, that's strange, there hasn't been any fatal accident down there recently, there must be some mistake."

One of the other aids, wanting to be helpful chipped in. His father, a retired PC worked as a Security officer in the same factory as Blodwyn. He phoned his dad and after a short conversation, put the phone down.

Ken Oxford looked up, "Well?" he asked.

The PC wished the ground would swallow him, "Dad tells me that Blodwyn hasn't had an accident, in fact he is looking across at the typing pool and she is busy working".

Any other time we may have seen the funny side but this was different, an outright betrayal of confidence. A quick search of Taffy's Section House room turned up a John Bull Printing outfit and several blank, half composed, telegram forms. Several days later, a tired, red rimmed Taffy returned to duty and we were all sworn to secrecy upon pain of immediate return to uniform duties.

"How did the funeral go Taffy?" asked Ken Oxford, exuding concern.

"Very well, thank you guv, it was lovely, lovely" replied Taffy in his lilting, Welsh accent.

"You're obviously still very upset," Oxford said, "the Chief wants to see you tomorrow but I think you should stay in the office tonight,"

"The Chief? What for guv?" Taffy asked.

Oxford didn't blink, "I think you'll be going on a board" he replied.

That night I watched Taffy with a mixture of admiration and more than a little irritation. He gazed sadly, forlornly into space and now and then, a slight trickle would course down his cheek to be quickly brushed away. The stiff upper lip, it was a masterly performance, worthy of an experienced trouper.

Next morning Taffy kept his appointment with his Detective Chief Superintendent. It was short, sweet and very much to the point. His guv'nor handed him two forms, "Take your pick, one's a discipline form, the others a resignation form, it's up to you."

It really wasn't much of a choice; Taffy took the only possible option and resigned on the spot. That was a formula I saw repeated several times throughout my service, no fuss, no messing about, no dirty linen washed in public, just the end of a career.

One of our more delicate tasks was to check out owners of cars whose index numbers had been recorded the previous night accosting toms working the Bayswater Road and Queensway areas. For obvious reasons a high degree of circumspection was needed when the checks were being conducted in a man's house and everybody did their best to avoid causing embarrassment to the subject. Sometimes however, they did nothing to help themselves. One particularly obnoxious individual brushed aside my request to speak to him privately.

"If you have anything to say to me you can do it in front of my wife, we have no secrets." Oh dear, that was definitely not the right response when confronted by detectives under intense pressure to trace and arrest a sadistic serial killer.

"In that case sir, perhaps we could begin by asking why a man answering your description and driving your car accosted a prostitute in Queensway last Saturday night and tried to forcibly drag her into your car." The questioning would then continue until such time as we satisfied ourselves the man was not connected to previous attacks and it was safe to eliminate him from the enquiry.

Did we catch the murderer? Well, let's put it this way. Our team traced minute silicone paint particles found on two of the murder victims' bodies to a paint spray shop on the Heron Trading Estate, Acton, where forensics were able to prove quite conclusively that four of the bodies had been stored before being dumped on the Thames bank side. A night security officer, with keys to the paint-shop, incidentally married to an ex prostitute, was brought in for questioning and released. His alibi for the nights in question was checked out and found to be false.

Enquiries showed he drove a small white van similar to one seen near the scene of two of the murders and he had been known to express his hatred of prostitutes in his local pub. He had the means and motive and could be proved to have lied about his movements at least on one of the nights of the murders. Big John sent him a message to report back to Shepherds Bush Nick that night; he never made it!

His suicide note stated he couldn't stand the pressure any more. The suspicions appeared to be born out when, following his death, the murders ceased and the squad disbanded for the last time. But 'Four day Johnny' a nickname given for the speed with which Du Rose usually solved his murders, could never claim the 'clear up' he undoubtedly felt he deserved.

Much later in February, 1972, Owen Summers, reporter on *The Sun* newspaper put forward the theory the killer could have been a disgruntled Police Officer who was thrown out of the Force having been convicted in 1962 of five cases of office breaking and sentenced to twelve months imprisonment. Prior to this, there were several strange incidents in which this individual featured that space precludes me from listing which certainly tended to support this theory. Was this the twisted mind of a psychopath deliberately playing a sick game with his ex colleagues, the ones who had disgraced him, had him thrown out of the job and imprisoned?

The man was interviewed during the course of the enquiry by John Du Rose and Detective Superintendent Bill Baldock. The latter held a low opinion of Big John's expertise, considered he should never have been called in on the enquiry and was more of a hindrance than help.

In the suspect's written statement he openly admitted the breakings for which he was convicted were by way of showing up his ex colleagues. Could these murders have been a continuation?

Despite Bill Baldock's best efforts, he was never able to place the suspect at the scenes of the murders, nor could he be connected with the dead women. In his closing report

Baldock concluded, "This man cannot be eliminated from the investigation and remains a strong suspect. The circumstances surrounding his mental history, knowledge of the area and background point to his being the killer".

This will remain one of crime's unanswered mysteries. Who was the serial killer? Was it John X or was it the ex policeman? Of course, without a trial there must always be room for doubt but it is a chilling thought the guilty man may still be alive although one would surmise, too old to commit any more heinous crimes.

I felt the killings could be the work of more than one man although I discounted some rather farfetched theories they were committed by pornographers making so called 'snuff movies'. Even Freddie Mills the boxer was put up as a possible suspect particularly when he was later found shot under suspicious circumstances.

Some wag on the Murder Squad reckoned it had to be one of the team who, after each murder was wound down and the 'special occasion' status removed, went out to do another to benefit from all the overtime we were clocking up. As for me, finding my social life severely curtailed for six months and the overtime payments flooding in I put the proceeds towards having a garage built upon my house in South Norwood.

D.I. Ken Oxford, John Du Rose's second in command, was undoubtedly an efficient officer but not a man I found I could warm to. He had a most disconcerting habit of studying Police Orders every Tuesday and Friday to see how many senior ranks had died, how many had retired or died or somehow fallen by the wayside and these were struck off a list he kept pointing to when his next promotion should fall due. He was an ambitious man and eventually went on to become Chief Constable of Merseyside.

There was a lovely story about Ken Oxford and James Anderton a.k.a. 'Holy Jim', the rather eccentric Chief Constable of Manchester Police both who allegedly harboured ambitions of eventual promotion to Commissioner of the Met.

'Holy Jim' found God big time and used his position as the Lord's prophet to conduct a war upon homosexuals, pornographers and villains in general. He had little time for defence lawyers he once graphically described as belonging to the 'Society for the prevention of conviction of the guilty' so in the eyes of myself and many like thinking colleagues, I guess he couldn't have been all bad.

Well, Ken Oxford and Holy Jim, both men with strong egos and highly developed beliefs in their own importance maintained a largely good natured rivalry. Ken was rather put out when, at a time when mobile telephones were still in their infancy, he was asked to phone Holy Jim on his new fangled toy. Anderton took the call in his car, gloating upon this technological prowess over his rival. Not to be outdone, Ken also invested in a mobile and one day both men were on different motorways headed for a conference at the Home Office in London when Holy Jim telephoned to Ken. Unperturbed, his driver answered the call, "Sorry Guv. but Mr Oxford can't take your call; he is busy on the other line!"

Chapter Eight

The more laws the less justice
Marcus Tullius Cicero 106 BC–43 BC

When it became clear the murders had run their course, the Squad was stood down and I found myself back at Mitcham; back to the more hum drum routine tasks of Divisional crime solving.

Whilst at Mitcham I had the first of many meetings with Detective Chief Superintendent Peter Vibart QPM. I would like to say they were all pleasant but that would be taking it a step too far. He was a giant of a man in every way, a man I look back upon with respect and latterly with affection. (that was only to come very much later after he retired.) Peter was a legend, he and his side-kick Tommy Butler served together on the Flying Squad or Sweeney as it was widely known. Peter, or PV as we called him, was a hard task-master, after all he graduated from a tough school. A deep scar ran down the contour of his jaw, a legacy of the days the Flying Squad tackled the vicious razor gangs that terrorised English horse racing tracks immediately after the war.

I shudder to think of the perpetrator's fate when he was nicked, the Squad didn't pussy foot around in those days.

Peter Vibart spent many years on the Squad and came to public notice at the time Gunter Podola was arrested for shooting Ray Purdy, an unarmed Detective Sergeant at Chelsea. Podola was eventually traced to an apartment block in Westminster when Peter and other Squad officers rushed the door, knowing an armed and dangerous man was inside. Unfortunately, some may think, the man was on the receiving end as the door crashed from its hinges and he sustained injuries to his face. This of course led to the outcry of Police brutality by the usual bunch of liberal do-gooders, many of who were working to their own agenda.

Mitcham was a happy nick, uniform and CID working harmoniously together as tended to be the case in most Stations. Every morning we had to telephone a sitrep (situation report) to Vernon, P.V's Divisional Clerk, containing details of every crime reported and every arrest affected over the past twenty four hours. Every legal aid report submitted would be subject to Peter's closest scrutiny. He didn't miss a trick.

As sure as God made little apples, P.V. would be on phone, "Vibart here matey, you have just submitted a legal aid report, page six, paragraph four, why did you say (do) that?"

Long experience had taught a copy of any submissions to Putney should be kept at hand for this precise eventuality and we always had a convincing explanation to hand. Not that it mattered one jot to P.V. "Well sir, ….."

"Don't you argue with me matey," the unmistakable stentorian voice would bellow down the phone, "come to Putney".

By the time we arrived at Putney and reported to the long suffering Vernon, the old man would invariably have forgotten he'd sent for us and Vernon would counsel a quick return to the patch before he bollocked us for wasting valuable time when we should be going out feeling thieves' collars.

I was living at South Norwood at the time, a pleasant enough cross country drive to Mitcham and actually got to spend some time with my young family which was something of a culture shock to us all. We worked the usual CID hours, six days a week, alternate early's from 9am to 6pm and lates, 9am to 10pm so the few early turns at home were a welcome respite. It is no small wonder that with the exception of Members of Parliament, statistically CID Officers had the highest divorce and separation rates of any occupation. I still have a vivid recollection one particular Sunday lunchtime, sitting around the family table and my youngest son Richard putting up his hand and saying "Excuse me Sir". Oh dear, was I doing something wrong? Rich has long since forgiven me for those parental crimes of omission.

I would like to think that since my retirement from the job I became a better father than the remote figure I had obviously been in those early days when I regret to say, I was married first and foremost to my work.

One afternoon, a dead body was found in a car on a notorious housing estate we dubbed 'Redskin village'. It earned that soubriquet from the columns of black smoke sometimes observed emanating from the outer casings being burned off stolen copper cable.

The man had been shot through the legs by a shot-gun and bled to death. We soon established the shooting took place in a villain's club in Tooting the adjacent Division and the thoughtless victim had driven back to Mitcham (despite his injuries) before popping his clogs. As luck would have it, it was on one of my designated early turns and I was looking forward to an early night for a change. Bill Monteith, the Detective Chief Superintendent at Tooting was contacted and satisfied there was nothing further we could do, D.C. Jim Parker and I booked off for the day. By the time I got home, the crap had hit the fan with a vengeance. The Station Sergeant at Mitcham was on the phone, "P.V. has gone ballistic, he wants you to report back to him at the nick, he's forming a squad."

"Tell him I'm not at home".

Even before the phone was put down, I knew that wouldn't satisfy P.V. and I was in the office the following morning at nine sharp just in time to receive my early morning greeting. "Come to Putney!" The familiar voice bellowed. Jim Parker my DC looked worried as well he might: Peter Vibart didn't take prisoners and this could be the end of a promising career.

Vernon ushered us into the great man's office. He was in absolutely magnificent form. For a full five minutes he harangued us nonstop, his great hands banging down upon his desk with such force the ink well jumped up and down. I could imagine the effect upon a guilty man under interrogation; it was nothing short of awe inspiring. I waited for the pause that experience had taught would shortly come and could have written Peter's next line, unfortunately directed at poor Jim Parker.

"Well, what have you to say?" Jim made the inevitable mistake of trying calm, logical reason; I could have told him he was wasting his time.

"I hope you don't think sir we would have booked off duty…" the rest of the sentence was drowned by a stentorian roar.

"Think, think, don't you try to tell me what I think matey, I know exactly what I think".

The haranguing continued unabated, perhaps even more clamorous than before for several more long drawn out minutes. Even Peter could not maintain that pace indefinitely and he paused for breath, now it was my turn for the high jump.

"Well, am I right, what have you got to say for yourself?" I put on a look of dumb insolence and played my trump card. "If you say so Sir".

Peter looked to be upon the verge of an apoplectic fit, he stared at me incredulously; this was the time I should have either agreed with him or argued the point, either way I would have been on a loser.

"If I say so sir" he mimicked, "If I say so, what do you mean, if I say so? Be direct man, be direct!" I kept my eyes fixed on an imaginary spot on the wall, "If you say so sir". The insolence in my tone said it all, other words were superfluous. Into those five small words Peter read the unspoken message loud and clear, "I don't agree with a word you're saying but you are the guv'nor so I'll just shut up and let you get on with it". Peter rose from his desk trembling with rage, "If you say so, if you say so, get out of this bloody office, I don't want to see your face in here again." Jim was rather subdued but despite myself I felt a faint air of triumph: I had equalled the Master at his own game and was sure this wouldn't be lost upon him. Later in my career I served with many senior officers, some for whom I had the utmost respect; contempt or indifference for some of the others. Peter Vibart fell squarely into the first category. Any lesser man would have disciplined me or had me returned to uniform but there was nothing petty or mean about Peter.

It is in the very nature of the job that inevitably, threats will be made upon your life by people you have put away. Most of these are just so much hot talk; I am a firm believer in the old maxim that threatened men live the longest. Only once were threats directed against my family and I took that seriously.

I nicked a small time dealer who had acquired something of a reputation as a hard man, for pushing cannabis to the locals. He appeared before the local Magistrates, was fined and given a suspended sentence. After my return to the nick, the Court warrant officer phoned me. “It’s probably nothing, but your prisoner has been rather mouthy, putting it around that he’s out to get you and if he doesn’t get you, he’ll get your family.”

Whether the man had the means or the bottle was beside the point, this was a dangerous precedent that couldn’t be overlooked. There was a small amount of property to be returned and signed for so that same afternoon I drove to his address in Tooting where quite fortuitously he was lying in the roadway, doing some repairs under his car. I tapped him gently on the sole of his foot with the toe of my shoe. He saw me and shot into his house bounding up the staircase two steps at a time. Coppers re-act almost instinctively when a suspect decides to run away. I gave chase, caught him by the legs at the top of the stairs and invited him gently to accompany me back down to the street level where he resisted.

A few choice words and punches were exchanged on both sides by which time a crowd had gathered so I really had no choice other than to nick him for assault on police. Just in time to get him charged and back again before the Magistrates’ Court closed shop for the day. Purists may argue that that rather unseemly brawl hardly amounted to an assault upon the police in the execution of their duty and who knows they may well be right? But the purists weren’t there. Whatever, he obviously saw the error of his ways, pleaded ‘guilty, the three months suspended sentence was activated and following his release he made sure he kept well away from Mitcham’s patch.

There were quite a few open spaces at Mitcham, including the Common and it was there I dealt with my one and only case of horse rustling. A businessman hacked into the Police teleprinter system and sent an’ all stations’ message reporting the theft of his daughter’s pony from stables in Banstead. A detailed description of the beast followed that obviously meant a lot to our equine loving friends.

After a quiet chuckle and some wild and quite fanciful speculation as to how our betters at the Yard would handle this breach of security we adjourned to the Burn Bullock pub for a quick beer before going home.

Our diaries would faithfully record such visits as follows, "I entered the Burn Bullock licensed premises and purchased refreshment for informant while seeking information re local thieves." This was one of the so called 'perks' of the Department as was the 'single refresher' food allowance for working over nine and a half hours and being unable to get home for a meal. Bearing in mind our average working week was around seventy hours and consolidated detective duty allowance based upon four hours overtime per week the Commissioner wasn't on such a bad number.

Eventually this came to an end when some interfering busybody from the Police Federation successfully negotiated a deal whereby CID officers were compensated for their overtime in the same way as the uniform branch. That was another small but significant nail in the coffin of crime detection. Whereas until then, CID officers had been expected and willingly worked overtime to do the job, often spending all mornings in court then the rest of the day and evening visiting scenes of crime, taking statements and occasionally even nicking somebody later that night, all of a sudden supervising officers were instructed to ensure CID officers worked an eight hour shift. Detectives were ordered to book off duty and hand the case to another officer who quite frankly was not au fait with enquiries taken to date and at any rate were busy working on their own enquiries.

The continuity so necessary in protracted enquiries was lost and with it the minute, often vital details or hunches the original officer had formulated were lost forever. Happily, that ridiculous state of affairs did not come into being during my time in the Department. When a murder or other protracted enquiry required more than the usual 'voluntary overtime' the Commissioner could designate the enquiry a 'Special Occasion' which meant CID officers were paid for their overtime in the same way as our uniform colleagues.

On my way back from Court one morning with George McCall and two aids, I spotted a pony two hundred yards away across Mitcham Common with what looked at that distance suspiciously like two 'pikies'. In the days before political correctness this was the name given locally to travellers or gypsies some of whom had been housed in 'Redskin village' the nearby council estate. I stopped the car and instructed the two aids to jump out. "There they are, nick them."

The aids stared at each other in amazement, "Nick who skip?" one asked not unreasonably.

"Don't you read the messages?" That's the stolen pony circulated over the teleprinter last night, do I have to do everything myself?"

George and I had a little chuckle as we sped off leaving the two aids in the middle of the common whilst we headed for the Queens Head pub for a liquid lunch. An hour later, we strolled back leisurely to the nick and there in the charge room were the aids, a pony and two prisoners.

"God you've done it this time Dave" George muttered, "this has all the makings of an unlawful arrest".

Well it so happens it wasn't, believe it or not it was a good result all round. The men were arrested, coughed and were charged. The aids were delighted with me for being handed a red ink entry for their diaries and one grateful gentleman and his daughter were over the moon at being reunited with their prize pony. I chuckled as I imagined P.V. reading the sitrep next morning 'two arrests for rustling'.

The businessman was a wholesale butcher who was so delighted at the assiduity, speed and efficiency with which we recovered his daughter's pony, the following day he arrived at the nick with four quarter sides of prime pig. I did my best to explain to him the rule upon accepting gratuities but he was quite persistent and well, what could one do but accept graciously? It would have been churlish to do otherwise.

Of course it wasn't all fun and games. Joey Pyle, a well known South London gangster decided to put the squeeze on our local casino. A team of his heavies descended every Saturday night and demanded £500 weekly protection. I managed to persuade the owners not to succumb to pressure but to face them out.

We mounted a surveillance operation and caught the team bang to rights with marked notes in their possession. I will never forget grabbing one of the team, Albert Cook by the arm and shouting out the shortened version of the official caution, "You're nicked."

He was six foot three plus and as strong as an ox. He raised his arm, bodily lifting me off my feet that were left dangling six inches off the ground. Not to be found at a loss for words I riposted with great eloquence and as much dignity as I could muster in all the circumstances, "You're still bloody nicked."

Nobody was more surprised or indeed relieved than I when, to lapse into popular vernacular, he came quietly. I promised this would not become a catalogue of glorious successes and there is a point to this story. Pyle, the gang leader, was well away from the scene of the action and unfortunately his right hand man, a tasty villain who had made threats and demands on previous Saturdays, for some reason was absent from parade when the job came off.

The following morning I paid an early morning visit and nicked him still in his bed at West Croydon. On the way back to Mitcham nick he made some rather incriminating observations that guaranteed his later appearance at the Old Bailey charged with conspiracy to demand money with menaces. From the time of the arrests until their appearance at the Old Bailey, we managed to keep the team in custody and as threats were made against the Casino staff witnesses, we all finished up housing the various witnesses at our home addresses. Fortunately things like witness protection programmes and safe houses have improved dramatically since those far off days.

Now to get to the point, there are many stories told about police corruption and as later events will show, some of these were fully justified. However, the majority of such allegations were not and this was my first real experience of a crooked approach.

London had more than its fair share of organised crime and there were one or two firms of solicitors who specialised in criminal defence work. Some were decidedly dodgy and employed 'legal executives', mostly ex coppers who had either been nicked or pushed out of the job for dodgy or corrupt practices. Some of these men used their experience of police procedure to pervert justice by rigging up false alibis and arranging for witnesses and jurors to be threatened and intimidated. We felt nothing but contempt for these toads who, as far as I was concerned, were the lowest of the low and traitors to a job and cause they had once sworn to uphold. One lucrative source of income for these rogues was to convince prisoners facing trial they had bribed Police officers to go easy, drop previous convictions or to change their evidence. In some instances no doubt they succeeded, but in the vast majority of cases this was pure fabrication and they were lining their own pockets. Having paid up like chumps, disappointed clients were hardly in a position where they could complain and lay themselves open to charges of bribery or attempting to pervert the course of justice. More than one solicitors' clerk made a lucrative living from this scam and of course it all helped to bring the job into disrepute.

In this particular casino case an ex copper, a slimy individual employed as a 'legal assistant', approached me. When certain we were on our own he came straight out with his proposition. "There's two grand in it if my man walks free". In those days two thousand pounds to a young detective with a mortgage and growing kids was a lot of money but I told him in no uncertain terms where he should go and did my utmost to ensure the prisoner's conviction.

At the Old Bailey the man and his fellow defendants were represented by an up and coming counsel named Ivan Lawrence, later knighted, who became a prominent member of the Conservative Party and their spokesman upon law and order. Ivan Lawrence was a brilliant advocate who made his reputation defending high profile murder cases such as the Kray twins, Denis Nilsen, and the Brinks Mat gold bullion case.

I am sure he will have the good grace to forgive me for saying much of his success was due to attacking the credibility of Police witnesses. No doubt he would counter he had good reason. I was to cross swords with him several times during my career. The highest tribute I could pay to him would be to say that if I was guilty of a crime there would be nobody I would rather have to defend myself than him.

Lawrence made great play of the fact his client was not present at the time of the original arrests and as best I recall left the jury in no doubt the incriminating statements attributed to his client were good old fashioned verbals, the product of my fertile imagination. I was dismayed when the jury acquitted the man and had difficulty controlling my temper when the toady solicitor's clerk approached me at the rear of the Court. "Missed out there, didn't we?" he crowed.

It was but small consolation knowing that somebody had not only had to pay expensive legal charges but also in all probability forked out two thousand pounds to the legal assistant. I hoped one day he would come a cropper. Unfortunately, as far as I am aware he never did.

As for Albert Cook and the others, they received hefty prison sentences that no doubt left the jury satisfied they had managed to satisfy all parties.

While in prison, Albert Cook's wife was purportedly having an affair with another ex con. This was considered to be a heinous act, a definite no go and it is not difficult to understand why. On the day of his release Albert put a knife through the man's heart and was sentenced to life for manslaughter. Knowing how easily that could have been me, I confess a grudging respect for Mr Cook who like myself, at least played the game according to the rules under which he had been brought up. To my mind he was much more a man than the toad who defended him.

Joey Pyle was one of the most feared members of the London criminal underworld. While not as well known as other notorious gangsters, Pyle was a close associate of both the Krays and the Richardsons yet somehow he always managed to escape imprisonment despite being arrested on more than fifty occasions for crimes ranging from murder, to robbery to drug smuggling. He was eventually sentenced to fourteen years imprisonment for drugs offences following a massive Police 'sting' operation.

At an early age his father took him on one side and supposedly said, "Son, you'd better make up your mind, you're either going to become a thief or a boxer, which is it to be?" He is reputed to have chosen the former saying, "Crime doesn't pay but the hours are better".

Whilst serving at Mitcham, Detective Inspector John Swain and his team from the Squad nicked John McVicar, a notorious criminal before he reformed, for armed robbery. At a search of the scene later, I found a home made mask, a woollen balaclava worn by one of the villains. John Swain always said he was glad it was me, a fresh faced youngster from Division who found it and none of his team from the Squad who would doubtless have been accused of planting it. At the Old Bailey I produced the mask in evidence. Judge Maude, a funny old coot, directed I put it on. To my dismay I felt a proper Charlie when finding the eye-holes in the mask came level with the centre of my forehead. This certainly brought a wry smile from John McVicar, sitting in the Dock admiring the performance. At the trial, I managed to save the day by tugging the mask down until my eyes were level with the holes, which was achieved not without some difficulty. The judge looked down from the Bench, "And quite becoming you look as well, officer". Coming as it did from Judge Maude that took some living down.

Not long after, we had another team of robbers on the patch, fingering a supervisor who was dropping off wages at various building sites every Friday night. One of the aids spotted the team and clocked the car number which a later check was found to be a ringer on a stolen motor.

The following week the building supervisor had even more company than before. There is always a fine line to be drawn between securing enough evidence to obtain a conviction and allowing an innocent person to be injured by letting a robbery proceed. It is policy always to risk losing a conviction than wait for the crime to be committed and an innocent person hurt or even worse. This was one of those occasions where it was an easy decision for me to take. The team had been clocked the previous week in a stolen car following the supervisor from building site to building site and were back on the plot again this week in the same car. We nicked them and they were taken to Mitcham where a search of the stolen car revealed pick-axe handles and a squeezee bottle containing ammonia.

In the charge room one face seemed vaguely familiar and it transpired he was one of the team I had arrested for the Woolworth's job at Croydon, several years earlier. He certainly remembered me immediately! Another trip to the Central Criminal Court and this time, much to my surprise the whole team pleaded 'guilty' and each received eight years. They knew exactly what they were up to, as did we.

One quick word on Identification Parades that in my book were often pretty hit and miss affairs, a subject to which I shall refer again later. Uniform officers nicked two tow-rags from Streatham who, at a time when copper was at a premium, broke into the local ironmongers.

After gaining entry, they retired to the all night café next door for tea before getting down to work. They spent the whole night at the scene bagging up every single piece of copper they could lay their hands on and then, before departing, obviously exhausted after a hard nights graft, returned to the café for a final cup of tea. As they loaded the bags into their van the local radio car crew making their way back to the nick to book off, disturbed them. Both men jumped into some back gardens and made off, followed by the slightly over-weight and physically under fit Police car crew. One of them got away, the other, jumped over a dozen or more fences and found himself in the Police Station yard where his collar was promptly felt. He didn't really have much choice and the next morning put his hands up, giving me a detailed statement under caution. The Streatham collator was able to supply the name of his usual companion in crime and I promptly arrested him and arranged for an Identity parade to be held at Wallington court where the other thief was due to appear.

With a marked degree of reluctance, the owner of the all night café, a mincing effeminate, was gently persuaded to attend court to see if he could recognise the suspect. The Court Inspector, who went to great lengths to see there was no chance of collaboration by witnesses, conducted the parade faultlessly. The witnesses were strictly separated from the suspect prior to the time of being led onto the parade.

My prize witness minced slowly down the line up, drawn from the local Council offices and to my surprise kept his eyes fixed firmly on the ground making no attempt whatever to scrutinise their faces. I was furious and under my breath vowed all sorts of dire consequences upon the man. Having walked up and down the line front and rear, he resumed his stroll, stopping immediately opposite the suspect. I took back all my ungodly thoughts until suddenly, the witness appeared to lose all interest in the suspect and concentrated all his attention on the man standing next to him. What a performance! He beckoned dramatically to the Court Inspector. I groaned inwardly. "Oh gawd, he's only going to finger the wrong man, I'll murder the little bugger".

With a flourish he then pointed unequivocally at my suspect. Later, when I came to take his statement I confronted him with his actions that seemed incomprehensible and would undoubtedly have weakened the evidential value of the identification. "Just what the hell do you think you were playing at?" I asked, quite reasonably under the circumstances.

"Well Mr Woodland, I know they always take the ties and bootlaces from prisoners to prevent them from topping themselves so I thought I'd check to see if I could spot anybody without laces in their shoes."

"But what about all that pantomime with the wrong man – were you taking the piss?"

"Oh, Mr Woodland, you'll never guess, the joke of the century, I looked up and down the line, saw the man who had been in the café and guess who was standing next to him? An old flame! I thought to myself, 'I'll make you sweat you bugger', what a carry on, didn't I do well?" On such firm foundations is our criminal justice system based.

One relatively minor case of housebreaking was to give me more satisfaction than many serious crimes from murders downwards that were later to come my way. It was just another routine job; to all outward appearances a burglar had climbed through an open ground floor window at the back of a modern maisonette and stolen an elderly lady's life savings which she kept in a biscuit tin under her mattress. Just shows, even in those days' people didn't trust the banks!

Routine that is until a closer examination of the flower beds outside the window showed no signs of footprints and there was no disturbance of dust on the sill. "How many people have keys dear?" I asked the distraught old lady.

"Only me and my daughter love, the house is new, I only moved in six months ago." The daughter was interrogated at some length and I don't mind admitting I gave her a hard time but somehow it just didn't ring true, it seemed most unlikely she would have stolen from her own mother and she naturally resented being treated as a suspect and let me know as much in no uncertain terms.

From closer examination of the two front door keys I noticed one didn't have a serial number and had obviously been cut from an original. It was a long shot but I decided to call on the house builders at Wimbledon and gave a lift to George McCall an experienced Aid to CID who was dealing with a breaking at a nearby Petrol Service Station. As George chatted to the garage proprietor, I waited outside, casually looking at the cars for sale on the forecourt. A chap in a builder's van was taking a close interest in one particular motor and by sheer coincidence his van had the builder's name on the outside where I was due to go.

Ten minutes later, I was in the builder's office, explaining my mission to the builder; namely to find which of his employees had fixed the door at Wandle Road six months previously.

"Oh, you're barking up the wrong tree there" he replied, "he has worked for me for over ten years and is as honest as they come!"

I checked the man out at CRO which confirmed he had no form. "Sorry to have taken up your time," I said, "but I'll just have a quick chat with him now I'm here." It turned out to be the fellow from the garage forecourt who was quite at ease and naturally denied being implicated in the theft. I searched his car, purely as a precaution and he apologised for the state of it. It was a long shot but I tried it on. "I suppose you'll be thinking of trading it in for something newer"

"No, I'm skint" he replied. That was it; the man had deliberately lied to me, why? "You're nicked sunshine" I said in best training school manner, grasping his arm and placing him in the back of the Police car. At the nick, I had some difficulty explaining to the Station Officer the grounds upon which I had deprived the man of his liberty but he was taken upstairs to the CID office where I questioned him for several hours, going over the facts, time and again but making little real progress save for a firm and growing conviction I had my man. Let me add to that remark: after a while in the job one's intuition sharpens and you instinctively know when somebody is lying (although that of course is gut feeling, not evidence and one is by no means infallible). This belief was reinforced by a call to the car forecourt where the dealer confirmed the man had asked for a discount for cash. Upon one thing the suspect was quite adamant; under no circumstances did he have any further keys cut. Confronted with both keys, the duplicate key quite obviously a blank, he made his first tactical error.

"Wait a minute, that's right, I remember now, there was only one key with the lock when I bought it and the lady specifically asked for two so I had one cut."

That was the only tenuous lead I had to justify his continued detention but the bit was now firmly between my teeth. A phone call to the builder gave me the name of his builder's merchant in Balham. By now the Station Officer and Duty Officer from Wimbledon were becoming rather agitated, the man had been in custody for over six hours with little realistic chance of being charged. I went to the builders' merchant in Balham where I put the facts before a sympathetic proprietor and luckily struck gold.

"I only supplied one key?" he said indignantly, "let me tell you Sgt I am a master locksmith, whenever I supply a new lock or key cylinder I always make a point of taking it out of its box, unwrapping the paper and showing the customer the cylinder and keys. There is no way I would ever supply only one key, I'd stake my reputation; which builder did you say the man worked for? " He scurried into his back room emerging some five minutes later, a triumphant look upon his face.

"Six months ago did you say? Here you are, just as I thought! I remember now the man definitely asked me for another key"

The locksmith produced an order from the builders, signed by my suspect that clearly showed the cost for one additional key requested; three in all. Faced with such clear and convincing proof, the suspect eventually made a written statement under caution and revealed where he had hidden the proceeds in a cupboard under the stairs. A quick visit to his home and the missing biscuit box and contents were safely in my possession. To find some corroborating proof like that is very satisfying as being the most convincing factor at a later date to disprove any allegations of impropriety or easily denied verbal admissions.

It was much later that evening when I returned to the loser's house where she was still in a state of shock being comforted by her daughter who, quite understandably was hardly overjoyed at seeing me again. "How much did you say you lost?" I asked.

"Oh, I don't know exactly dear, about £500 altogether".

I produced the biscuit tin, "Does £777 sound better?" I asked.

What a remarkable transformation; this was her life's savings, the legacy she hoped to pass to her grandchildren, stolen by a heartless thief. From sheer abject misery she was suddenly transformed as though a heavy burden was removed from her shoulders, laughing through her tears.

I can say in all modesty, during an extremely active Police career, I arrested more people than I care to remember for every kind of crime and I have recovered stolen property amounting to hundreds of thousands of pounds but nothing ever came close to giving me the same feeling of satisfaction as seeing the smile upon that old lady's face. If I had ever doubted the reasons I became a copper, that one job revealed it all. Inspiration? Luck? Perseverance? What did it matter; it's the outcome that counted.

The next morning, prior to taking my prisoner to Court the victim's daughter called at the nick and asked for me. "Oh well, now for the complaint" I thought as I went down the stairs to see her.

"Mr Woodland, you gave me a hard time yesterday, accusing me of nicking my mum's savings". What could I say? It was perfectly true; you can't make omelettes without breaking the occasional egg. If a complaint was the outcome, I could live with that.

"Well I'd just like to say we're proud of what you did, it's good to know you would take so much trouble over an old lady, I've talked it over with my hubby and we want you to accept this." She reached down into her shopping bag and produced a bottle of Johnny Walker whisky. As I have made perfectly clear earlier, regulations make acceptance of gratuities a disciplinary offence. On the point of refusing I recalled the words of one of my old war time heroes, Wing Commander Douglas Bader, "Rules are made for the blind obedience of fools and for guidance of the wise."

One other amusing incident arose when Winston, a young Jamaican, was arrested for theft from an off licence in Mitcham. A strong athletic chap, he jumped the counter and helped himself to the contents of the till. As he bounded out of the shop he ran straight into the path of a patrolling area car which was how I came to meet him one morning at Mitcham nick. Winston, one of nature's characters was brought up in the slums of Kingston, Jamaica. Having fallen foul of the local constabulary on too many occasions, like many of his compatriots he decided to chance his arm in England where 'the filth' were decidedly gentler.

In his rich Jamaican accent he smiled and addressed me, "You know mon, when I get to de Court I'm going to tell de Judge you treat me real bad and beat me about."

"Winston, you're a bloody liar".

"I know dat man, but what's de point of being a thief if you ain't a liar too?" Good point! Next day in Court, Winston, doubtless on legal aid, was represented by Counsel.

"Your worships, I ask for a remand and that my client is remanded on bail pending his next appearance"

The Bench Chairman looked at me expectantly, "Any objections to this man being granted bail officer?"

"Yes Sir, strong objections, this man has been arrested and convicted on five occasions in this country and on the last three deported to Jamaica at the end of his sentence. I have not the slightest doubt that should you bail him now he will reverse the procedure." Even the Chairman and prisoner joined in the laughter that swept the Court and poor old Winston remained in custody until such time as his next sentence was served after which he again returned to his native land at the taxpayers' expense.

One day I sat in the office catching up with the ever increasing paper work when the phone rang. "Vibart here, drop whatever you are doing, get yourself over to Surbiton and sort out all those breakings matey."

Although up to my neck in unfinished business at Mitcham, there was certainly no point in arguing the point with PV and within half an hour I was in the CID office at Surbiton reading up the Crime Book. I called in the aids. "O.K. do you have any ideas who is working the patch?"

One of them popped up like a chump, "We've got a good idea who it is skip, but we don't have any evidence. There's a little team of layabouts that seem to spend most of the day in the Charrington Bowl in Tolworth."

"Have you had them in?"

"No skip"

"Then book the bloody car out". Ten minutes later we parked up at the Charrington Bowl and the aids pointed out four yobbos sitting at the bar. That seemed to be as good a place to start as any and I strode up to them. "O.K. you four, you're nicked on suspicion of burglary and I'm taking you to Surbiton Police Station".

CRO searches showed they all had form, some juvenile findings of guilt and a few convictions for petty theft, taking and driving away and similar offences. One of the four was obviously worried and I concentrated my attention upon him. It took an hour during which I impressed the inevitability of conviction on them when forensics had examined their clothing and footwear, when fingerprints were taken and compared with marks found at the scenes and their houses searched for stolen property. He made a full written statement under caution implicating his fellow prisoners in the series of housebreakings.

That confession was the key I needed to break down the others' initial denials and it was very gratifying that evening to finish up with all four charged with numerous offences of housebreaking to which they eventually pleaded 'guilty' and were convicted.

Relaxing later with the aids in a local pub, I found that the previous weekend there had been a serious wounding at the Charrington Bowl and reading the witnesses' statements later saw a description of the main offender matched that of a local Mitcham hoodlum with form for gbh. I trotted back to Mitcham and picked up George McCall. We swooped into Redskin Village, arrested the violent suspect who was taken to Surbiton, and charged him with causing an affray and gbh, charges upon which he was subsequently convicted. All in all not a bad days work.

The following morning found me back at my desk in Mitcham at 9am when the phone rang. "Vibart here, what are you doing at Mitcham matey, I thought I told you to go to Surbiton and get stuck into those breakings".

I leaned back in my chair, a smug, self satisfied look upon my face.

"We've sorted all that out as you asked sir, it's all on the morning sitrep; four arrests for several breakings, and oh, by the way an arrest and clear up for an affray and unrelated gbh. for good measure."

That was the only time I believe I ever managed to get the last word in with PV, after a few muttered grunts the phone went dead and I got back to my bloody paper work.

One other small incident happened in the aftermath of my little excursion to Surbiton. Returning a few days later to the Charrington Bowl, Tolworth to take statements, I saw a man in the car park whose face I vaguely remembered. He came striding across towards me and held out his hand, "Hello mate, remember me? We had dinner at Villa de Cesari some time back, remember now?

Of course, then I remembered, the man was one of the pornographers present on the occasion a vain approach was made for me to join the Dirty Book Squad. Shortly after, a man I recognised immediately came striding up, Detective Inspector Alton, a member of the later disgraced squad. "What the fuck are you doing here?" he demanded, "piss off".

It was quite clear to me the reason that Alton was there and I wasn't going to be spoken to by a man I was sure was corrupt and had in all probability arranged to meet the pornographer to take a bribe.

"I don't need to tell you what I'm here for Mr Alton, I'm doing my job, more to the point you should ask yourself just what you are up to".

Alton was one of a handful of crooked police officers convicted of corrupt practices when the balloon eventually went up upon the Dirty Book Squad's activities and sent to prison with his fellow officers.

Mitcham proved a good training ground and when the time came for me to go on a promotion board for 1st Class Detective

Sgt., Peter Vibart showed his true colours. Despite the cheeky insubordination I had shown over the years, he looked beyond all of that and unhesitatingly recommended me for promotion. Believe me, coming from him that meant a lot.

My next move was to the big time, Chelsea. Elated as I was to be posted back to Central London this next move was destined to prepare me for the higher ranks. It was also the time when I found myself working under the command of crooked cops and experienced at first hand the defects in the criminal justice system that allowed so many guilty people to evade justice, a true case of 'Chelsea Blues'.

Chapter Nine

Law controls the lesser man,
Right conduct controls the great one
Mark Twain 1835–1910

There couldn't have been a greater contrast moving from suburban Mitcham to the sophistication of Chelsea, a world apart. Promotion to 1st Class Detective Sergeant in May, 1967, brought a subtle change in role that made the move even more challenging. As understudy to the Detective Inspector, the new position demanded a more supervisory role.

Chelsea was a large Sub-Division stretching from the World's End through to Belgravia, bounded by the Thames to the South and Knightsbridge to the North. It was a busy patch and for administrative purposes was divided into two separate CID Offices; BD1 to the East incorporating most of the Kings Road, Sloane Street, and Knightsbridge areas and BD2 to the West bordering onto World's End and Fulham. I was attached to BD1, the posh end.

During three busy years at Chelsea I served under no less than six Detective Inspectors so from necessity I became the central stabilising factor in an ever changing spectrum. Of those six, one died through a heart attack, three were promoted, one arrested, convicted and imprisoned for corruption, and one disciplined and reduced in rank.

I virtually ran the office with thirty CID officers and thrived on the experience. There were two Detective Chief Inspectors but most of their time was taken up with administrative and supervisory tasks and of course investigating complaints against Police officers which was fast becoming a fashionable trend.

My Detective Superintendent at Chelsea was Fred Lambert, a thorough gentleman, copper of the old school and straight as a die. Fred taught me a lot. On my very first day at the nick he ordered me to book out a car and we went to a suspicious death in a basement flat just off the King's Road. It turned out to be a straightforward suicide of a Swedish man who had taken a massive overdose of painkillers. What differentiated this from many similar jobs I encountered through my career was that this one happened about a week or so earlier and the body had been left to putrefy in the closed apartment with the central heating left on. Maggots were literally oozing from the mouth, ears and other orifices. The stench was overwhelming and stayed on my clothes and in my nostrils for several days afterwards.

I drove Fred to the mortuary at Horseferry Road where an autopsy was performed. He studied me closely to gauge my reactions but despite my stomach churning, I managed to keep a deadpan face. At the conclusion, we went back to the canteen at Chelsea nick and he bought me breakfast, eggs swimming in fat and greasy bacon. Don't ask me how but I swallowed the lot and Fred grinned – I had passed the first test.

Fred Lambert served in the army during the Second World War and joined the Met after being demobbed in 1946. After being in uniform for less than a year he was selected for the Department, served on Division, and then on The Flying Squad for eight years. To have achieved such swift promotion was testimony by itself to his dedication and intelligence. He was involved in many notorious cases including that of Gunther Podola who shot and killed D.S. Ray Purdy in Kensington in 1959. Fred's detective ability identified Podola as the murderer and led to his arrest and subsequent execution.

Mr Lambert was one of several senior officers for whom I had the greatest admiration and it was tragic the way he was targeted by corrupt senior officers and forced out of the job; but more of that later.

On 19 September 1967, Claudie Delbarre, aged 18 years, a French 'au pair', was found murdered in her bed-sitter in Walpole Street, Chelsea. Death appeared to be caused by cerebral haemorrhage caused by blows to the head. A forensic examination at the scene found two glass tumblers that were submitted to Fingerprint Department at the Yard. Fingerprints found on one of the tumblers belonged to an American, Robert Lipman, arrested a week previously for possession of cannabis. Fred Lambert hurried to the Hotel address given by Lipman but the bird had flown the morning of the murder to Amsterdam and thence to New York. Liaison with the FBI traced him to a psychiatric hospital in the States from where he was eventually extradited.

At his trial he raised the defence that he was on a drug induced trip, remembered nothing and could therefore not be guilty of murder. After protracted legal arguments he was convicted of manslaughter and sentenced to six years imprisonment.

It has been said a good East End copper can always adapt to the West End whilst the transformation from West to East is harder. One thing didn't change, a crook remained a crook and the basic tenets of coppering remained the same. As one old lag once said to me "Shite is shite the world over – it's only the flies that change."

Chelsea was an ideal training ground where any remaining illusions I may have possessed were rapidly shattered. This was a world of utter calumny where deceit and treachery was widely practised; a man's word counted for nothing and dog voraciously ate dog.

I found it fairly easy to blend into cosmopolitan Chelsea but never quite managed to overcome my aversion to the rather loud, braying hooray Henry's and Sloane Ranger types that frequented the watering holes of Chelsea and Belgravia. As far as I was concerned the law was the law and everybody was equal before it. What a joke. How naive can one get?

Of course, working within a community that had so much outward display of wealth brought its own policing problems and the manor had its fair share of predatory robbers and con men ever on the lookout for mugs and easy pickings.

Whilst at Chelsea, I met perhaps one of the most successful confidence tricksters of all times, Charles Percival da Silva. I was investigating the activities of a crooked Peer, Lord Moynihan of Leeds, and my enquiries led me to a well known pub, The 'Star', Belgrave Mews, Belgravia, a known hangout of nobility and crooks. Paddy Kennedy, the foul mouthed manager, delighted in insulting the clientele who in turn found it tremendous fun to be the butt of his insults.

The pub had a reputation and had been used by a variety of upper class Bohemians including Princess Margaret and John Aspinall, the gambler who at one time was suspected of being the paymaster for the Great Train robbers and later on of having masterminded the disappearance of 'lucky' Lord Lucan.

Champagne Charlie was born in Ceylon of a wealthy family, came to England after the end of the Second World War and was renowned for the frauds he pulled off within the wealthy establishment he regarded as being fair game for his scams. On one occasion he walked into a London Bank, purporting to be a high ranking official in the Ceylon Consulate negotiating a contract to buy a fleet of fishing boats for his Government. So eloquent was he that he managed to walk from that Bank with £90,000 in cash before the Manager discovered he was a victim of the silver tongued con man. There was nothing small or petty about Champagne Charlie.

West End Central Police once asked me to check out a man he had given as a reference when opening a bank account. I traced the man, Johnny Adams, a newspaper seller with a pitch outside Knightsbridge Underground Station. "Did you give a reference to the Bank for a man called Charles de Silva?" I asked.

"That's right guv," he cheerfully admitted.

"But you said you had known Mr De Silva for many years and he had conducted numerous financial transactions with you that he had always honoured."

"That's right guv, he bought a newspaper from me every day!"

It's said you should never attempt to con a con man but I decided over a series of meetings to try and buck the odds. Charlie de Silva was a veritable treasure house of information, he knew many of the top villains in London and I tried over a period of years to cultivate him as a potentially useful informant. While I gleaned much useful background information over seemingly innocent chats where he imparted useful snippets, it was only several years later he intimated he may have some useful information regarding some forged plates for American Express Travellers cheques. When the job eventually sprung, I was holidaying in Spain with my family and despite his making efforts to contact me he never succeeded.

Whether he was merely trying to use me as insurance or whether he was genuine I will never know as he was arrested and committed for trial to the Old Bailey. Whilst on bail he telephoned me and said, "Dave, you must help me, I just can't stand going back to gaol, it would finish me."

Much as I would have liked to help him there was no way I could intervene and I told him this with a heavy heart.

Charlie was an intelligent, articulate man with a wealth of amusing stories, but there is a line over which one cannot cross. There is an old villains saying, "If you can't do the time, don't do the crime" and that was the situation with poor Charlie. He booked into the Divan Hotel in South Kensington under a false name, took an overdose of sleeping pills washed down with half a bottle of gin and went to meet his Maker.

A successful writer once told me the formula for writing a bestselling book was to include plenty of sex. As he explicitly explained, "Sex sells books." Well, in the aptly named swinging sixties there was certainly plenty of that around in Chelsea. For some reason or other many ladies fancied policemen – or could it just have been anything in trousers?

Sorry, I am afraid there are no kiss and tell stories in this account, no titillation, but a couple of amusing incidents illustrate my point and I'm afraid dear reader, you will have to content yourself with them.

A no doubt apocryphal story circulated regarding a certain DCI, (Detective Chief Inspector) at Chelsea, later destined to become a senior detective at the Yard, who accompanied the investigating DS to a burglary in Cadogan Square. The loser, a gracious titled lady invited the senior officer upstairs into her bedroom where she went to great pains to point out where the thieves had obviously gained entry through a window. The DS, patiently drinking tea below was quite surprised at the time taken until some ten minutes later, a rather red faced senior officer descended followed by the lady with a satisfied smirk on her face. As the DCI was offered tea by the maid, the lady insisted upon showing the Det. Sgt the probable point of entry.

Ten minutes later he too came down the stairs looking somewhat red and dishevelled. After taking all the relevant details for the Crime Book the lady graciously showed the two officers to the front door and as they left, turned sweetly to her maid and said, "Well Gladys, not a bad morning's work, one postman, one milkman and two policemen."

We were now firmly into the era of the swinging sixties yet before the advent of aids, the medical sort that is, there was a lot of it about and it caused havoc with marriages. It was a hard drinking, hard working environment and many a good officer fell by the wayside for one reason or other. One particular young D.C. (Detective Constable) rather fancied himself as a man about town with an eye for the ladies. He became smitten with a rather attractive young member of the Chelsea set to whom he naughtily claimed he was a barrister at law and the local Detective Inspector. All went well for several weeks until obviously flushed with post or possibly pre-coital insanity; he foolishly proposed marriage and the smitten young lady invited him home for the weekend to meet Daddy. Having excused his absence from home under the pretext he had an out of town escort duty, our gay Lothario arrived at Daddy's rather sumptuous mansion in Hertfordshire where he was proudly introduced by his beloved to her doting parents. It was quite natural for Daddy to want to know more of his prospective son in law and he was invited into the drawing room for sherry. "So young man, I understand you wish to marry my daughter?"

"Um, yes sir"

"She tells me you are the Detective Inspector at Chelsea, rather young aren't you?"

"Well yes, sir, I've been very fortunate in my career to date."

"She also says you are a qualified barrister, tell me young man, what chambers are you in?"

"Chambers sir?"

"Yes young man, chambers, which Inn of Court?"

There was an embarrassing silence only broken by Daddy, an eminent Judge of the High Court and a personal friend of the then current Commissioner of Police.

"You sir are a cad and have offered your hand in marriage to my daughter. I can overlook the fact you are a mere Detective Constable, more to the point you are a married man with two daughters, I suggest you leave this house immediately and do not dare to contact my daughter again."

The following morning, a crestfallen DC was called in front of Bob Huntley, the Detective Chief Superintendent where he tendered his resignation in preference to being served with disciplinary papers and sacked.

Well, that's enough sex for the moment at least, now to get back to the nitty gritty. I certainly couldn't complain about the variety or volume of crime and during my three years I went through the whole gamut ranging from murder enquiries, robberies, arson, blackmail and rapes. It was all grist to the mill and although our home lives of necessity suffered, it was one of the most exciting and self-fulfilling periods of my career.

Whilst at Chelsea, I lost any remaining and lingering doubts I may have held about the majesty of the law, the administration of the criminal justice system and the way it could be manipulated. In particular several cases brought home to me the inadequacies of the jury system and also the limited value of identification as a reliable means of detecting crime.

Anybody who has seen that excellent film "Twelve Angry Men" will have a good insight into how the average jury reaches their conclusions and can be manipulated. Fortunately since my working days, much has been done to eliminate some of the major deficiencies in the jury system. Investigating rape has never been easy; to bring a successful case we needed clear corroboration such as bruising, teeth marks or other injuries, forensic material and an immediate complaint to Police. There was a natural tendency born of experience, for allegations to be treated with a degree of suspicion, particularly if the supposed victim was a person of easy morals or a chequered past. In these circumstances it was not unusual for such allegations to be written up in the crime book as 'No Crime- insufficient evidence to substantiate.'

This was not chauvinism or even laziness on behalf of investigating officers but the reality of knowing just how difficult it was to get juries to convict in these cases. Added to the terrible ordeal defence counsels so often put victims through by way of searching and humiliating cross examination in the witness box, they could be aggressively cross examined about their previous sexual history. Indeed, victims have complained to me their ordeal in the witness box where they were forced to go over detailed descriptions of the incident itself, were as traumatic as the original rape. Lastly of course, an allegation of rape is easy to make and can be made for a variety of reasons but the effect upon an innocent person is disastrous.

One such allegation of rape that stands out in my memory involved Robin Gray, a barrister. Gray was a particularly obnoxious, greasy, individual who frequented nurse's dances and preyed upon impressionable young nurses easily taken in by his suave, urbane mannerisms and undoubtedly lulled into a false sense of security by his profession.

Gray first came to my attention when a young German nurse living at Hendon went into the local nick to complain of rape. Gray met her at a local nurse's dance, charmed her with his urbane, polite conversation and invited her for coffee in his sumptuous Cadogan Gardens apartment. Safely inside the flat, the girl described in graphic detail how his whole demeanour suddenly changed and he placed her in fear of her life by threatening her with violence unless she complied with his perverted sexual practices. Once safely back in the Nurse's home the hapless girl tearfully confided in her roommate who insisted she complained to Police. Unfortunately before this happened, she subjected herself to several baths to cleanse her body from the unwelcome contact and of course by doing so, destroyed any possibility of finding forensic evidence.

The local DS believed her account and took a very detailed statement but in the absence of any corroborative detail, with reluctance he marked it up as 'not recorded as a crime, insufficient evidence to substantiate."

As the alleged offence occurred on Chelsea patch a copy of the Crime Book entry was sent to BD (Chelsea Police Station) for record purposes.

That is where the matter would have rested had not an identical incident occurred the following week with a young

Swedish nurse in Clapham. Same method, same result and again a copy of the allegation was sent to Chelsea for record purposes. The details of how the offences were committed were just too identical to ignore; a classic carbon copy.

I arranged for both girls to be brought to Chelsea where the experienced WDS (Woman Detective Sergeant) Thelma Wagstaff, interviewed them separately. One vital fact we needed to establish was whether there was any possibility of collusion and we were both satisfied they never knew each other previously and their stories were true. Both described the apartment in detail and remembered not only the precise address but also the first name of their assailant, indeed, identification was never an issue. They both described in detail the furnishings and bed covers in the bedroom where the attacks took place, where he kept a jar of Vaseline used in the assaults, the drawer where he kept the pornographic literature and how they were threatened with a horsewhip.

I say that in hindsight, this happened more than fifty years ago and without any written notes, precise details of necessity may be slightly blurred. What was in no doubt and perhaps the most striking fact was the way they quite independently described his facial transformation from kind friendly urbane gentleman into a snarling vicious animal, oblivious to their pleas for mercy. Both girls considered themselves fortunate to escape from that flat with their lives.

That evening, with a colleague, I paid a visit to Cadogan Gardens where the door was opened by Gray. Having seen the fear and heard of the degrading experience he had subjected these two girls to, it would be fair to say I wasn't feeling well disposed towards the man. We announced our identities and despite his protests, pushed past him into the flat. He followed closely afterwards, actually muttering something about an abuse of his rights. The layout of the bedroom, the Vaseline, the books, the horsewhip were all where described. I told the man the nature of the complaints made by the two girls, cautioned him and despite his protestations, handcuffed him and placed him unceremoniously into the back of the Police car, quite accidentally banging his head upon the car roof as I did so.

An eminent QC who defended in many famous criminal trials once said to his instructing solicitor, "I don't care what the bloody fool has done, what did he say when arrested?"

Verbal admissions under caution made immediately after an arrest played an important role in crime investigation and it was calculated in those days more than 40% of cases leading to convictions in the courts relied heavily upon such involuntary confessions.

Despite his legal training, Master Gray was apparently unaware of these statistics for in the back of the Police car he blurted out, "It must be quite obvious these two girls have conspired together to implicate me".

It goes without saying that Gray elected trial and eventually was arraigned before the Judge at the Old Bailey upon an indictment specifying two separate counts of rape.

British justice is full of strange anomalies and I certainly met with some of these during the forthcoming proceedings. The most important as far as the prosecution case was concerned is the fact that evidence of similar conduct to that charged may be adduced to show a propensity of the accused to commit that particular type of offence and also to negate any defence of mistake, in short, by proving 'system'. Clearly in this case the similarity of complaint and the conduct of the accused in the commission of the rapes were vital to rebut any claim of willingness made by him against the complainants. I was quite prepared to be challenged upon the verbal admission; after all it was par for the course in all criminal defences where a plea of 'not guilty' is entered.

However my first inclination that not all was destined to go smoothly came before the jury was sworn in. Prosecuting Counsel took me on one side. "Officer, if this chap is convicted, don't you think we can overlook the fact he is a barrister?"

I stiffened, "No way, he deliberately used his position to gain the confidence of these girls and I shall say so at the appropriate time".

Counsel looked quite embarrassed at the vehemence of my response but I was irritated enough not to leave it there. "I don't suppose you would be suggesting that if the defendant was a Police Officer"

The jury were sworn in but before the indictment containing the two counts was read, Defence Counsel leaped to his feet. "My Lord, before this case continues, I wish to address you in the absence of the jury."

This in itself was not uncommon when a question of law had to be decided. The Judge raised his eyebrows but ordered the usher to conduct the jury into the jury room. "My Lord, I respectfully ask that this indictment be split and my client be charged upon two separate counts of rape by separate juries".

"Upon what grounds?"

"My Lord, if one jury hears both cases upon the same indictment, the prejudicial effect will far outweigh the evidential value".

Prosecution Counsel rose, "My Lord, may I have five minutes to take instructions."

At the rear of the Court, the Prosecutor addressed me, Well Mr Woodland; do you have any objection to the counts being split?"

"Objection? Of course I have a bloody objection, each case effectively corroborates the other, if the counts are split and each is heard by different juries the whole thing will be nothing short of a farce, we may just as well go home now." Despite a half-hearted objection by the Prosecutor, the Judge allowed the counts on the indictment to be split and tried separately before separate juries.

To rub salt in the wounds, in order that neither jury be aware of the second charge, the whole of the prosecution case was dissected and any references to the second rape were ordered to be removed from the evidence. This was allegedly to be fair to the victim but out went that telling but incriminating admission, "It must be quite obvious these two girls have conspired together to implicate me."

Two separate trials then took place in front of two separate juries but of course it was a foregone conclusion. In both cases the defendant successfully claimed that sex took place with consent and in the absence of marks, bruises or other forensic evidence, the jury quite rightly acquitted the defendant who walked from the dock with a smirk of triumph on his face.

Should the judge have made the decision to split the counts on the original indictment? Where a defendant can be shown as having a desire to commit a particular type of crime, such as paedophilia, such proof is not merely limited to commission of the same kind of offence but could include any evidence that made it more likely the defendant had behaved as charged. After all, isn't the whole purpose of a criminal trial to seek the truth? In my view the judge should never have split that indictment but joined the two counts and allowed the jury to decide upon the facts, after all that is why we have a jury system. I was left with the clear impression that the nature of the defendant's calling had influenced the Court; of course I could be wrong.

'Justice must not only be done, it must be seen to be done' is an old legal maxim as is 'every man is equal in the eyes of the law'.

Really? I don't think so; some people appear to be more equal than others.

To my mind, those two young foreign girls, guests in our country, certainly didn't get the justice they expected, deserved and were entitled to.

Isn't it about time we started to consider the victims of crime and applied a little more common sense to the absurdity of some of these more archaic legal shibboleths?

Chapter Ten

"Justice will not be served until those who are unaffected are as outraged as those who are."

Benjamin Franklin 1706–1790

On 8 December 1944, Captain Ralph Douglas Binney, CBE, Royal Navy, died from injuries received when bravely and alone he tackled two armed men robbing a jewellers shop. To honour this courageous act Captain Binney's fellow officers with others founded the Binney Memorial Awards for civilians who in the face of great danger and personal risk followed Captain Binney's example and steadfastly upheld law and order.

Some twenty three years later, shortly after my move to Chelsea, in July, 1967, an armed robbery took place at the National Provincial Bank, Sloane Street, Chelsea. During the course of the robbery, Anthony Fletcher, a brave passerby, tackled the gunman but was shot down and killed in cold blood. Mr Fletcher was dubbed the 'have-a-go hero' by the National Press. Despite intensive enquiries, regrettably we never brought Mr Fletcher's killers to justice and I am sure the £1,000 award given to his widow was but cold comfort.

The job brought me into contact with people from all walks of life and in doing so taught me a lot about human nature. Some of the crimes we investigated were bizarre to say the least; one of those that stick out in my memory was the arrest of a woman for committing rape.

'Borshtch 'n' Tears', a well known restaurant in Beauchamp Place was owned by one Benno Taylor who raped a young American girl while his girl friend, Rosalind Jardine helped to hold her down. It caused quite a fuss at the time as the victim was the daughter of a U.S.Senator and the American authorities quite rightly do not take kindly to their Senators' daughters being raped. In March, 1969, Taylor was convicted of what the judge described as a particularly brutal rape and sentenced to nine years imprisonment. The girlfriend Jardine, being a principal in the first degree to the commission of a felony gained the dubious distinction of also being convicted of rape and she was sentenced to a suspended sentence of two years imprisonment; Not a nice one to have on your curriculum vitae.

Another Chelsea character was Susan, owner of a smart basement drinking club in Beauchamp Place. She refused to serve two drunken Glaswegians who left, threatening to burn the place down. They returned later and threw a canister of burning petrol down the basement staircase.

The men were traced and arrested and a petrol service station attendant gave a very clear matching description of the men. Try as I might, he could not be persuaded to give evidence. After all, why put up with having to take time off work, make statements, go to Magistrates' Court, and eventual trial and risk being pulled to pieces by defence lawyers? Better by far to steer clear of all that. This refusal weakened the case which depended to some degree upon initial denials and the verbal admission of one of the accused under interrogation.

At the Old Bailey I received a pretty severe grilling from Defence Counsel. He successfully convinced the jury my questioning had been so prolonged and persistent the admission had been made through convincing his client he was guilty; in short, I had brainwashed him. Counsel put it to me that I had induced the admission by his client in the same way that Ivan Pavlov, the famous Russian psychologist had conditioned dogs' behaviour in laboratory experiments. Well it was a novel defence and obviously impressed the jury as both men were acquitted. All that as any seasoned detective will concur, is accepted as being par for the course. What astonished me even more than the acquittal was when I went back to the club later to return some exhibits. Susan, sat resplendent in her usual position by the bar, drinking champagne.

After I had returned the exhibits she beckoned me over and said in her well modulated Chelsea accent, "Darling, do me a small favour, don't come here again, it disturbs the patrons and gets my place a bad name." I walked out of there full of righteous indignation but looking back at the incident now I can't help but have a quiet chuckle to myself.

It was just another pretty straightforward robbery when a Rolex watch representative was attacked by two men as he left his flat and his sample case carrying many thousands of pounds of watches was stolen. In this particular case we had two eye witnesses, both professors at the nearby Imperial College who came back to the nick and helped draw up Photo-fit pictures of the assailants. A DS recently transferred from Notting Hill nick saw the photo-fit impressions "Good God, that's the spitting image of Kenny Smith and Sammy Harvey from the Hill, no doubt about it."

The pair were previously unknown to me but I had often seen their photos upon internal police bulletins as being active robbers. Both men were swiftly nicked. The ensuing enquiry was conducted with scrupulous fairness. In this particular case, despite their previous known records, the main evidence was from the two independent professors who quite unhesitatingly picked out the two suspects in an identification parade.

This was supported through evidence that both men were known to associate together but of course that had to be presented in such a way that no inference could be drawn that their previous association was when they had embarked and been arrested upon previous joint criminal activities. Never let it be whispered we have displayed prejudice against the poor hard working criminal classes. Kenny Smith was convinced he had been done up like the proverbial kipper. "You've stitched me up" he accused me, "those two witnesses are coppers and that ID was bent"

The men appeared before Judge Michael Argyll at The Old Bailey. Their defence counsel was a doughty, determined advocate, as convinced as were his clients that the Identification Parade had been fixed. He had me in the witness box for more than a day, vainly trying to induce me to concede it was just possible that the parade was flawed and that I had manufactured evidence including a 'verbal' against his clients. Now in the 'bad old days', such an attack upon the character of a prosecution witness should have been sufficient to allow a defendant's previous convictions to be admitted in evidence but of course, in these more enlightened times, although legally this could still be done, it rarely was as of course 'the prejudicial effect would far outweigh the probative value' and we all know by now we mustn't be too harsh on the poor prisoner must we?

On the third day I went back into the witness box to endure what I thought would be another grilling when Defence Counsel jumped to his feet.

"My Lord, I have to tell you I can no longer act for these defendants."

The whole court was stunned. Very occasionally this can happen when a principled lawyer, aware he has been lied to by his client, feels morally unable to continue to represent him. Not I might add a frequent occasion or one I had experienced before. This was certainly not the situation here. Judge Argyll demanded an explanation. "My Lord, I am defending these two men upon legal aid and I cannot afford to waste any more time on this case."

The Judge was almost lost for words. "But you have a duty, both to justice and also to your clients in this case."

"I also have a duty to my family and I am afraid that takes precedence."

With no further ado, this paragon of the law picked up his brief, placed his law books under his arm and stalked out of the Court despite Judge Argyll's warning he would report his unprofessional conduct to the Bar Council. A new counsel was appointed, the trial continued. Both men were found 'guilty' and sentenced to five years imprisonment. I couldn't help but feel that having been abandoned by their brief in that fashion they hadn't received a fair crack of the whip even if they were guilty.

Chelsea was my introduction to the legendary Aussi mob. Their exploits were often recounted with a degree of admiration by officers who had dealt with them. They were a cheeky, brazen lot and as I learned later in my career, to dismiss them as mere shoplifters was far from the truth. Although some of the team had quite violent criminal records in Sydney, they didn't resort to violence on this side of the pond and in consequence were never given particularly high priority in the nicking stakes. They were also quite careful to cultivate drinking associates in the local CID a fact that again to my chagrin made my future dealings with them more complicated. This wasn't a question of out and out bribery or graft, although no doubt they were up to that as well. Their cultivated relationships extended to being invited to Police Boxing dinners and the like.

Two of the hierarchy in the team were identical twins, Jimmy and Cecil Lloyd. Legend had it that not only had Nature endowed them with a natural aptitude for crime but more importantly a close facial and physical resemblance that was uncanny even for identical twins. It was rumoured they could almost read each others' minds. They were in their mid forties and whilst Nature has a way of reducing the resemblance with the vicissitudes of time, diet and manner of life these had made little or no effect upon the twins.

As is so often the case, folklore tends to blur that thin line of distinction which separates fact from myth and this was very much the case with the Lloyd brothers. Earlier in their careers Cecil conducted a particularly brazen sneak theft of a tray of rings from a jewellers shop in one of the larger provincial towns. The local constabulary took a rightful civic pride in maintaining a low level of crime on their patch and naturally resented the incursion of villains from the smoke. Immediately after the theft was reported, road blocks were mounted and checks conducted at railway and Bus terminals which resulted in Cecil being nicked about to board the early evening train back to London. He received a pretty gruelling session with a burly local DS who was unable to glean the location of the missing rings nor would Cecil divulge where he obtained the three grand in bank notes found in his inside jacket pocket. Despite the usual promises, threats and cajolery they never identified the fence to whom he had obviously disposed of the loot before having his collar felt.

Within the week, a slick London solicitor with the aid of substantial sureties secured Cecil's release on bail pending his committal for trial. When Cecil's fingerprints and details were received at CRO a helpful Det. Sgt from Method Index phoned the local constabulary with the express intention of warning them of Jimmy's existence and the potential threat this may pose to a successful conviction.

The local DI made it quite clear they were not country yokels and he would brook no interference from the Yard or anywhere else for that matter. It was his job and he suggested rather forcefully that everybody knew the whole of the Metropolitan CID were bent and he thanked them to keep their noses out of his business.

It was only when the case came for trial that Cecil sprung his so called 'ambush defence'. At the very end of the trial when it was too late to prove otherwise, he revealed that at precisely the time the ring snatch took place, he had an appointment with a local bank manager and had arranged to withdraw £3,000 against the security of the London branch to make a cash offer on a Bentley car advertised for sale locally. Needless to say he didn't keep the appointment but presumably his brother did. The rest as they say is history. After all it was Cecil standing trial not his brother Jimmy. It's true, you win some and you lose some and I must say that with people like the Aussies there was never any ill feeling if they managed to get away with it.

That was certainly the case with another well known Aussie, Victor Kruse who switched a paste imitation bracelet from a display at Kutchinsky's jewellers in the Brompton Arcade as an accomplice diverted the shop assistant's attention by posing as an aggressive drunk who burst into the shop.

It was only later that evening, as the stock was being checked and replaced for the night that the swap was discovered and Police in the shape of young DC Wilkins at Chelsea was detailed to investigate.

The shop assistant gave an excellent description of the offender and of course the accent used soon alerted Taffy Wilkins he was dealing with one of the notorious Aussies.

CRO had composed an album of known Aussie thieves and with the aid of this hand out, the shop assistant immediately and without any hesitation picked out Victor Kruse. Taffy circulated Kruse 'suspected' in *Police Gazette* and his photo distributed to every Police Force in the country.

Several months later Victor was picked up by Police in the Midlands and an elated Taffy collected his prisoner and brought him back to Chelsea. They returned late on Saturday evening and the witness could not be located so with much reluctance, the decision was made to bail out Victor with substantial sureties to return the following week to stand upon an Identification parade which he did with his brief, a slightly dodgy solicitor. Before the parade started, Kruse asked to see the CID officer in charge and he was ushered into my office with his solicitor. "I hope your witness is not going to identify my client" was his brief's opening gambit.

"I'm sure you do" I responded cordially "we shall have to see, won't we?"

"I don't think so," piped up Victor, "because if he does your DC will have fingered me to the witness first and he'll be out of a job in next to no time."

The man sounded quite confident and I realised something was amiss and allowed him to continue.

"You see, the other day I went into Kutchinsky's with me brief here, and I asked that witness I saw in your waiting room just now if they sold batteries for me watch. Well, he hadn't seen a battery watch before, said they never had call for them. He asked me where I got it so I told him I bought it in Australia where I come from. Now, he didn't recognise me then so if I'm pulled out on a parade today there's bound to be some awkward questions asked, get my drift?"

I certainly did and turned questioningly towards his brief who nodded in agreement. "Please wait here for one minute!" I asked and went into the waiting room to confront Taffy. "Taffy, don't eff me about, tell me straight, have you shown your witness those photos again today"

Taffy hesitated, "Well yes skip, it's been some time now and he needed to refresh his memory."

That is strictly improper where a suspect can be placed upon an identification parade. I said some very rude things to poor Taffy and returned to the Detention Room, mustering all the dignity I could under the circumstances. "Well gentlemen, it appears we can take this matter no further, Mr Kruse you are free to leave, no doubt I shall be seeing you again soon."

Those words were miraculously prophetic as Victor left the nick, went straight round to the Marlborough Arms pub to celebrate his good fortune with a few double scotches. When he came out, he decided to go into the local supermarket for a packet of bacon, reverted to true form and slipped it into his coat pocket. A sharp eyed store detective witnessed this and within no time Victor found himself back in the same nick being charged with the heinous crime of shoplifting a packet of bacon. As he told me later, "To tell the truth Mr Woodland I was so embarrassed at being nicked for a bit of ham I just wanted to plead and get it done and finished without me mates knowing." A year or so later, I was sorry to hear that Victor had been killed in a car crash in Belgium, a country regularly frequented by the Aussie team.

Chelsea may be a little village but events in the outside world had reverberations on my patch. In July, 1968, the Baathist party in Iraq seized power in a coup d'état when Colonel Saddam Hussein burst into the Presidential Palace and held a gun to President Arif's head. Over five hundred supporters of the old regime were put to death in a bloody coup in the night of the long knives. Arif and many of his party members fled to London where they were granted political asylum.

The following year Saddam was appointed President and sent a team of twelve Army officers to London with orders to assassinate many of the deposed President Arif's leading supporters.

M.I.5 made Special Branch aware of these developments and a Detective Chief Superintendent from Special Branch came to Chelsea to brief me upon the whereabouts of one of these assassins and emphasised the danger he presented. The man was holed up in an apartment in Elvaston Place, SW7 and we were requested to maintain observation, identify and arrest the man who was known to be armed and dangerous. The need for a positive result to avert any assassination attempts was impressed upon me. A DS from Special Branch (SB) was assigned to my team and as an authorised firearms officer I drew a Smith and Wesson revolver with six rounds of ammunition from the Station safe. Firearm offences are something that many coppers have to deal with at some time in their careers.

At Elvaston Place, with the Podola incident very much at the forefront of our minds, we didn't waste too much time upon unnecessary formalities, the apartment door was unceremoniously kicked in and the man, an Iraqi Army Major, swiftly arrested. Despite a search of the living room, kitchen and toilet areas, all we found was an empty Webley revolver carton; obviously the gun was concealed elsewhere.

Meanwhile on my instructions the SB Det Sgt and an aid to CID searched the bedroom again with no success. This was quite contrary to the information we received and I said to the team, "It must be here somewhere, let's search again, this time more thoroughly". I searched the bedroom again and found a revolver hidden underneath some clothing in a bedside cabinet.

Back at Chelsea nick I recounted the facts to the Station Sgt. accepting the charge and produced the revolver. I could hardly believe my ears when the Det Sgt from SB glared accusingly at me and interposed, addressing the Station Officer, "Excuse me Sergeant, but I searched that bedside cabinet and that gun was definitely not there, it must have been planted."

I confronted the man in anger, "Just whose bloody side are you are on?" Turning to the bewildered Station PS I said, "Sorry skip, it just goes to show this plonker didn't search thoroughly enough".

Hurried telephone calls to the Yard resulted in the Detective Superintendent from SB coming down hot foot. The hapless Det Sgt was taken into an office and spoken to. Five minutes later, the Superintendent emerged, grim faced and apologetic.

"Sorry Dave, but the man insists the gun wasn't in there when he searched the room and will stick to that if we go to Court. I agree he couldn't have searched properly but the important thing is the Iraqi is in the country illegally and we can deport him without causing a diplomatic stir, that is, if you don't mind dropping the firearms charge."

What could I say? At least we had got our man, he was deported with no fuss and an assassination attempt averted. Despite the allegation of planting evidence made by a fellow officer, I am quite sure the prompt action I took in removing a dangerous man from the streets had prevented the assassination of some innocent person. I must confess though, to a slight feeling of satisfaction when several weeks later I read in Police Orders that a certain Det. Sgt. from SB had been returned to uniform duties in the sticks. Hopefully a little spell directing traffic at South Mimms would work wonders with his eyesight.

Chapter Eleven

Truth is never pure and rarely simple
Oscar Wilde, The Importance of being Earnest

By this stage in my career I was beginning to despair of the way in which the criminal justice system could be manipulated or abused. Should anyone still harbour any lingering doubts on that score let me recount the story of Billy Thornton and Barry Feathers, two young tearaways from World's End, Chelsea who managed to find themselves recorded in the annals of Method Index at CRO by specialising in something called 'housebreaking by artifice' or gaining access to premises by deception, in their case as bogus window cleaners.

Ennismore Gardens is a quiet, pleasant little back street in Chelsea with some rather quaint but select mews type houses. The house in question was owned by a charming retired couple in their eighties, he being ex- City broker and she a still most attractive Scandinavian lady with exquisite bone structure who in earlier days must have been a quite exceptional beauty. Their quiet, well ordered retirement was rudely interrupted one day by our bold heroes Billy and Barry who knocked on the front door.

"Clean your windows lady?" asked Billy with a cheeky grin.

"Bless me, is it that time again already? Where is the regular cleaner?"

"Oh he's got a touch of the flu; he's asked us to do his round until he's better like". Without more ado, the two men were admitted to the house. Within five minutes flat they were in the upstairs bedroom where during the subsequent prosecution it was alleged they pocketed over ten grand's worth of jewellery before beating a swift retreat through the front door.

"Goodness gracious, are you finished already?" the lady of the house asked.

"No lady" was the sharp response, "we're just going round the corner to pick up an extension ladder to do the upstairs windows, as this one ain't long enough." Exit stage left Billy and Barry purportedly with ten grand of tomfoolery (£10,000 of jewellery) in their pockets, all in all not a bad afternoon's work.

This is where Photo Albums room and Method Index at Criminal Record Office proved their worth. The rationale behind Method Index is the proven theory that villains tend to stick to one proven method of crime and repeat it, time and time again. Under the various sub divisions of burglary is 'housebreaking by artifice – bogus window cleaners.'

Our two heroes were well represented having been arrested several times previously for this particular type of offence and incidentally having been acquitted more times than they were convicted. Their photographs, together with other bogus window cleaners known to frequent the Chelsea area were shown to the victims who made a partial identification.

That evening I booked off duty leaving it to the late turn CID officers to pull the suspects in for questioning and placing them upon a formal identification parade. The next day, fresh from a good night's sleep I was back in the office early and collared Taffy Wilkins.

"Did you nick them Taffy?"

"Oh yes skip"

"Good, well done, where are they, in the Detention Room?"

"Oh no, we had to let them go"

"You did what?"

"Well, they denied it and we couldn't get hold of the witnesses so we let them go."

I knew the two officers well, they were certainly not corrupt, just lazy and I let them know my feelings in no uncertain terms. I called over Robin Constable, a sound and efficient officer. "Robin, book the car out, we've got some villains to nick."

Within an hour, both suspects were back at the nick loudly protesting their innocence. Now, question and answer under caution is quite an art, and it isn't made any easier when your suspects are able to tell you that not only had they denied the offence to those other nice officers last night, but that after being released they had enjoyed a social chat and drink with them in the Marlborough Arms pub around the corner. Oh dear, trouble at Mill?

Persistence proved its own reward and bit by bit both men realised we were not quite as accommodating as those kind officers they met the previous night. Whilst denying the theft, they made slight but important admissions. Yes, they had cleaned the windows. Tick that box – no need for identification parades. Yes they had been in the bedroom, yes they had left without finishing the job and no, they hadn't even asked for payment. Tick those boxes: placed at the scene of the crime; motive; opportunity.

These answers and the limited time scale from when the lady had last seen the jewellery and subsequently found it stolen with no intervention by any third party plus just a modicum of good old common sense was more than enough in my book to convince any jury and they were nicked and charged with housebreaking by artifice. Some chance!

Both men appeared before the Inner London Quarter Sessions before that grand old stager, Judge Ossie McLeay Q.C. who was admired and respected by counsel, police and even villains who appeared before him. Well perhaps not the villains, maybe feared would be more accurate.

Ossie could tell how many beans made five and he didn't like thieves, especially when caught bang to rights, not only wasting valuable court time but also causing innocent victims to undergo the ordeal of having to give evidence and being cross examined. Naturally, their previous convictions for similar 'bogus window cleaner' housebreakings could not be disclosed to the jury.

The trial followed the usual pattern, the same old accusations of verballing' being levelled against Police and of course defence counsel made great play of the fact they had been arrested the previous night and released without charge. Despite that minor set-back, they did themselves no good in cross examination and were at a complete loss to explain why they had scarpered from the scene before completing the job and even more telling and to the point without seeking to be paid. Nevertheless it was a pretty open and closed case, at least that's what I thought but of course I hadn't reckoned on the jury, bless them.

Experience had long taught me to know the jury's verdict even before the foreman was asked. Invariably, if they acquitted they would look directly at the prisoners in the dock and turn away from the investigating officer.

If it was a guilty verdict, the reverse would apply. I think everybody in the courtroom including the defendants were more than just a little amazed when the jury returned with a verdict of 'not guilty'.

Ossie McLeay, almost beside himself with anger, instructed the clerk of the Court to read out the mens' previous convictions all of course committed by with exactly the same method. I watched the jury with some bemusement; they just didn't know where to put their eyes. The judge addressed the prisoners, still in the Dock, scarcely able to believe their good luck.

"Well, you heard what the jury said; now get out of my Court."

As they skipped quite jubilantly from the Dock bleating the usual words of praise for the wonderful English justice system, the judge leaned over to the Clerk, glared at the jury and in a whisper loud enough to ensure it was heard, said in a disgusted tone, "And I hope they all get their houses broken into."

Outside the Court, the jury foreman approached me.

"It was your fault we acquitted" he mumbled, shamefacedly.

I bit my lip but gazed at him in utter disbelief. "Oh yes, and just how do you make that out?"

"Well, they said they left the house to get a longer ladder, why didn't you check to see if their ladder would reach the upstairs windows?"

I kept my cool; it was not really my job to discuss the verdict with a juror but couldn't resist my response.

"Listen my friend, you have just come up against two professional thieves, the judge was professional, the Police are professionals, the lawyers are professionals, the only bloody amateurs are yourselves, now don't waste any more of my time with your stupid effing questions."

What was the purpose of that little story? Oh yes, the jury system is a lottery, just one of its many weaknesses is it allows convicted thieves to do jury service provided they hadn't actually done too much time inside which of course is only after they have several convictions after their name. Perhaps it is time at least in some cases to replace the jury by a panel of lawyers or honest citizens. Until that happens, miscarriages of justice will happen all too often.

That would have been the end of the story except for one small but vital detail. Not content with their acquittal, late that night, doubtless fired up with drink, our two heroes banged upon the door of the elderly couple causing them some consternation.

"What about our money then" shouted Billy.

"Money?" queried the husband tremulously.

"Yes, money, you heard the jury, we were acquitted, what about the fifty bob for doing your bloody windows?"

It doesn't take too much to imagine the effect upon that elderly couple, to put it simply; they were terrified out of their minds. The next morning when I heard what transpired, I telephoned the men's solicitor complaining of their outrageous conduct.

"I don't believe a word of it Sgt. Woodland; this is just more of your lies."

I took no exception to this unwarranted rebuke, from the outset their solicitor, a very decent man probably more at home handling property conveyances and the like, but not terribly practiced in criminal law and the ways of the ungodly, had fallen for their story hook line and sinker and genuinely believed his clients to be innocent.

"Believe it or believe it not, that is precisely what happened and I'm telling you here and now, within six months your clients will be nicked again".

The man could hardly believe his ears, "That's outrageous, how dare you threaten them like that?"

"That's not a threat, just a statement of fact, they just can't help themselves and when they do, I shall be waiting for them."

I put the word around to my local informants and as luck would have it, almost six months to the day I received a telephone tip off from a snout.

"Thought you may be interested Mr Woodland, Billy and his mate are down the World's End Café, trying to knock some hookey gear out."

Ten minutes later, I casually strolled into the World's End café where Billy and Barry were sprawled out, doubtless enjoying a well earned cup of coffee before going down to the Labour to collect their dole. Their car was parked outside. "Hello Mr Woodland, nice to see you again".

"Hello Billy, that your car outside?"

"You know it is"

"Open the boot then, let's have a look inside"

Billy reluctantly opened the car boot and inside was a parcel containing a load of silverware subsequently identified as being stolen from a shop-breaking at Beauchamp Place the previous week. He put on as brave a face as he could muster; it was either 'hands up' time or put up a fight later in Court. Naturally, he chose the latter.

"Bit early for Christmas ain't it Mr Woodland, my brief warned me you would stitch me up within six months".

At Chelsea nick, Billy turned to me, "I don't suppose I can make a phone call to my brief"

"Course you can Billy, you know your rights by now."

Billy dialled a number, "Hello Mr Poynder, Billy Thornton here, you remember you told me that Woodland would stitch me up within six months, well he has, I'm at Lucan Place nick, can you come and bail me out?"

Within half an hour, Mr Poynder presented himself at the front desk of Chelsea Police Station; he always appeared somewhat florid of complexion but this time he was redder than the carnation he invariably wore in his smart pin striped suit, well after all this was Chelsea.

"This is disgraceful Sgt Woodland, what is it this time?"

I quietly explained the facts to the near apoplectic solicitor who was clearly unimpressed.

"And what pack of lies, are you coming up with this time?"

My eyebrows raised a fraction as I opened my pocket book, "Well sir, when I told your client he was being arrested and I cautioned him he did make a reply, 'My brief warned me you would stitch me up in six months.' Did you say that Sir?"

Poynder looked startled, "Surely you don't have to mention that Sgt?"

"Come now Mr Poynder, you're not asking me to alter my evidence are you?"

The lawyer glared malevolently at me and stalked out of the front office, much I must confess, to the amusement of the desk sergeant who had heard the exchange.

"Mate of yours Dave?" he enquired solicitously.

As it happened that rather telling response to his solicitor could never have been given in Court as it would immediately have alerted the jury to the effect that the prisoner had previous convictions and that would never do would it? But as I thought, Mr Poynder was a decent chap and obviously hadn't had much experience dealing with the criminal class. Some half hour later, after the charging and fingerprinting had taken place I took a telephone call in the CID office from a more affable sounding Mr Poynder.

"Ah, Sgt. Woodland, I have given this matter a great deal of thought, I don't think it would be either in my interests or those of my client if I were to represent him in this matter, it could prove most embarrassing."

"Quite right Mr Poynder, if I may say so, a very wise decision."

By one of those strange coincidences, when the case came for trial at the Inner London Sessions the two men found themselves arraigned before one Judge Ossie Mcleay who was no doubt delighted to renew their acquaintance.

Despite their earlier protestations of having been stitched up, they both pleaded 'guilty' to receiving stolen property and received nine months imprisonment which they richly deserved. At least, I thought so and so apparently did the learned Judge. As usual, Billy had to have the last word. "Nine months Mr Woodland? Do it on my head. Not enough for you eh?"

"Don't worry Billy; I'll still be here when you come out."

It so happens I was, but Billy decided perhaps Chelsea and the World's End was a little hot for him. Within two days of his release he moved across the water to Battersea where no doubt he felt safer to pursue his ungodly ways. If by any chance you should ever come to read this Billy and you have turned your life around and led a blameless life since then please forgive me for dragging up the past, I will gladly apologise.

1968 was a year when the whole world appeared to be erupting in anger. In April, the American Civil Rights leader,

Dr Martin Luther King was assassinated and a wave of riots spread through the black areas in over one hundred American cities including Louisville, Baltimore and Washington DC.

In the same month, Conservative MP Enoch Powell made his strangely prophetic anti- immigration speech 'Rivers of blood' which cost him his career and sparked off demonstrations all over England including one by London dockers in support of him.

French students rioted in Paris because... well that's what French students do isn't it? These were joined by nearly two million workers, this swiftly escalated to ten million workers, two thirds of the French workforce.

It seemed the whole world was striking and protesting about the American war in Vietnam and this culminated in bloody clashes in London as crowds tried to storm the American Embassy in Grosvenor Square. The Metropolitan Police responded to the violence and thousands of Police Officers were drafted into Central London to combat it. I was one of those officers.

The day saw hours of street fighting between police and demonstrators during which there were many injuries on both sides and two hundred demonstrators were arrested. Some demonstrators managed to get into the US Embassy and reached the ground floor. They were most fortunate not to have gone further as armed US marines were stationed on the first floor with orders to shoot anybody going further into what was effectively United States territory. I was one of a contingent of uniform and CID officers posted around the West End to prevent any groups breaking away from the main demonstration and causing collateral damage.

Totally oblivious to the chaos and confusion reigning outside, I was detailed with two other officers to sit in the reception area of The Dorchester Hotel to deter any straying rioters, after all, we wouldn't want any of our Middle Eastern visitors disturbed, would we? As we sat whiling away the time with tea, afternoon cake and the occasional gin and tonic with the security personnel, riots and mayhem were going on less than half a mile away. Oh well, somebody had to do it I suppose.

Chelsea Police Station was soon to feature in the National Press for other reasons we could all have done without. In 1969, Mick Jagger and Marianne Faithful were living in Cheyne Walk, Chelsea. Jagger was often the subject of press comment for his admitted drug abuse. It was not therefore surprising when in June, as a result of information received; DS Robin Constable obtained a warrant to search the house for drugs. What follows later has been the subject of conjecture and dispute. In all events Jagger was arrested, appeared at Marlborough Street Magistrates Court and was fined £200. It has been said this incident was the result of two conflicting cultures during the swinging sixties. Jagger alleged that Robin offered to drop the charge for a £1,000 bribe. This allegation was repeated at the conclusion of the court case and investigated by Commander Bob Huntley, Central Office.

His investigation concluded "The very serious allegations against three of the officers are made by a very intelligent, shrewd and well known public figure with many influential friends. On the other hand he was being dealt with by an astute and experienced detective who led a thoroughly and carefully briefed team. The matter finally comes down to the word of Jagger against that of Detective Sergeant Constable and is clearly a matter to be determined by the Director of Public Prosecutions."

Bob Huntley had recently been Detective Chief Superintendent at Chelsea during which time he had been Robin's senior officer and well knew his worth. It was inevitable this type of situation would sometimes arise but Bob clearly played a straight bat – too straight some may think. He could have mentioned that Jagger had previously been convicted of drugs use and had openly bragged in press interviews of his addiction to drugs and this would have been fairer to Robin. He could even have pointed out the effects a drugs conviction could have upon an international artist if in future he wished to travel to U.S.A.

In all events the DPP decided there was no case to answer. Such allegations are easily made but irrespective of the ultimate conclusions they do nothing to further a detective's career, however unsubstantiated or unfounded they may be.

It was during the late sixties that we all awoke to the realisation that drug trafficking was becoming a major factor in the increasing levels of crime caused by junkies having to feed their habit. It also resulted in another type of criminal, one that was inherently more intelligent, more articulate and had access to a fast developing industry intent upon defending people arrested and charged with drugs offences.

That first line of defence indeed often the only defence open for anybody arrested for this type of crime was to allege planting of evidence by the Police. This inevitably led to clashes with the National Council for Civil Liberties (NCCL) which had been set up before the Second World War to tackle infringements of personal liberty. It became relatively common for drug addicts and persons charged with possession to turn to NCCL for aid and this in turn led to a belief by some NCCL officers there must be an underlying body of Police officers who routinely turned to planting drugs to secure convictions.

We shouldn't overlook the fact NCCL didn't always get it right and in those days was closely associated with the Paedophile Information Exchange, opposed all new child abuse legislation. They openly lobbied for the right to sleep with children arguing that it was their civil liberty to do so. With such strange bedfellows, perhaps it was not unusual NCCL should regard the police, part of the Establishment, as a legitimate target.

In those days, a detective was only as good as his information and it was vital to enter that dangerous area of cultivating informants. One such man was Gary Rhodes, ex South Africa Police who purportedly was sacked after an African National Congress suspect he was interrogating in Pretoria allegedly committed suicide by jumping from a second floor window.

Well, talk is talk and such rumours and innuendo are the easiest way to blacken somebody's character. Obviously Rhodes managed to blot his copy book somewhere along the way, upset somebody quite high up as his reputation preceded him and in London he soon found that door after door was closed against him. He once confided to me he thought it was either the notorious Bureau of State Security (BOSS) or UK security services that were queering his pitch. After a few years in London he turned to crime, always petty con tricks and it wasn't too long before his collar was felt.

He seemingly led a charmed life for although arrested several times had only chalked up one previous conviction for fraud. Hardly a top flight villain but a useful one for all that and several tasty snippets were thrown my way. Basically, the majority of scams are pulled against greedy people looking to make a fast buck without asking too many questions. It has often been said a fraudster can never defraud an honest man.

Before his last conviction he decided to do a 'nut and gut' defence' which to the uninitiated means pleading mental problems, looking for a 'Section 60, Mental Health Act' result and being sent to a Hospital for treatment. Whilst on remand he was sent to Cane Hill Hospital where during a session of group therapy, he sneaked out with a young woman patient, had sex in the woods and was nearly returned to Brixton Prison where the porridge was decidedly lumpier.

How ironic it was that through Rhodes I found I had failed a promotion board for Detective Inspector before being officially notified. As he confided to me in the bar at Royal Court Hotel, Sloane Square, "You've had too many Number ones (complaints) and one is still unresolved; keep your nose clean and you're through the next board."

I wasn't too pleased receiving the news in this fashion from a criminal, informant or not but later found that apart from throwing me the occasional tit bit, he was also working for a senior CID officer at the Yard and this could well have explained his charmed life and higher than usual acquittal rate.

Chapter Twelve

Justice is always violent to the party offending
For everyman is innocent in his own eyes.
Daniel Defoe 1660–1731

Basil Street is a charming road just behind Harrods where an elegant South African courtesan Anne Defries lived. She was in her early forties, tall, slim and blonde. Any man would have been happy to be seen in her company. Anne was most discreet, operated independently within her own apartment, living within the laws of the land and servicing a small but discreet number of clients who ranged from High Court judges, politicians, bankers and a scatter of well heeled business men.

Anne would never have come to the notice of Police had she not fallen foul of a blackmailer. Willy Gallagher was a tough wee Glaswegian villain with form for housebreaking, robbery and violence. Whilst practising his chosen profession he came across the diary in which rather indiscreetly Anne kept names and telephone numbers of her clients cross referenced against their own personal sexual peccadilloes.

This made Willy very happy as he could see the potential that little diary held out to supplement his income by offering his services to Anne as a paid minder. Upon his first return visit Willy had his wicked way with poor Anne then went away two hundred pounds richer while leaving her to contemplate his business proposition. Unfortunately for him, Anne was made of sterner stuff than Willy expected and she called Police.

Which all goes to explain what I was doing hiding in a bedroom closet of a high class hooker whilst my colleague Robin Constable was more uncomfortably squashed under the mattress of her bed hoping against hope that no violent spring movements would further restrict his limited breathing. It was rather unfair, Robin was a powerfully build 6'3" giant but that was one of the very few occasions I exercised the privilege of rank. Fortunately Willy was very punctual and arrived at the appointed hour to clinch his new found partnership agreement.

Although Willy obviously had blackmail on the agenda, far more urgent considerations were clouding his entrepreneurial judgement and Anne had little difficulty in guiding him into the bedroom. Timing here was of the essence and happily Anne was smart enough to hold his passions in check long enough for him to repeat his demands for money. Here was a perfect example of where to give a formal caution was a somewhat unnecessary preliminary to the unfolding drama. Willy knew who he was, he knew why he was there and there could be little doubt in his mind who I was as rather dramatically I threw open the closet door and uttered once again the classic phrase, "Police, you're nicked."

Poor Robin eased himself stiffly out from under the bed and we frogmarched a rather unwilling Willy to my red Ford Corsair for which, did I mention I was paid nine-pence three farthings a mile?

As we passed The Admiral Codrington public house, which incidentally boasted an impressive one hundred and three different makes of Scotch whisky, Willy broke free from Robin's grasp and made a spirited exit from the rear of the fast moving car. Within the space of a minute there were three bodies rolling about on the pavement exchanging kicks and punches in the heat of the moment.

It was an unequal contest and Willy was unceremoniously dragged back to the car and dumped on the back seat with Robin, a heavy chap, sitting quite effectively upon his head. Order having been restored, I resumed a more leisurely drive back to Lucan Place nick when two Police cars, sirens wailing and lights flashing passed me at speed.

This is a perfect example of the danger of relying solely upon identification evidence. The Police cars were responding to a "999" call from a concerned citizen who telephoned the Yard to report he had just witnessed two Mediterranean men brutally assault and kidnap a man outside the Admiral Codrington pub and forced him unwillingly into a white Mercedes car which drove off at high speed. Both Robin and I were from good old Anglo Saxon stock and I would have thought it would be hard to confuse my red Ford Corsair with a white Mercedes.

Despite these reservations, identification with all its defects, still plays a major role in crime investigation and will always continue to do so. Fortunately now, with the advent of DNA and enhanced forensic capabilities, facial recognition can often be supplemented with safer and more scientific means of identification.

Homosexuality, part of the way of life in Chelsea was pretty low down in our priority stakes. Unfortunately, homosexuals' life styles were such they would often come to our notice as the victims of crime.

One night I was called to a particularly nasty stabbing in a first floor mews flat behind Sloane Square. The flat owner, Adrian Hall had been badly slashed around the arms and neck and stabbed through the stomach several times with a knife, his apartment resembled an abattoir, and there was blood everywhere. Next to him was another man, also with knife injuries but obviously not so life threatening. Both men were rushed by ambulance to casualty department and Adrian taken straight into the operating theatre. After treatment during which he was given copious blood transfusions, he was placed into Intensive Care where the doctors were convinced he would not last the night. It's a strange thing about crime investigation, contrary to what one sees portrayed on TV, generally speaking what appears at first sight to be the obvious solution often turns out to be the right one. Bearing that in mind, I made a beeline for the second injured man and when I was at last able to speak with him realised he was not the perpetrator but another victim. The pair had been indulging in some mutual homosexual shenanigans when they decided to spice matters up by having a 'ménage a trois.'

As any good mathematician can figure out, that required a third party so they made haste to the Kings Road to a notorious gay pub conveniently nearby. There they met up with this nice little Scots laddy that appeared only too happy not only to partake in an evening's fun but to earn a few pennies into the bargain. They were not to know Archie Duffield was working to a slightly different agenda. He positively hated queers and made his living by robbing them but then of course they were not to know that; at least not just yet. The three retired to Adrian's flat, stripped off and were having a most enjoyable romp on the floor until spoilsport Archie changed from being a nice obliging little Scots laddy into a raving homicidal maniac intent it appeared upon disembowelling his new found friends.

This wasn't in the spirit of the evening and the two victims, realising they were fighting for their lives, put up a spirited resistance causing Archie to flee, but not before he had inflicted grievous bodily harm upon his playmates.

Of all the crimes most difficult to detect, statistically the chance encounter where neither party is known to the other is possibly the hardest to crack, especially in a busy metropolis like London where everybody goes about their business and really doesn't want to get involved. It wouldn't be very easy to break through the 'omerta' operated by the gay fraternity.

Happily, back at the nick another of Adrian's affairs had dropped by to enquire after his health. Now, while I, or any other hairy copper wouldn't get very far asking questions in a gay pub, Oscar certainly would. Not only would Oscar help, he was willing to do whatever it took to bring Adrian's attacker to justice. There is a form of freemasonry amongst the gay community and within a few days, Oscar was back to see me, this time with a name, Archie Duffield.

The gay pub was a useful stamping ground for Archie and in the past he had propositioned several habitués. Had Adrian not had other more pressing things on his mind and made a few discreet enquiries first, he would have learned of Archie's far from unblemished reputation, in fact the landlord had barred him from the pub.

Unfortunately for Adrian, that night a relief manager had been left in charge. After a quick visit to CRO and comparison with fingerprints left at the scene, Archie was soon identified. He had a long history of violence and convictions for preying upon the gay community.

When the fingerprint boys turned up Archie's prints on a beer bottle in Adrian's flat and he had been positively identified by photograph by both victims I felt there was sufficient evidence to circulate him 'wanted' for attempted murder in *Police Gazette*.

Adrian made a remarkable recovery, and a full and very chilling statement of that night's events. You just wouldn't believe the things people get up to; at least I hope you wouldn't! Sooner or later Archie was certain to come to notice of Police and so it came to pass. Within weeks, a telephone call came through from Strathclyde Police to the effect Archie had been nicked and was awaiting my presence in Barlinnie Prison, Glasgow.

If one should ever be tempted to take to crime, if nothing else please take one word of advice; don't get nicked and finish up in Barlinnie Gaol it is seriously not good for your health. If you do, don't for goodness sake give the gaolers any lip, it just isn't advisable. Glasgow may have been awarded as Europe's City of Light some years back but certainly in the seventies it was a place best avoided and the wee hard men that frequented the bars and dives of the City centre were notorious for their violence and love of a fight. In those days at least, that extended to some of the warders in Barlinnie gaol and considering the nature of some of their inmates, could you really blame them?

I flew to Glasgow with one of my aids, Billy Prentice, a Scot, to act as my interpreter. Poor Archie was in a sorry state when I reached the gaol having been foolish enough to be lippy to one of the screws. "Oh Lord" I thought as I perused his badly bruised face, "isn't this going to look good when he appears at Marlborough St Magistrates Court?" – More allegations of police brutality.

It was a bitter cold, raw night, snow falling and an icy gale blowing. Being a warm blooded Sassenach I had the foresight to bring a thick sheepskin coat, just the job for an escort back from the frozen north. Bill Prentice, a highlander, was shivering in a thin raincoat but that served him right he should have known better.

I put the handcuffs round Archie's wrists and we walked out to the plane for the journey back. He was also underdressed for the weather, being clad in a thin cheap suit and open neck shirt. His face and lips were literally blue with the cold and he was shivering uncontrollably. Now in those far off days I realise I couldn't have been all that mean and bad, for despite the atrocity of his crime, I couldn't help but feel sorry for the poor wretch facing an uncertain future.

Quite involuntarily, I slipped off my sheepskin and draped it over his shoulders. After mounting the plane steps Archie turned to me, "Do you know Mr Woodland, that's the first kind thing anybody has ever done for me in my life."

Poor blighter, if we only knew just half of what turns people that way.

"Now Archie, you know you're nicked, you know you're going down, how are we going to do this, easy or hard?" Archie looked at me quizzically. "You won't have a very comfortable flight back in those cuffs, if you give me your word we can take the cuffs off here and now but make no mistake, they go back once the plane taxis down at Heathrow, are you going to behave yourself?"

A grateful Archie agreed, despite the circumstances the three of us had quite a pleasant trip back and no doubt contrary to every regulation in the book we shook off the pervading cold with a wee dram or two of the hard stuff.

Back at Chelsea nick, after fingerprints had been taken and Archie formally charged we retired to the CID office where I guessed Archie was sufficiently mellowed to open his heart which he did. It was a copy book statement under caution, no prompting, no prodding, just the occasional pause for another drop of the amber water of life.

Archie appeared at the Old Bailey, was convicted of attempted murder, deemed to be insane and sentenced to be confined to a secure mental institution. Months later, I received a letter from Archie in Broadmoor thanking me for all I had done for him and telling me how happy he was, three good meals a day and would you believe it, he was playing cricket that afternoon. Not all of my clients have been that grateful.

Chapter Thirteen

The more sand has escaped from the hourglass of life,
the clearer we see through it.
Niccolo Machiavelli 1469–1527

Many paedophiles have themselves been victims of abuse in the past. They are often seemingly upright members of the community such as school teachers, scout leaders and clergymen. Of course one may argue, this is one reason why people with this propensity enter such occupations but that is not necessarily always the case.

Sitting in the DI's office one day and minding my own business a Turkish gentleman was ushered through to see me. He was acting as unofficial guardian for a thirteen year old Turkish lad, studying English at an expensive private school just off Cadogan Square. Mr Ali recounted how the School's headmaster had allegedly sexually assaulted the boy. As it appeared the boy was a willing participant – I suppose on a scale of one to ten this would have registered around the four mark but was exacerbated by the fact the alleged offender was in a position of trust over a minor. If there was any credence to the allegation, it was the sort of behaviour that needed to be discouraged before it escalated higher up the scale. According to the boy's statement he was in the habit of masturbating with such regularity and intensity he damaged a particularly tender part of his anatomy which in consequence was sore and bleeding. Being somewhat naive and far from home, the boy had reported to the Head's study for morning sick parade.

Having examined the afflicted part, the Head massaged in a soothing cream that, whilst reducing the inflammation, was so soothing it caused the young man to ejaculate, much, it would appear, to the mutual pleasure of both parties. Thereafter, under the pretext of preventing a recurrence of the soreness, the Headmaster instructed the boy to return to his study every morning which he did willingly and the treatment was repeated. This went on for some two weeks until the lad casually mentioned the matter to one of his more worldly wise classmates who realised this was not a recognised treatment as laid down in Mosby's medical dictionary and spilled the beans to Mr Ali. After hurried conferences with the boy's father in Turkey it was decided he should be withdrawn from the school and a complaint made. There was only one small problem, because of the specific circumstances under which this alleged offence had been committed, the boy's father was quite reluctant for him to attend Court and give evidence. Indeed, the whole thing was considered to be something of a family disgrace. Evidentially, this presents some difficulties to an investigating officer. Apart from the natural reluctance for the boy to have to repeat his ordeal in court, there was the slight matter of corroboration.

A Doctor's examination didn't take the case any further forward against the accused individual. Of course, I suppose a visit to the School and a private talk with the Headmaster may have frightened him into desisting from such practices but for how long? How could one be certain this was an isolated case or was this just the tip of an iceberg? (no pun intended)

Clearly the matter needed to be resolved so, without more ado and in a manner which no doubt in this day and age would have resulted in questions being asked in the House, I went with my trusted sergeant to the school to interview the Headmaster. The subsequent conversation went rather like this: "Good morning Sir, I am Detective Sgt. Woodland from Chelsea Police Station. Are you Mr Smith? You are? Good, well get your hat and coat on mister, you're nicked."

Now poor Mr Smith obviously wasn't well acquainted with Police procedures and formalities for if he had been he would have said words to the effect, "I ain't saying nuffink till I've spoken to my brief."

Coming as he did from the more refined world of academia and obviously not having been educated through the medium of "Z" Cars or "The Sweeney", Mr Smith obediently put on his hat and coat and accompanied me to the nick at which stage

I read him his rights and informed him of the nature of the complaint.

As anybody with even a modicum of common sense will rapidly grasp, the words of the official caution have a habit of bringing home to the accused the gravity of the matter and the advisability of not further complicating the issue by the simple expedient of telling the truth. On the contrary, it is a direct inducement to do the reverse namely deny the matter and then at some later stage to do one's utmost to wriggle out of a very awkward situation by whatever means open and that of course includes making very wicked allegations about the conduct of the awful policeman who has placed you in this predicament to begin with.

With the ordinary common or garden villain this will usually result in keeping one's own counsel until a very skilled and expensive criminal lawyer has thought up a plausible defence; by making an allegation of ill treatment, planting, verballing or whatever seems the most effective counter attack. It is a very rare occasion indeed when a lawyer, obviously thinking of all those lovely legal aid certificates and the mortgage on his house, will advise his client to actually tell the truth. That could lead to a quick plea of 'guilty' and subsequent loss of earnings to learned counsel. Sod the truth, that must not feature in the equation.

Poor Mr Smith of course wasn't up to all the niceties of these little games and initially merely resorted to an unconvincing denial of the boy's story. It is in times like this when one feels obliged to offer advice to the uninitiated. "Alright," one might be tempted to say, "You claim the boy is lying, perhaps we can put that to the test by calling in every other boy at the school and seeing whether they have had any similar experiences."

That's usually the time when a small tear forms in the corner of the eye, a sob suppressed and in a halting voice the question is asked, "What will happen to me?"

Now Judges Rules are very clear upon the point that no hope can be held out or any inducement made to persuade an accused person to admit an offence. Quite right too, what would the poor lawyers do without any clients to defend? However, in such cases as this, when one's advice is asked for it does behove the officer to explain in layman's terms, the workings of criminal law procedure. In a situation like this for example, a man could plead 'not guilty' and elect trial before a jury.

In the rather unlikely event he is actually convicted, he could finish up with a term of imprisonment, especially if the Judge is having a bad day with his gout or liver. On the other hand, a man of previous good character, who elects for summary trial before a Magistrate and has the good grace to save a witness the ordeal of repeating his statement in open court by pleading 'guilty', may actually get away with payment of a fine. I guess that just about sums it up. As verbal admissions are almost invariably later denied, a written admission under caution is by far the better, cleaner option.

In the end, that was the route chosen by Mr Smith, it certainly wasn't for me to reveal the hesitation on the part of the boy's father in far off Turkey to allow his son to remain in England for a trial or even to give evidence in Court for that matter.

To my mind, whilst one may have felt a certain degree of sympathy for Mr Smith, may I be forgiven for being old fashioned enough to believe his liking for small boys was such that he should never be allowed to remain in a position of trust over vulnerable children. Mr Smith went before the Magistrates' Court, pleaded 'guilty' and was fined £1,000.

We didn't have a Sexual Offenders' register in those days and of course this was not part of the bargaining process but it was felt best all round that Mr Smith should relinquish his post at the school and retire to the West Country and this is precisely what he did.

Mr Ali, the guardian, was most impressed by the efficient manner in which the Metropolitan Police had handled the matter as was the boy's father who turned out to be a wealthy industrialist in Istanbul. Having been informed the parents would like to see and thank me personally, I decided to take some annual leave and travelled to Istanbul for a week's holiday. It was a fascinating city and I had the good fortune of seeing it before the natural courtesies extended to any traveller were blunted by hordes of budget tourists, many taking advantage of the Turks' inherent hospitality to strangers.

The highlight was my invitation to meet the young man's family in the Hilton Hotel. To my surprise, I found the whole of the upper restaurant, with breath taking views over the Bosphorus and the City by night, had been reserved exclusively for the whole extended family approaching eighty members. During the course of a quite remarkable banquet, complete with cabaret and belly dancer, many family members were introduced to me personally and thanked me for resolving the boy's ordeal in London and just as importantly preserving the family honour. I like to think I was a good ambassador.

And that good reader is how I joined London's Metropolitan Police and saw Istanbul. Perhaps there is something I should explain to people who are naturally intrigued or even dare I suggest obsessed by the thought of police corruption. Police regulations clearly forbid the acceptance of gratuities and quite properly so. However, there is a world of difference between a gratuity and corruption. I would define the latter as doing, or precluding from doing something it is your duty to do in return for some form of reward. That, no sensible copper would countenance.

Of course that view doesn't correspond too closely with the Discipline code which would take a slightly more jaundiced approach. However, we are talking the language of common sense and in this particular case, my dinner at the Hilton Hotel was offered and accepted post event, the case was done and dusted and I had no qualms whatever in accepting the invitation. If by way of distinction, one asked for or even expected to be invited to dinner prior to arrest and conviction that would be totally wrong and therein lies the difference. Of course the air flight was a different matter and I felt it proper to offer recompense for that aspect of the trip.

Much is made about the supposed antagonism that exists between the uniform and CID branches. To some extent this is understandable and their two functions are so different; the one more concerned with the prevention of crime through a visible presence on the streets and the latter to detect and arrest once crime has been committed. That said, there is and must be close liaison between the two and the following incident illustrates the point.

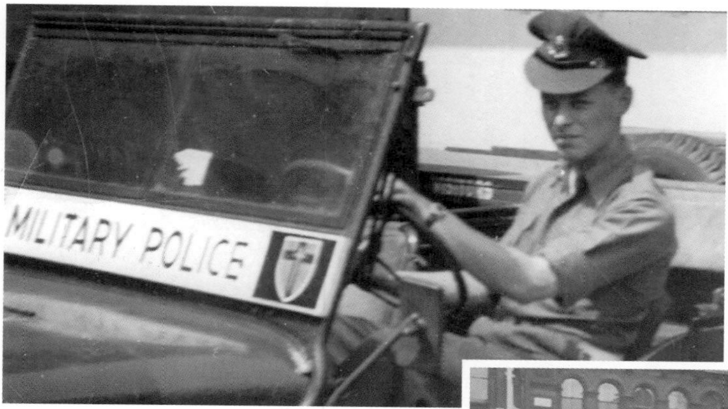

Author, L/Cpl RMP, Germany 1956.

PC 555 "C", 1957.

Aid to CID promotion party, 1959.

DI Ian Forbes. (*Dick Kirby Collection*)

Memorial to PC George Clark. (*Lee Sheldon and Linda Rhodes, authors of* The Dagenham Murder)

Hendon Training School, 1960. Second row from top: Author, second left; Luis Ghio, fourth from right. Front row seated: DI Forbes, third left; DI Clarkson, second from right.

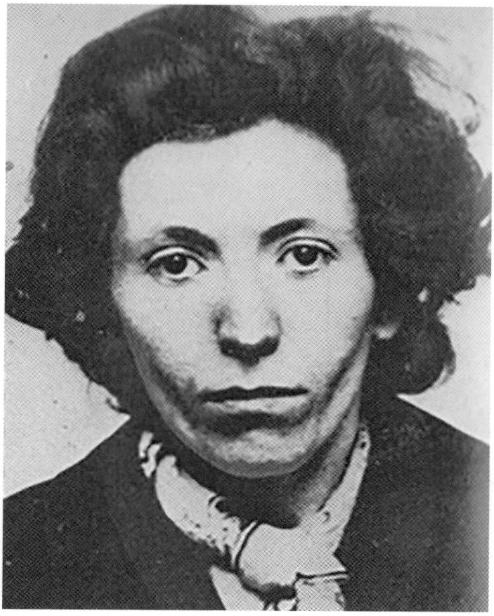

Hannah Tailford (victim), nude murders.

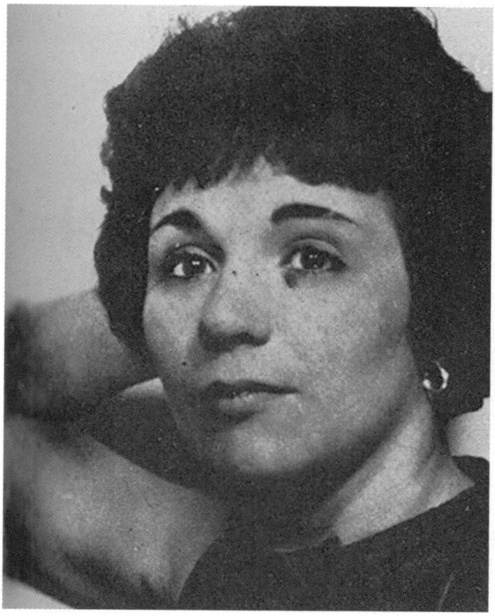

Bridie O'Hara (victim), nude murders.

DCS Du Rose, Det Supt Baldock, DCI Oxford and DI Crabbe, Nude Murder Squad, "F" Division. (*Ernest Allen/Associated News/Rex*)

Official photograph of the author following commendation at Criminal court for arresting three criminals for demanding money with menaces, "V" Division, 1966.

Lord Moynihan. (*Getty Images*)

Grosvenor Square riots, "C" Division.

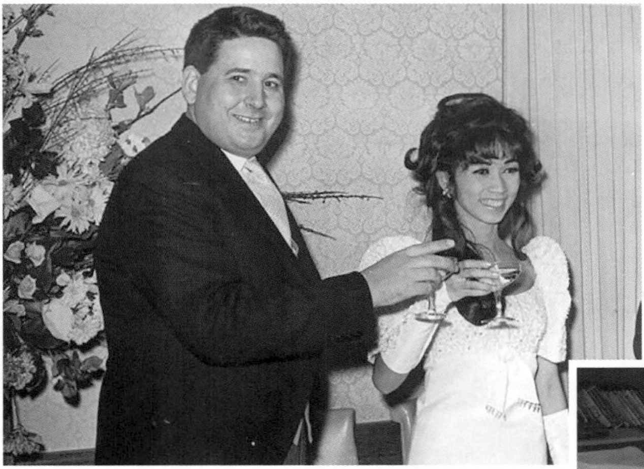

Lord Moynihan with his wife.
(*Getty Images*)

Foil printing machine,
"B" Division, 1971.

The Aussie Team – diversion theft. (*Adam Shand and Full Box Productions,* The Kangaroo Gang – Thieves by Appointment)

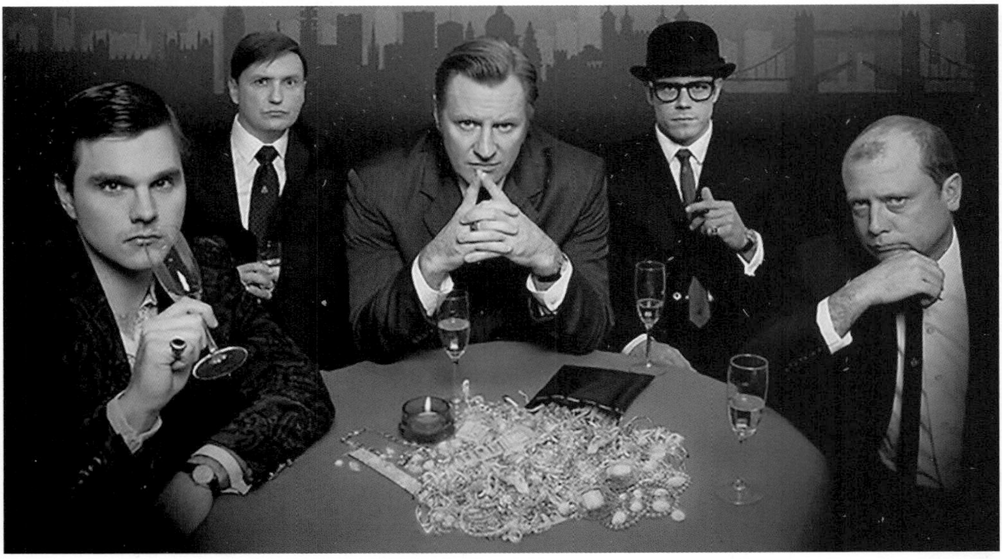

The Aussie Team – diversion theft. (*Adam Shand and Full Box Productions,* The Kangaroo Gang – Thieves by Appointment)

DI Woodland and DCI Bill Croucher. (*Jim Smith Collection*)

Commander Dave 'The Kipper' Dilley (*Jim Smith Collection*)

DC Jim Smith, C11, in observation van. (*Taken from* Undaunted *by Jim Smith*)

Certificate of service.

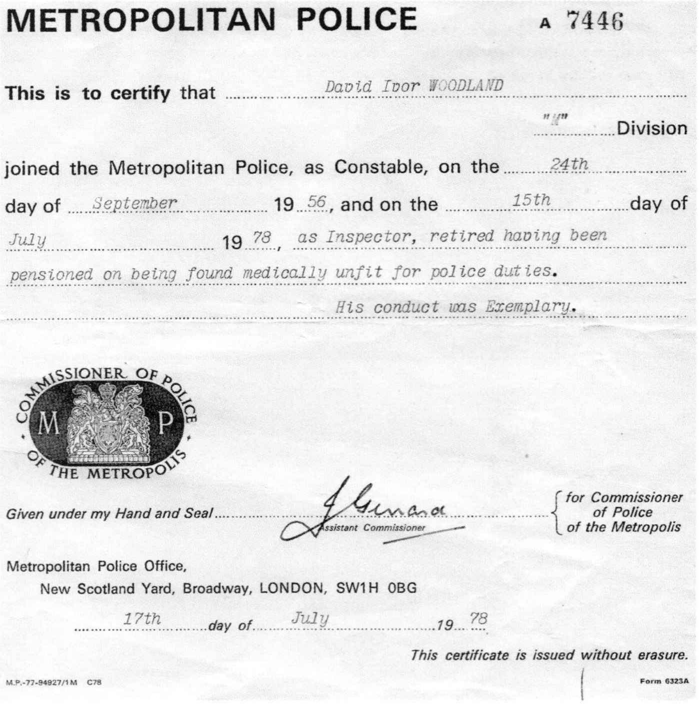

METROPOLITAN POLICE A 7446

This is to certify that .... *David Ivor WOODLAND* ....

"M" .... Division

joined the Metropolitan Police, as Constable, on the .... 24th ....

day of .... September .... 19 56, and on the .... 15th .... day of

July .... 19 78, as Inspector, retired having been

pensioned on being found medically unfit for police duties.

His conduct was Exemplary.

COMMISSIONER OF POLICE M P OF THE METROPOLIS

Given under my Hand and Seal .... Assistant Commissioner .... *for Commissioner of Police of the Metropolis*

Metropolitan Police Office,
New Scotland Yard, Broadway, LONDON, SW1H 0BG

.... 17th .... *day of* .... July *19* 78

This certificate is issued without erasure.

M.P.-77-94927/1M C78 Form 6323A

Dick Kirby – ex Det/Sgt Flying Squad and Serious Crime Squad. (*Dick Kirby Collection*)

In 1969, Chelsea was plagued like other Inner London areas by a series of armed raids upon Post Offices. It soon became apparent this was the work of a team of Irishmen whose methods were quite simple but effective. Full frontal walk-in brandishing a gun, a demand for a bag to be filled and then have it away within minutes. One particular morning the team appeared in the Kings Road and were spotted by Aids keeping observation in the area. After a punch up and chase in Kings Road, two Irishmen were arrested and brought to Chelsea for interrogation. We soon established that one of the men who got away was a tall Irishman named Eamonn O'Donnell, ringleader of the gang, who hailed from Dublin's fair city.

Chelsea was always a busy nick and when the prisoners were brought to the Station there was a problem housing them. All the cells and detention rooms were full of prisoners and suspects and I arranged for one of the men to be brought to the D.I.'s office for interrogation. Please do not believe that interrogation in London Police Stations bears any relation to the image so vividly portrayed in film and crime novels. There were no brutal beatings, no third degree or physical abuse. Yes, there may have been 'good cop/hard cop' scenarios but all in all it was very much a psychological contest where the objective was to seek the truth and where appropriate eliminate a suspect or elicit an admission, part admission or even revelation of a damaging fact that would convince the prisoner of the inevitability of conviction.

This could swing the balance in favour of the interrogator and induce a state of mind in the prisoner where he felt the urge in his own mind to co-operate in order to mitigate the consequences of his actions when he finally appeared at Court. All these admirable objectives needed to be achieved in strict compliance with Judges Rules. The important point to establish in this particular case was not the prisoner's guilt. This would be achieved by witness statements and evidence from the Police officers affecting the arrest at the scene.

What I needed to establish quickly was the whereabouts of Eamonn to search his address before he had the opportunity of disposing of valuable evidence. It was at that precise moment the Station Officer told me there were two very irate Irishmen from Dublin who wished to speak to me. One of the first things we established through a quick call to Special Branch was to satisfy myself whether or not these two characters or indeed members of this particular team whose identities were by then known, had any connections with the IRA (Irish Republican Army) who at that time were active in London.

The men confided to me that Eamonn had run off with their sixteen year old kid sister, they had flown to London to find her and they were very keen to have words with Eamonn and convince him of the error of his ways. They were two strapping six foot three men oozing menace and if you will excuse the vernacular, built like brick shit-houses. I certainly would not relish confronting them should they get nasty.

I explained I may actually have the key to their search next door in the D.I.'s office and it could be to our mutual interests should we discover Eamonn's whereabouts.

D.C. Wilkins was guarding my prisoner in the D.I.'s office. The door was slightly ajar and this gave the prisoner a glimpse of two large, angry men outside who were desirous of furthering their acquaintance with him.

After quite an exhausting morning, I felt the need for a quick comfort break while the prisoner contemplated the possibility of an early reunion with his fellow countrymen. It goes without saying that under no circumstances would I have allowed this to happen but then of course the prisoner might not necessarily have been aware of this fact and the presence of these men could just help to weaken his resolve.

Ten minutes later, feeling as fully refreshed as one can from a canteen coffee; I was surprised to see Taffy Wilkins sitting at his desk immediately outside the D.I.'s office in deep conversation with the two Irishmen having left the suspect unguarded.

The statement I made later to the investigating officer explained that as I opened the door to the D.I.'s office, I was knocked off balance by a fist in my face which caused a bruised and cut lip and as I struggled to my feet the prisoner opened the first floor window and dived out into Lucan Place. A hue and cry was raised but he was off like a long dog and we never recaptured him.

All of this put me in something of a personal predicament. The following week I was due to go on a promotion board at the Yard for substantive DI and with an unresolved complaint hanging over my head this was clearly a non starter. There was time for a little damage limitation. The two Irishmen were driven back to Heathrow Airport and put on a plane straight back to Dublin. Any unsympathetic investigating officer from A.10 Branch may well place more sinister motives over my actions, put two and two together and make six.

Fortunately as mentioned earlier, there was a good working relationship between uniform and CID with the result that the uniform Commander who apparently held me in some esteem, appointed Superintendent Ken Newman to serve me with a discipline form 163 alleging that 'through negligence you allowed a prisoner to escape from Police custody'

Well, Mr Newman investigated the complaint against me; his report was on the Commander's desk before the week was out. I was completely exonerated and went before the promotion selection board which I am pleased to report I passed.

Supt Newman served in the Royal Air Force during WWII and upon cessation of hostilities joined the Palestine Police as a detective in Special Branch until the Force was disbanded in 1948. I suspect that at that time the Stern Gang was operating in Israel and the murder and hanging in orange groves of British soldiers was a pretty heavy number to contend with.

He then joined the Metropolitan Police and by 1971 was promoted to Commander at New Scotland Yard. There is an apocryphal story that one afternoon he was sitting in his garden and his wife was reading a Police publication. It was at the height of the IRA bombing campaign in the Province and she remarked, "Oh I say, they are looking for a Chief Constable for the Royal Ulster Constabulary, I wonder what idiot would apply for that post."

He looked up quietly and said, "Well actually I have." Mr Newman was successful in his new role and helped turn the RUC into one of the most efficient Police Forces in the United Kingdom. Upon his return to England he was knighted and in 1982 appointed Commissioner of the Metropolis where he is credited with implementing many major reforms before retiring in 1987.

Chapter Fourteen

Pigs and Lords must be well bred –
Old Catalan saying.

1968 was quite an eventful year one way or the other. 'Tricky Dickie' Richard Nixon became president of USA, Britain launched its first Polaris submarine, Russian tanks rumbled into the streets of Prague, London Bridge was sold to an American Oil Company and Enoch Powell made his rivers of blood speech. As for me? I met Lord Moynihan of Leeds.

Anthony Patrick Andrew Cairnes Berkeley Moynihan, Lord Moynihan of Leeds, was an ex Coldstream Guards Officer and Liberal Peer, a pillar of respectability one may be tempted to assume. Not so. His principle occupations were bongo playing, fraud, brothel keeping, drug smuggling and informing. In short, he was an out and out rat of the first water and it fell to me to launch an investigation into his criminal activities which effectively outlawed him from England until his reported death in Manila in 1991 at the age of fifty five.

Moynihan, reputed to have married five times and to have fathered several children was held up by critics as the best argument for abolition of the hereditary peer system. I first ran into 'Tony Moynihan' at Chelsea CID while investigating the fraudulent activities of one Charles Harold Lee. Lee, writing from Frankfurt, opened Bank accounts, formed several shell companies and through fraudulent trading and false pretences obtained many thousands of pounds worth of credit, airline tickets, antiques and other property. He had been assisted by references supplied by his good friends Lord Moynihan and a crooked solicitor called Jimmy Newton.

My initial enquiries concentrated upon the references Lee supplied and I was not too surprised to find Lord Moynihan was the subject of several police fraud investigations in the past.

More to the point, whenever it appeared likely his collar would be felt Moynihan invariably wrote letters to the Commissioner of Police on House of Lords notepaper complaining of Police malpractice and victimisation. Reading the minutes on the Police dockets I was disgusted to find this was usually sufficient to close the matter and this only made me the more determined to dig deeper.

I'm afraid this was but one of many such examples of gutless leadership from the top that every working policeman encounters some time during his career.

At one stage Moynihan was employed by the notorious slum landlord Peter Rachman and drove him around London in his maroon Rolls Royce whilst, with a squad of heavies and Alsatian dogs, he employed strong-arm tactics and terrorism upon unfortunate tenants he wished to evict. Nice people!

As for Jimmy Newton, a quick check showed that although in the Law Society Register, he did not hold a practising certificate and he was strongly suspected of being involved in the notorious Fire Auto Marine Insurance Company fraud with Dr Emil Savundra. This man referred to by David Frost as 'the reviled insurance swindler,' was sentenced to eight years imprisonment but no charges stuck against Newton. But of course, that is one of the hidden perks of the job for those rare members of the legal profession that deliberately use their understanding of the frailties of the law to feather their own nests.

The deeper I dug, the more it became apparent the major beneficiary of the 'Lee' frauds was Moynihan himself and it didn't take me too long to suspect the reason nobody except a small clique of fellow conspirators had ever claimed to see Lee was because he didn't in fact exist and was the product of Moynihan's fertile mind. This realisation presented an interesting forensic challenge, namely, how to go about proving that somebody did not exist.

First port of call was obviously to Frankfurt on Main where Stefan Wolferman, a most helpful chief of Police checked the West German Aliens Department Records but found no trace of the elusive Lee. However, from letters received in London purporting to have originated from Lee in Frankfurt, Stefan traced the address and found it to be a Theatrical Agency representing Moynihan who in turn acted for Filipino cabaret artists in Europe. A list of these artists corresponded with the names on airline tickets valued at many thousands of pounds that Lee had fraudulently obtained to bring Moynihan's performers from the Philippines to Europe and friends to his forthcoming wedding.

It hardly took much detective ability to reason that if Lee existed, he would possess a passport. I spent many long hours in Passport Office, Petty France where I uncovered no less than six genuine 'Charles Harold Lee' passport applications. By a painstaking process each of these were traced and eliminated from my enquiry.

My initial suspicion was now materialising into hard evidential fact but certainly not enough to justify lifting Moynihan at that stage. When I eventually moved he just had to be caught bang to rights. I traced several Bank accounts operated in London by the fictitious Lee and also accounts owned by Moynihan. I suspected that all of Lee's deposits matched withdrawals from Moynihan's accounts but how to prove it?

At this stage I confess to a little subterfuge. The Bankers Books Evidence Act 1891 granted Courts power to allow Police to inspect the bank accounts of persons against whom 'proceedings had been instituted.' This was fine but a typical chicken and egg situation. As was the situation in this case, proceedings could not be instituted until the evidence was available yet so often, until the accounts were examined it was impossible to obtain the evidence to commence proceedings.

Justice sometimes needs a little nudging, particularly in criminal law matters and I applied to Marlborough Street Magistrates' Court for a warrant to arrest the non existing 'Charles Harold Lee'. This was granted and then, with a flourish, having 'instituted proceedings' I presented the magistrate with a handful of applications to allow me to examine Lee's various Bank accounts.

Somehow or other, amongst the 'Lee' bank accounts I must have quite inadvertently slipped the 'Moynihan' bank account applications which were all duly signed by the Magistrate. These were successfully executed despite the efforts of one particular Bank Manager who tried his best to prevent my getting access to Moynihan's account details and more to the point marked his card as to the ongoing investigation.

I then painstakingly charted the various money transactions between the various accounts which showed precisely as I had expected. The very day that specific sums were withdrawn from Moynihan's accounts, the same amounts were deposited into Lee's account and then, over a period of time, the money was gradually repaid into Moynihan's account. Once the accounts were set up and established, the fun began. My banking friends inform me that in the trade it is called 'teeming and lading'.

The net was slowly tightening and one evening, I sat in the Detective Inspector's office at Chelsea, piecing together a strong evidential case against Moynihan. By this time I had already sent an interim report to the Director of Public Prosecutions outlining the facts collated to date.

A rather flushed looking Station Officer burst into the office interrupting my train of thought. "There is one very irate Peer of the Realm outside who is demanding to see you immediately".

"Thanks Skip, give me a couple of minutes then wheel him in". It was rather unfortunate at that particular moment all my team were out of the office on enquiries and I already knew enough about the slippery Lord to appreciate the first thing I could expect was a written complaint to the Commissioner and allegations of harassment or even worse.

Moynihan's father was arrested years ago for importuning in a gent's urinal at Piccadilly Circus and before appearing before the Court, had committed suicide. Since that time, his son had developed an almost pathological hatred of Police and made many unsubstantiated allegations against various Police Officers. It was a pretty safe bet he would make no exception for me and that eventually proved to be the case. I placed a small, pocket dictating machine onto record mode and slipped it into the top of my partly opened desk drawer. Not very professional, but certainly better than nothing and all I could do on the spur of the moment.

The Station Sgt. showed the blustering Lord into my office and beat a hasty retreat. He obviously sensed Forms 163 (complaint forms) flying around when the eventual complaint was lodged and wisely made himself scarce. Moynihan was beside himself with rage, his eyes popping from his head, veins standing out on his forehead, he banged his fist upon my desk and in a blustering tone demanded, "Are you Detective Sergeant Woodland?"

Satisfied I was the subject of his wrath, he demanded, "How dare you? You have been examining my private Bank accounts, the Commissioner of Police shall hear of this, you have no right whatever."

I let the man finish ranting and calmly showed him the signed Bankers Book application.

Five minutes later a very subdued Lord Moynihan, by now doing his best to ingratiate himself realised he was getting nowhere and turned for the door. By now he was all charm and smiles. "You know Sgt., you remind me of my good friend Bobby Butlin."

I fired a parting shot at the fast retreating figure. "Lord Moynihan, my enquiries are far from complete at this stage and until they are, I have no intention of questioning you, however, once I do I suggest it would be in your best interests to have a lawyer present."

I heard his feet echoing down the hall as I pulled out the dictating machine and wound it back. Perfect, it had recorded every part of the meeting leading from his entrance to my office to his rather subdued exit. I called in the Station Officer, placed the tape into an envelope, sealed, timed and dated by us both. The following morning I took the tape to the Engineers Department at Denmark Hill where a full transcript was made of the conversation. It's called insurance and as subsequent events showed, it proved a sensible step to have taken.

A week later a legal gentleman came to Chelsea Police Station and left a sealed envelope, addressed to myself, with the Station Officer. As chance would have it, I was in the vicinity and had my first glance of Jimmy Newton as he scurried down the steps of the nick into Lucan Place.

The letter from the noble Lord informed me that as I was obviously set upon persecuting him he had no choice but to leave the country.

When he did leave, it was in a Rolls Royce Silver Cloud motor car obtained from Meads of Weybridge, a Rolls Royce showroom, upon the strength of a worthless cheque drawn upon Chase

Manhattan Bank, Monrovia, Liberia. When I subsequently interviewed the unfortunate car salesman it transpired he had been given the whole works including dinner at the Café Royal and a visit to the public gallery in the House of Lords whilst Moynihan made a speech advocating that Gibraltar be returned to Spain.

Very occasionally, in those far off days I was blessed with rare moments of lucidity. I had plenty of typed letters and signatures from Charles Lee, many purportedly written from Germany. Now for obvious reasons all records relating to complaints against the Police are jealously guarded. It was no easy matter and required a little imaginative thinking but through some devious means or other I managed to wheedle the carefully guarded complaint dockets relating to Moynihan from General Registry at New Scotland Yard. I removed the letters of complaint sent by Moynihan to the Commissioner and submitted these to the Forensic Science laboratory at the Yard and they eventually returned them to me with a comprehensive report. Bingo, not only could they prove all the letters were written upon the same typewriter but they were typed by the same typist!

It didn't take too long to trace Jacky Daniels, Moynihan's part time secretary, who confirmed that all the letters, including all the 'Lee' letters posted from Frankfurt, had been dictated to her in London by Moynihan, signed in her presence, typed, then posted by himself from Germany. Things were decidedly warming up.

Moynihan married yet again, this time to one of his Filipino dancing troupe in London. The many thousands of pounds of airline tickets obtained upon 'Charles Lee' cheques were used to ship his friends and business associates in from Asia and Africa for the wedding as were the lavish hotel and restaurant bills incurred by the generous Peer.

I obtained samples of Moynihan's latest wife's handwriting that were examined by a Scotland Yard handwriting expert. He testified the letters 'C' and 'L' from the 'Charles Lee' signatures as being totally consistent with the new Lady Moynihan's handwriting. Almost game, set and match I would say. Notwithstanding, there were several others involved in the conspiracy and one by one I arrested them and they were committed for trial to the Old Bailey. In addition to Jimmy Newton aka James Maurice Nicolas Newton the bent solicitor, were Carlo Spetale, James Waldron, a small time crook and Peter Scaramanga, a well known confidence trickster.

Peter, like so many of his ilk, was a likeable rogue and when he learned I was close to feeling his collar he voluntarily admitted himself to the Royal Holloway Infirmary, obviously preparing himself for what we called in the trade a 'nut and gut' defence. In brief this was a Court Order under the Mental Health Act, committing a defendant to a Mental Hospital for treatment.

It was early in the evening when I arrived at Virginia Water to interview Scaramanga and knowing he was caught 'bang to rights' he regarded his arrest philosophically. "Before you bang me up old chap, why don't we go and have dinner together?" he suggested. I thought about that one before replying. It was late, I was tired and hungry and knew the ensuing paper work at the nick would keep me occupied to the early hours of the morning, I agreed. "O.K.Peter, but there's one condition"

"What's that?" he enquired.

"I pay for the meal; I don't want to be nicked later for aiding and abetting fraud."

It was a deal and Peter Scaramanga proved a convivial, informative and entertaining dinner guest. He was full of amusing anecdotes but of course it made no difference to the end result, Peter knew he would be charged and convicted with the rest of his fellow fraudsters.

Now, several years before this, indeed before my involvement in this particular case, Moynihan had persuaded one Samuel Tyler Dodd, an ex con, (criminal) his valet and former batman in the Coldstream Guards, to stage a simulated burglary at his country seat, Rock Cottage, Dymchurch. After the deed was done, Moynihan disposed of the house contents and successfully claimed upon his insurance. He arranged for Dodd to leave the country and paid his air fare to Lagos, Nigeria, and his stay at the Federal Palace, Lagos, all with dud cheques of course.

Dodd had several previous convictions for burglary and theft and Moynihan counselled it would be advisable for him to stay out of the country until the heat died down. It is highly indicative of the man's nature, that when Moynihan reported the alleged breaking to Police, to give a flavour of authenticity, he had the gall to name his manservant as the culprit. It reminded me of the story of the scorpion crossing the river on the frog's back. A warrant was obtained for Dodd's arrest and after spending a fortnight at Federal Palace Hotel, Lagos, a place where Moynihan provided not only cabaret but also high class call girls for the country's elite, he received a phone call from his master advising him it was safe to return. What of course he didn't know was that Moynihan made another call to Police and as Dodd stepped from the plane at Heathrow Airport he was promptly nicked and charged. There is loyalty and loyalty but that was just too much. He made a full confession to Police outlining the circumstances and implicating Moynihan.

The Police officers from Paddington Green believed him as did the Attorney General who took over the prosecution which finished at the Old Bailey in March, 1967 before the aforesaid Mr Christmas Humphreys QC who didn't buy that defence at all.

"You have decided in your defence to besmirch the fair name of a Peer of the Realm" he thundered at the unfortunate Dodd, "a man of honour who took you in and you deceived him. You gambled and you were gambling high, You knew full well the risk you took of undertaking such a defence and you knew full well the penalty should your defence fail, you will go to prison for five years."

Evenutally Moynihan's accomplices all appeared at the Old Bailey and as chance would have it, were arraigned before Judge Christmas Humpreys.

Moynihan himself was not there, of which more in a moment.

There was more than just a little poetic justice in all this and it was fit and proper that Mr Christmas Humphreys learned at first hand just how honest and upright the noble third Lord Moynihan of Leeds actually was. This latest trial was the ideal opportunity to do so.

Richard duCann, Q.C., Prosecuting counsel outlined the case against the prisoners. "My Lord, this is a case of Hamlet, without the Prince of Denmark".

He detailed the case, emphasising Moynihan's prominent role, referring to him as "The evil genius." The other prisoners were convicted and sentenced to imprisonment. What did they receive? After all this time I honestly don't remember, it wasn't really important. My mind was still concentrating upon bringing 'The Prince of Denmark' to justice. I sometimes wondered what the Judge must have felt and how he would have reacted had Moynihan been arraigned before him.

Moynihan was given refuge by General Franco in Madrid. Franco held Moynihan in high regard as before his fall from grace he made several speeches in the House of Lords advocating that Gibraltar be returned to Spain. Franco obviously didn't quite understand the British way of doing things; had the reverse happened in Spain, Moynihan would undoubtedly have been placed before a wall and shot. My concern was to trace the man and the first step was to obtain an extradition order from Bow Street Magistrates' Court making him liable to arrest in any country which had an extradition treaty with U.K.

My best lead to trace his whereabouts was the Rolls Royce and I arranged for all Rolls dealers in Europe to be circulated with details of the stolen car. Sooner or later he would have to have it serviced. Sure enough, the following year Moynihan put the car in for service at Salamanca Garage, the Rolls Royce distributor in Madrid.

Through Interpol Headquarters in Paris I made a formal request to the Spanish Police for Moynihan to be arrested. The reply eventually came back. They had made exhaustive enquires but Moynihan was not in the country. What rubbish, I sent another cable giving his address in Hotel Cuzco, Madrid. It so happened that by a happy coincidence several of my wife's relatives lived in Madrid which made things much easier.

After many months I received another official response repeating that Moynihan was not in Spain. In desperation I sent yet another cable, this time with a copy of a Spanish newspaper report complete with photograph showing Moynihan had received a civil decoration 'The order of Don Quijote for signal services to Spain' from the hands of General Franco himself. Strangely enough, I received no further replies from the Spanish Police and I felt his award appropriate although I was clearly the one tilting at windmills.

It became quite apparent that while the aging dictator lived, Moynihan was safe in Spain and not being properly equipped for an international kidnap attempt, I tried a more subtle approach. The only way to feel the noble Lord's collar was to get him out of Spain into a more accommodating country and what better place than Germany, where Police Chief Stefan Wolferman would be only too willing to execute the International arrest warrant.

The National Press had taken a very close interest in the Moynihan story and I was plagued with reporters looking for a fresh lead. Somehow or other, Brendan Mulholland from Sunday Express obtained Moynihan's address in Hotel Cuzco and several reporters went to Madrid to interview him. There has always been an uneasy truce between Press and the Police and in general, experience had shown they were not always to be trusted and would do anything for a headline. Fortunately Brendan was one of that rare breed who could be trusted. I knew that several years earlier, he and a fellow reporter Reg Foster were committed to prison for contempt of Court when he refused to divulge the name of his informant, an act I considered admirable. I felt quite secure in dealing with Brendan and we developed a mutually advantageous working relationship upon this particular enquiry. The Press got their interview with Moynihan and when reporting the story disclosed that Moynihan alleged the reason he fled the country was because I had demanded £50,000 to drop the case against him.

As Moynihan said to the reporter, "Because I believe in God and England, I told him to get stuffed". Several years later that allegation by itself would have been sufficient for me to have been removed from the enquiry, immediately suspended and an internal investigation begun. Fortunately, we had not yet entered that era of paranoia and I was summoned to the Detective Superintendent's office to see Fred Lambert.

Fred pushed the newspaper across the desk and I glanced at it with some amusement. "All nonsense guv, fortunately I have a tape of our conversation and what is more the DPP (Director Public Prosecutions) already has my report so any rubbish about dropping the case is sheer poppycock, it's now in his hands."

I produced the transcript of the taped conversation which Fred read then visibly relaxed, "Just as I thought Dave, but our masters at the Yard wanted reassuring, I told them I was quite sure there was nothing in it", he paused, chuckling, "I told them if it had been true your price would have been at least two hundred grand".

One of Moynihan's close associates was a car dealer, Anthony Harding who acted as Moynihan's personal assistant and was clearly up to his neck in the Rolls Royce fraud and several similar ventures. I lifted him early one morning and took him to Chelsea Police Station where, after being confronted with convincing evidence of his involvement, he made a detailed written statement of admission under caution. Harding, caught between a rock and a hard place didn't really have much choice. He confirmed meeting with Moynihan in Madrid and admitted that Charles Harold Lee was a figment of Moynihan's imagination. Moynihan was aware I had interviewed his secretary, Jacky Daniels and with his lawyer they concocted a story that I threatened her into making a statement as her husband was black and he could then claim this was a racist police persecution. Interestingly, until that day I wasn't even aware that Mr Daniels was black but then after all, that wouldn't be the first or last time the race card was played in criminal investigations.

It also amused me when Harding disclosed in a detailed statement that Moynihan had asked his brief whether I could be bribed with £2,000 but he replied he had already made enquiries and I could not be bought off, at least not before adding two noughts to the equation!

Moynihan then offered to pay any individual who was prepared to testify I had been bribed and was willing to make a complaint to the Commissioner but his brief assured him that was too difficult to arrange. Nice for a change to actually get this all in writing before a complaint was made and the usual messy internal enquiry began.

I attended a conference at DPP office, Buckingham Gate with Mr David Hopkins, DPP Department and Richard Du Cann QC. It was decided that on balance, Harding would serve better as a prosecution witness than a fellow defendant. I was in no hurry to communicate this to the man, he was too useful and too close to being able to finger Moynihan so for the time being it was judicious to allow him to sweat a little.

With Moynihan safely protected in Madrid, it was time for a few unorthodox Police methods. By now the man knew his Rolls Royce was a giveaway and with the aid of Stefan Wolferman in Frankfurt, I concocted a little ploy to winkle Moynihan out of the country to Germany.

Moynihan had expressed interest in a top of the range Mercedes and a fake deal was set up for him to travel to Mercedes headquarters in Germany and exchange his Rolls Royce for a less conspicuous set of wheels. Moynihan appeared to be about to buy the scheme, hook line and sinker and the German Police were standing by to arrest Moynihan when he arrived. Unfortunately, at the last moment he got cold feet about leaving his safe sanctuary so my cunning plan came to nought.

I saw no reason why Moynihan should continue to enjoy his ill-gotten gains and had no hesitation in giving the car's precise location to the poor car salesman from Meads who stood to lose his job. I suggested that perhaps with a set of duplicate keys, log book and insurance, he may well be able to re-possess the Rolls and repatriate it to England. This he successfully accomplished and as he crossed the French border heard a Spanish news radio report upon the 'theft' from the noble Lord that officially was not in the country. There was absolutely no truth in the rumour circulating at the time that I was the co-driver. You don't believe me? Check my diary.

I kept pressing the Spanish Police and eventually it became something of a diplomatic nuisance to them. General Franco arranged for his old friend President Marcos in the Philippines to give Moynihan refuge. Indeed, later Moynihan often referred to Marcos as 'my old drinking chum'.

Manila became a good career move for Moynihan who opened a string of brothels, one of them 'The Yellow Brick Road', only a hundred yards from the British Embassy whose officials were powerless to act as there was no extradition treaty with The Philippines. As Moynihan said later to one of his chums, "I just sit back and collect the money; the girls do all the work."

It was a dot on the card that sooner or later Moynihan would blot his copy book and he managed to do so in spectacular fashion by being implicated in the murder of one of his ex-wives' latest husband. Fortunately for him, Marcos shielded him from prosecution but by this time he was so involved in drugs and prostitution he was unable to follow one of his guiding principles in life which was later found on a brass plaque in his office in Manila and should have served as his epitaph. 'Of the thirty six ways of avoiding disaster, running away is the best'.

By this stage Moynihan's drug running activities attracted the attention of the American Drugs Enforcement Agency and when faced with the prospect of arrest he reverted to true form. He traded his freedom for that of his old friend, Howard Marks, reputed to control a sixth of the world market in marijuana. Marks was an interesting man who always contended that cannabis should be legalised and it is to his credit he would never indulge in other, harder drugs. However, Moynihan in accordance with his own twisted code secured his own immunity in exchange for secretly taping his friend and eventually gave evidence at Mark's trial and conviction in Florida. This afforded the noble Lord immunity from arrest in the States where he was regarded if not as a hero then at least as a useful asset to be protected. Howard Marks of course had a slightly different more jaundiced view and in his book, *Mr Nice* which became a best seller said of Moynihan with good cause, "He was my friend, I felt terribly betrayed, he is a first class bastard".

I never did bring Moynihan to trial; he returned to the safety of the Philippines and made his base in the 'Yellow Brick Road' where he eventually died. At least, that's what the records show but – who knows? I would believe it if his body was exhumed and DNA tested. Moynihan actually boasted that in the 1980s he returned to England on a false passport and watched the MCC at Lords.

Upon promotion to Detective Inspector, doubtless because of the publicity surrounding this case, I was invited to meet Commander Ernie Millen at New Scotland Yard who offered me a post in the Fraud Squad but my eye was set firmly on the Flying Squad and I declined the offer with thanks. I had maintained my self imposed schedule and was to become one of the youngest Detective Inspectors at Scotland Yard. My modest ultimate ambition was to become a Detective Superintendent on the Murder Squad at New Scotland Yard. That of course was before the wheel fell off the wagon and I was unwittingly caught up in the maelstrom that swept like a whirlwind through the Yard when evidence began to emerge of organised corruption within the highest echelons of the Criminal Investigation Department. Just what the heck was I getting myself into?

Chapter Fifteen

The first method of judging the intelligence of a leader
is to look at the men he has around him.
Niccolo Machiavelli, 1469–1527

Like many of Chelsea's cosmopolitan, ever shifting populace, Daniel Vegas lived by his wits. Having purportedly had many brushes with the law in Caracas, a very dangerous thing to do by the way, he felt it better for his long term health to immigrate to Europe where by and large keepers of the peace were relatively civilised and certainly presented no threat to life. Not that he had any time for the law. Whilst he treated its representatives with the utmost contempt, he took every precaution not to come to their notice. The anonymity granted in a large city allowed him to flourish as he trod precariously along that very thin line which separates the entrepreneur, which he fondly considered himself to be, from the out and out crook. Vegas travelled to Europe on a false passport which ensured his past peccadilloes didn't prevent the Gaming Board in London from granting him a licence as a croupier after the usual due diligence checks had been made.

He wasn't the sort to take regular employment of any kind but a gaming licence was a key to that demi-monde where he felt most comfortable, rubbing shoulders with the rich and famous whilst enjoying the company of the inevitable little coterie of poseurs, crooks and gangsters that always seemed to hang around them.

Vegas was tall with the dark swarthy looks that made women of all ages as attracted to him as he was to them. All he asked was they had plenty of money and were generous; not too much you may think for the pleasure he gave to them. He picked his ladies carefully to ensure that after contributing handsomely towards his well being they were not the type or more to the point were unable to go running to the Police to complain. When he realised this looked likely to happen, a little gentle blackmail was often practised until he found another meal ticket.

All in all, life was good for Daniel at least until I blundered into it. His amorous escapades afforded him an expensive, rented apartment off the Kings Road where he lived with his wife, a fiery Venezuelan girl who fortunately for him was unaware of just exactly how the rent was paid. I say fortunate, for had she known, her upbringing and instinct would most probably have resulted in a little judicious rearranging of his more tender parts.

Vegas could have continued to live his charmed life for some time had he not become rather careless with his choice of female company. I'm by no means a betting man but I might have wagered that sooner or later something just had to go wrong.

Upon one such encounter, the lady concerned had fallen for him in a big way, in fact it would be true to say she was totally infatuated with the smooth tongued Latin lover. The only trouble was she happened to be married to a jealous gangster who not only found his marital rations severely curtailed but even more disastrous, their joint bank account was becoming depleted to help pay for her new boyfriend's extravagant lifestyle.

It was only after a couple of heavies were recruited by the cuckolded gangster to persuade him of the error of his ways that I came into Daniel's life. It was inevitable that my career choice brought me into direct contact with the seamier side of life and some of the denizens that frequented it. If a detective is doing his job properly he sometimes learns about crimes before they actually happen and through a well placed snout I got wind of trouble brewing on my patch. Now even low lives like Daniel are entitled to the protection of the law and although a part of me was tempted to think that in this particular instance natural justice may result by allowing nature to take its course, another part, happily the more responsible side of me, considered it my duty to remember the words of Sir Robert Peel who founded my little firm back in 1829, namely the primary object of an efficient Police Force is the prevention of crime and it is only when that has fallen down that people like me are sent to pick up the pieces.

So, full of boy scout zeal, early one afternoon I made my way to the Pheasantry club in the Kings Road where I was greeted fairly unenthusiastically by the proprietor, surrounded by a group of heavies who towered menacingly over me and certainly didn't seem overjoyed to see 'old Bill' (police) in their little domain.

"You've got a fucking nerve showing your face in here Mr Woodland" he put it succinctly but much to the point.

"I think it would be wise for you and I to have a little chat privately, Billy" I said with just the slightest touch of hesitation in my voice caused no doubt by my Adam's apple jumping up and down with a will of its own. Why on earth did I put myself into stupid situations like this?

Well, we had our little chat and it didn't pass unnoticed that Billy was just as keen to know who had grassed up his plans to revenge himself upon the gay Lothario who had taken such a diabolical liberty with his nearest and dearest as he was to make idle conversation with 'the filth' on the subject of Mr Vegas.

As quietly and diplomatically as the present circumstances dictated, he was left in no doubt whatsoever that should anything befall the unfortunate Mr Vegas on my patch, a posse of Old Bill, headed by yours truly, would concentrate all their dedication, numerical advantage and undoubted venom into making life very difficult for all concerned. The message wasn't lost upon him. "Got your drift Mr Woodland, but it's down to your lot to sort him and if you don't we will."

Let's just say I left the club a little wiser about Vegas and his activities than when I entered which is the reason I went on a fishing trip to Marlborough Street Magistrates Court and came away clutching an invitation to visit Mr Vegas at an ungodly hour of the day.

I'm never at my best at seven in the morning and certainly not at my conversational best in short I tend to be bloody taciturn and confine myself to the bare minimum of social niceties. As the front door was opened by a tousle haired, silk dressing gown clad Vegas; I flourished a piece of paper before his rather bloodshot eyes.

"Police, I have a warrant to search these premises" I said barging past him. A search of the drum (house) produced two passports, one Argentine and the other Venezuelan both in different names. The only similarity was the identical photo of a rather suave looking Daniel Vegas staring back at me from both documents.

Well, I've heard of dual nationality but different names? Hello, hello, that just couldn't be right I reasoned to myself. More intriguingly in the back spare bedroom was a peculiar piece of machinery, not unlike a one armed bandit in weight and appearance. I scratched my head, it was obvious from the expression on Vegas's face he was far from overjoyed at my find and my sixth sense told me I had hit the jackpot but what on earth was it?

A search of a desk drawer revealed a manufacturer's leaflet that produced the answer. Forgive my ignorance but this was the first time in my life I had stumbled across a Marshall Series 3, toggle type marking machine with front roll leaf auto feeder, electric heating, and dial regulator fitted with an automatic sliding table movement. The leaflet informed me the machine had been supplied by John T Marshall Limited, a wholly legitimate company in Essex Road, North London which subsequent enquiry revealed to be specialists in making machines for gold blocking, novelty stamping and plastic marking.

In another drawer I found some sheets of gold foil and blank plastic chips in different colours and shapes. To be more precise, not all the chips were blanks, all had a top hat design on the face and on closer examination some bore the name of "Cazenoves Club" on the reverse side.

The chips ranged in value from £5 to £500. I turned to my partner Robin Constable, "Crikey Robin, I think we've hit the jackpot here, this looks like a counterfeiting operation, never had one of those in the back of the book before."

Strictly speaking the Cazanove Club was on neighbouring "C" Division covering the West End of London and protocol demanded I hand the case over to them. However, this was a little bit out of the ordinary and understandably I was reluctant to let it go. Vegas came straight to the point, "Look officer, can't we do a deal?"

Now, as we all know by now, that's an offer I have had made in many ways and in differing forms but I always had a stock response. "Sure we can do a deal"

Robin Constable grinned wanly, he knew precisely what was coming, and he'd heard it all before. The man visibly relaxed; perhaps it wasn't so different in London to Latin America after all. "How much will it cost to straighten this little misunderstanding up?

"Two hundred grand".

"What? The man gasped; I must confess I always enjoyed the look of total disbelief on their faces when I reached that stage of the act.

"Mr Vegas you've only just met me and you are asking me to put my job on the line for you, you just have to be joking. My job and pension are worth far more to me than that, but of course, if you would like to contribute two hundred grand to my retirement fund here and now perhaps we can talk business, now don't waste any more of my time, get yourself dressed, you're nicked."

Back at Chelsea nick I telephoned West End Central and obtained the name of the owner of Cazenove Club who lived in nearby Belgravia. The owner, Mrs De Freitas, being a very sensible lady, telephoned West End Central CID to verify who I was and only when satisfied on that point agreed for me to call round to her apartment to take a statement. She told me that over the past few weeks the Casino had lost literally thousands of pounds, that this had been reported to West End Central Police who up to that time appeared to have done very little about it. It obviously didn't take too long for them to find out my interest for within minutes of my return to Chelsea I was called upstairs to see Detective Superintendent Fred Lambert.

Fred was one of the fairest guv'nors I had the pleasure to serve with, one of the old school he was later brought in to salvage the *Times* corruption enquiry investigation. "Nice job Dave, I hope you've got that guy cold." I didn't reply, sensing there was more to come. "I understand you've been doing a bit of poaching"

"Sorry guv, I don't understand" I replied warily.

Fred was never other than matter of fact, "Don't bullshit me sergeant, I've just had the Detective Superintendent from West End Central on the phone, seems you are investigating his Casino fraud, he's had a team working on that for two weeks and he's less than happy."

I felt unapologetic, "Well they don't seem to have got too far to date"

Fred relaxed, "OK Dave, you've had a good result but I've promised you'll hand the prisoner over to CD. [West End Central]"

"I'd hand it over straight away but the venue of the offence is clearly here in Chelsea."

Fred looked up despairingly, "You just convince me how the venue of a casino fraud in the West End is on this patch and I'll go along with you."

"Well guv, this is obviously an organised criminal set up, I agree the venue of the casino is on C.D's ground but this is a conspiracy to defraud and one of the acts in that conspiracy took place here in Chelsea, so it makes sense for me to continue the investigation and eventually charge the man with conspiracy to defraud within the jurisdiction of the Central Criminal court. At any rate the red ink and clear up will look better in our Crime Book than in CD's."

Fred leaned back in his chair, a bemused look upon his face.

"That all makes sense Dave, I'll go along with that, now get on with the job, don't hang around here."

I didn't need any prompting and made for the door, but before I got there Fred pulled me up sharp, "Just remember this Dave, you're not a one man Police Force".

I grinned as I turned the door handle, "No guv, but it certainly seems like it sometimes." I hastily closed the door behind me upon the broadside I knew this would evoke.

Later that evening I called into the Cazenove club, Lower Grosvenor Street. I don't particularly like Casinos and all they stand for but despite myself couldn't help being impressed by the sheer magnificence of the interior, the thick pile carpets, crystal chandeliers, heavy velvet curtains creating an air of timeless elegance and opulent decadence.

Mrs De Freitas showed me into her office and examined the gaming chips I had brought with me. "Hm," she said appreciatively, "these are really good. They are standard type gaming chips made by Christy and Jones in Las Vegas. This particular type is known as the 'Top Hat' chip, and they are the ones being passed off in my Casino. As you can see there is a pattern of top hats and walking sticks indented along the rim, that's how they got their name. It's a popular chip used in several casinos in Las Vegas and also in London." She looked across at me anxiously,

"I just can't understand where your prisoner managed to get his hands on these blanks. For obvious reasons the moulds and dies for these little beauties are preciously guarded." She looked up at me melodramatically, "I think you must be looking for a Mafia connection somewhere along the line."

Wow, I wouldn't mind having a clued up lady like that on my team. After taking a witness statement and partaking of an extremely overdue but well worth waiting for meal, I made my way thoughtfully back to Chelsea.

The next day I reported my findings to Freddy Lambert and later that afternoon he sent for me. "Well Dave, I think you are right about the mafia connection, I've just had lunch with the FBI agent posted to the U.S. Embassy. It would seem that Christy's went out of business several years ago and sold their moulds and equipment to another reputable Las Vegas firm. Apparently they all went walkabout and there is a strong suspicion, nothing more, that they were acquired by the mob. This is the first time any have turned up on this side of the Atlantic."

Strange, I had long felt there was far more to Mr Vegas than met the eye but the FBI arranged for his fingerprints to be run through their computer in Washington and that hadn't thrown any further light upon his true identity. That is of course unless in the murky world of international crime it was convenient for the man to be protected and I was only told what suited the FBI.

One more interesting little snippet emerged on this job however. About a week after the original arrest, I had a most unexpected telephone call from Billy at the Pheasantry Club.

"Well Mr Woodland, nice to see you've kept your side of the bargain now I'll keep mine. One job and that's that, we're square – I'm no grass."

I could hardly believe my ears, a villain who actually kept his word. "One of the geezers mixed up with the ponce you nicked is Tony Raffini, a hard case from Brooklyn; I hear he's up to his neck in the gaming chip scam. Oh, and by the way, watch your back, word on the street is you are due to be set up." With that comforting thought Billy walked out of my life I never saw or heard from him again. Sometimes that's the way deals would be done involving informants in those old unenlightened days.

There was yet another strange little twist to the Vegas saga. My enquiries into his activities showed him to be involved as a front man at "211" Club in Balham, south of the water, which was part owned by Freddy Foreman, aka 'brown bread Fred,' the self styled godfather of British crime. The title 'godfather' was justly deserved. A close associate of the Kray twins, apart from the occasional armed robbery he admitted murdering Mad Frank Mitchell and Ginger Marks and was a known hit man for the Krays. As was the case with Joey Pyle, both men operated protection rackets at clubs and casinos and they both had strong contacts with notorious New York Mafia families.

Many years ago, the "211" Club was called Hamilton House, owned by Lady Hamilton, Admiral Nelson's mistress. It was now a casino with a restaurant and bar on the ground floor. The club was officially opened by George Raft who arrived for the ceremony in a Rolls Royce owned by the notorious Ronnie Kray. It was not long after that on a return visit, Raft was refused entry upon his arrival at Heathrow Airport upon the grounds of his association with the Mob, in the States.

At the Club I introduced myself to the manager who seemed confused. "I don't know why you're bothering; two of your lot were down here last night making themselves busy."

"I don't think so" I said, what were their names?"

"Oh, they didn't give any names at first, just said they were newspaper reporters and for a price they could help sort out any problems Mr Vega might have with old Bill. That was bollocks Mr Woodland, I know a cozzer (policeman) when I see one so I gave them a drink and asked them to sign into the visitors' book, want to see it?"

Of course the names were phoney but the writing of the signature was quite unmistakable to my mind, I had seen it time and time again. It belonged to a certain senior officer at Chelsea Police Station who had taken more than a passing interest in my progress in this particular case. It was even written in that rather distinctive black biro ink which, although quite uncommon in those days, had just become standard issue to the job. I was furious, this was obviously an attempt to sabotage my enquiry but in a strange way it was gratifying to know that even villains had no time for a bent copper. I always did my best to keep my distance from that certain officer but it wasn't easy when we worked in the same office and he was senior in rank.

A few days after my visit to "211" Club, I was typing in the CID office at Chelsea when that certain senior officer came in and put his arm on my shoulder. "What's the matter Dave, you've been very quiet lately, by the way, how are you getting on with the casino enquiry?"

I swung around in my chair and looked him straight in the eye, I had always been wary of the man and his reputation had preceded him to Chelsea. Rumour had it he was as thick as thieves with a certain dubious Regional Crime Squad Sgt with whom he went clubbing.

"Do you know what, some bastard in this office is trying to sabotage me and has been down to the "211" Club posing as a newspaper reporter." The man looked at me wide eyed and innocent, "No, you're kidding."

It didn't go unnoticed: he didn't even bother or think to ask me where the "211" Club was.

"No Sir, I'm not kidding and what's more I know just who that bastard is and the identity of his bent mate from the Regional Crime Squad, it's just a matter of time before they are both nicked, I'm having the Visitor's Book from the Club examined for forensic evidence and a copy made of their signatures for comparison purposes."

That certain senior officer blanched at the ferocity in my voice, turned on his heel and marched smartly out of the office. As for me, what you know is one thing, what can be proved is another, I knew I hadn't a hope in hell of taking that particular matter any further. Of course I confided to Freddy Lambert exactly what had transpired. Very shortly afterwards the man was posted from Chelsea and I later learned he was demoted and forced to leave the job rather hurriedly not long afterwards.

As for Vegas, to this day I will never know just who he was or where he really came from. That was one of the troubles with Divisional CID work. As soon as one job was completed it was on to the other, without the luxury of possessing the necessary time to concentrate upon follow up enquiries. There were just not enough hours or days in the week. However, he did appear at the Old Bailey, was sentenced to five years for conspiring to utter forged instruments and for passport offences and ordered to be deported at the end of his sentence.

The Court directed that immediately upon his release, he be handed over to Immigration officers and escorted from the country. Where to? Who knows? I had done my bit and Venezuela or could it be Argentina or even North America was welcome to him. There wasn't the slightest doubt in my mind that tip off at the Pheasantry Club leading to the early morning turnover in Chelsea had quite unwittingly led to my foiling or at least curtailing a Mafia based plot to flood United Kingdom casinos with forged gaming chips so, job well done.

Oh yes, the set up that Billy from the Pheasantry Club had warned me about. I will never know for sure whether or not there was any connection but during the months that Vegas was in custody and awaiting trial at the Old Bailey I had a strange phone call at the nick in consequence of which I made my way to the Chelsea Potter pub just off the Kings Road one lunch time. I gazed with some curiosity at the man sitting at the end of the bar, a glass of Guinness in his hand, a *Daily Sketch* newspaper lying on the counter in front of him. "I'm Woodland, you just phoned me?"

The man nodded and tried to catch the barmaid's attention.

"That's right; Peter Cook at Paddington suggested I call you if I had anything on your Manor. Teachers isn't it?"

"You seem to have done your homework, what's your name?"

"Just call me Freddy".

"Do you work for Sgt Cook?"

"Let's just say I've put a few bodies his way"

I grunted non-commitally, "Hm, how's Cooky doing these days?"

Freddy shrugged, "OK, he's on a board for DI shortly so he's pushing for a few results. You interested in a pusher?"

"Could be, what is it, shit?" (Cannabis)

"No, this is heavy; the man's pushing high grade cocaine."

I leaned closer to Freddy and caught a stench of putrid breath, obviously coming from some rotten, discoloured teeth.

"Hm, could be of interest, tell me more".

"Well, I'm meeting up with the guy this weekend at the Royal Court Hotel; he's got a heavy parcel to trade".

Now, to tell the truth, like most of my contemporaries, I hadn't had much involvement with drugs at that time but I knew there were plenty of scams being pulled. "Do you know the scene?" I asked "there are plenty of cowboys at it nowadays."

By way of answer the man rolled up his sleeve and I saw the scabs, sores, and collapsed veins of a main liner. "Satisfied?"

"OK, what's the deal?"

"Easy Mr Woodland, I want a piece of the action and there's no way I can score into this deal myself, it's just too big".

"So, let's get this straight, what you want is to set this guy up then expect some of it to come back your way once he's nicked, is that right?"

"You've got it; I've got a habit to feed somehow"

What very little I did know about junkies was they were notoriously unreliable and would sell their mother's soul for a fix. Quite frankly I was surprised that Peter Cook was running one as a snout. Still, that was his business, he had been in the job long enough to know what he was doing. Something just didn't add up, if he was snouting for Cook why on earth was the man offering to work for me? Even if the meeting was at Royal Court Hotel, it could just as easily have been one of dozens of Hotels or clubs in the Inverness Terrace area of Paddington.

The whole thing just smelled of a set up but I decided to play along. "Have you actually seen a sample?"

"Sure, it's definitely high grade, very pure; would you like to see some?"

"Well, I would like to have an analyst's report first, there's plenty at the con, punting everything from alabaster to icing sugar, I don't want to show my hand if anybody's trying to set you up as a patsy."

Freddy seemed rather irritated at the way things were going, I wasn't actually biting his hand off.

"OK, I'll get a packet and ring you tomorrow, and then perhaps we can get down to some business."

I walked back to the nick, the whole thing smelled and Billy's warning at the Pheasantry Club was still fresh in my mind. Why would a snout proposition a copper he didn't even know and suggest he be paid off with prohibited drugs? It stank to high heaven. I rang Paddington CID and asked to speak to DS Cook. "Sorry skip; he's on annual leave, touring Scotland by car." I cursed under my breath; Force regulations required that police officers registered their holiday address in case they had to be recalled suddenly for Court or any other reason. Consequently, 'touring by car' prevented many well earned vacations from being interrupted.

"OK thanks" I replied, "by the way, how did Pete get on at the disciplinary hearing last week?" The DC on the other end was only too happy to impart the latest gossip.

"Well, he wasn't very happy, he was reprimanded for thumping that prisoner and fined £2 a week for twenty six weeks for making a false entry in his diary. He's just hoping those vindictive bastards don't shove him back into uniform in a few weeks, which would really finish him."

"Reprimanded? Are you sure?"

"Course I'm sure skip, we had a whip round for his fine last week, and in fact it's in last Fridays Police Orders under 'fines and other punishments."

"Thanks a lot," I said, replacing the phone thoughtfully on the hand set.

Quite unknown to me, on the eighth floor of New Scotland Yard, Frederick Rogers was recording his official complaint to the Duty Chief Inspector at A.10 Complaints Branch. "Let's get this straight, what you are alleging is that Detective Sgt. Woodland from Chelsea Police Station stopped you in the street, discovered some drugs on you and demanded £100 to drop the charges, is that right?"

Rogers nodded, "He told me to phone him tomorrow when I had the money." After making a detailed statement, Rogers was given full instructions as to any future meetings and thanked profusely for his public spirited action in rooting out corruption in the Police Force.

The following morning Rogers telephoned me at Chelsea. "Mr Woodland, Freddy here, I've got that packet you asked me for."

Chief Inspector Barrett put down the extension phone in A.10 Department and turned off the recorder. He had heard enough.

Back at Chelsea, Freddy Lambert stretched out in his padded armchair and gestured to me to sit. "What's the trouble Dave?"

"Dunno guv, it's more a feeling that I'm being set up and I don't quite know what for." I gave Fred a word for word account of the meeting with Rogers. "Well, you were warned this might happen, it's a pity you can't check it out with Sgt Cook, have you shown the meet in your diary?"

"Oh yes, and charged an incidental for the drink I bought him. That's another thing that doesn't add up; he told me Cooky was going on a promotion board shortly but that's not possible, he's just been disciplined and reprimanded so that will bar his promotion for a couple of years at least."

Half an hour later Fred Lambert and I drove to the Police Communications Centre at Denmark Hill where I was introduced to DCI Linn. "How's the dirty tricks business Geoff?" Fred asked amicably.

Linn was friendly enough but not a man to indulge in small talk, he was obviously totally engrossed in his work and much reminded me of the quartermaster "Q" in the James Bond stories.

"Just look at these sir, long range binoculars with built in camera, it will take 60 prints that can be blown up to show a wart on a man's nose at 200 yards, now with this light intensifier it even takes perfect pictures at night time, we got it from the Army in Northern Ireland you know."

Fred looked suitably impressed, "God, it's not safe to have a meet anywhere nowadays, not even in a ploughed field, stripped bollock naked and even then you would have to check he didn't have a microphone secreted up his back passage."

Linn, gratified by the response, allowed himself a ghost of a laugh, "What can I do for you sir?"

Fred came straight to the point, "This is Dave Woodland, he's one of the good guys, I think somebody's trying to set him up, do you have one of those neat little voice actuated cassettes with a throat mike?"

"Sorry sir, they are all out with A.10 Branch"

Fred groaned, "That's a sign of the bloody times, there's more coppers chasing after coppers than there are nicking villains." Linn nodded sympathetically, went to a cupboard and rummaged around inside. "There's something here that might do, depending upon the range"

He produced a minute radio transmitter, smaller than a cigarette carton and two clip on neck ties with pea size microphones concealed in the knot.

It wasn't long before Rogers phoned to meet me again at the Chelsea Potter pub. Needless to say I didn't keep the meet. A Det. Sgt and myself spent a very boring but necessary two hours in the Prisoners' property store checking receipts and that is where a very pissed off C.I. Barrett from A.10 Dept. eventually found me, still fortunately wired up to prevent any damaging statements being attributed to me. The man didn't capitulate gracefully and made a point of searching my desk in front of the whole office and painstakingly checking out my diary and pocket book to no avail.

Eventually he gave up in disgust and stalked from the office in high dudgeon with his bag carrier trailing forlornly behind him. A whistled chorus of Colonel Bogey wafted after the two retreating figures then we all went out to the 'Blenheim Arms' and had a well earned wet.

Oh yes, Freddy Rogers, well of course that wasn't his real name and when quite fortuitously he was nicked in the King's Road by a couple of aids a few days later with some cannabis in his pocket we found out who he really was. He had quite a lot of form but interestingly enough his last arrest had been at

Paddington and even more interesting in view of his antecedents, he had got away with a suspended sentence. It didn't come as much of a surprise to me to learn the arresting officer in that case was none other than that certain senior officer who shortly afterwards had been posted to Chelsea Police Station.

In fact, if the truth was to be known, nothing much could surprise me anymore. It goes without saying that had I fallen for the trap set for me while Vegas was still on remand, the charges against him would have been dropped and one particular individual would have undoubtedly earned a nice little bonus. I made the reasonable assumption that in return for leniency, Rogers was recruited as a grass (informant) by that senior officer who saw an opportunity of using the man as a means to making that bonus. Just how low can a man stoop and in what other walk of life could one encounter such infamy?

Chapter Sixteen

Quis Custodes Ipsos Custodet?
(Who will Police the Police?)

The advent of Sir Robert Mark as Commissioner of Police for the Metropolis was the most significant factor to occur during my Police service. That one event had a profound effect, not only upon me but on policing throughout the United Kingdom, still being felt more than forty years later. Although this is primarily a personal account, the impact Mark made upon the CID was so overwhelming that any memoirs failing to take this into account would be fatally flawed. Likewise, any account not dealing openly and honestly with CID corruption during the 1960s and 1970s would be equally incomplete.

During 1967, following a series of Police force amalgamations Robert Mark, the Chief Constable of Leicester City Police was appointed Assistant Commissioner of "D" Department, at Scotland Yard. In his illuminating account 'Doing the business' Dick Hobbs, a Research Fellow at the Centre for Criminal Research, Oxford University, (Clarendon Press 1998) contrasts the necessarily entrepreneurial role of the detective with the role of the uniform officer which, by tradition and training is based more upon the militaristic model. The appointment of eleven of the first eighteen Commissioners from senior military personnel reflected and shaped the militaristic nature of the organisation and Mark fitted quite naturally into this mould.

There were several incidents during Mark's career such as the Spaghetti House and Balcombe Street siege where he successfully used the Army in joint police and military operations. It was almost inevitable that Mark, would clash head on with the CID and clash, he most certainly did. In the words of Hobbs, '*Mark arrived at Scotland Yard as a provincial with a reputation for dogmatism and self publicity. He received a predictably icy reception.'* That was an understatement. Indeed, from his own account he was virtually ostracised by his three fellow Assistant Commissioners and his duties, covering a dogsbody of control over a variety of minor matters such as welfare, recruitment, buildings and dogs must have been a shattering blow and infuriating to the self esteem of an ambitious officer who had previously held his own command, albeit in a small provincial force. This rather sorry introduction to the Met. set the scene for the confrontation that followed.

By anybody's standards, the 1960s were a pretty exciting period. After the austerity of the war England was enjoying a revival of former, hedonistic times. This euphoria affected every level of society and newspapers were full of the antics of the rich and powerful. It was somewhat ironic that the scandals that rocked society in the sixties and seventies, implicating Peers of the Realm, judges, television personalities and even foreign Royalty ultimately infected the forces of law and order themselves in particular those police officers charged with the task of enforcing laws relating to vice and pornography. When the great, good and powerful in the land show complete lack of morality, is it any wonder that on occasions those they delegate to rule behave equally badly?

As a young Detective Sergeant operating in the outer London suburbs, I came very close to being sucked into the vortex of organised graft and corruption which swept through one particular section of the Force. One evening I was invited with my wife to dinner by Ernie Carver, a junior officer with whom I had served both at Cannon Row and Wimbledon Sub-Divisions. My surprise at the venue was as nothing when I saw the composition of the other members of that dinner party.

Villa de Cesari, on the Chelsea Embankment was an unlikely meeting place for policemen and I was quite taken aback by the opulence and wealth so apparent in the clientele. I was introduced to some of my fellow diners that included Detective Superintendent Bill Moody and a Detective Chief Inspector from the Obscene Publications Branch, New Scotland Yard.

As the evening progressed, I became more and more uncomfortable as I gleaned the identity of some of the other guests. These included John Mason and 'Big Ron' or Ron the Dustman as he was referred to. They were clearly all top distributors of pornography, obviously with a close and intimate relationship with the senior policemen charged with curbing their activities.

By the time main course was served the reason for my invitation was quite clear. This was a vetting procedure, a parody of a selection board, I was actually being head hunted or recruited to join the 'Dirty Book Squad' as it was rather dismissively referred to throughout the job. I was growing increasingly uncomfortable and as the brandies were being served at the end of the most expensive meal I could remember, my invitee, Ernie took me on one side. "Dave, now's your chance to join the big time", he glanced towards his boss, Bill Moody.

"The guv'nor likes you; you are well thought of in the job and are going places. There's a place waiting for you on the Squad if you just say the word, what you see tonight is just a taster, you can make a fortune."

It didn't take two moments for me to make up my mind but I was also conscious of the potential dangers a refusal could entail. Powerful enemies at the Yard could mean the end of my career and at that time, despite obscure rumours that were all part of Police canteen culture, nobody had any idea of just how far up the chain of command the rot had reached. As later events showed all too clearly, my reticence was well founded as the corruption spread like a cancerous growth to the highest echelons of the Department.

"Thanks for the offer Ernie, let's sleep on it," I said as noncommittally and nonchalantly as possible under the circumstances. Sure enough the next morning, the telephone rang. "Well Dave, what do you think?"

"Ernie, we've known each other for several years and I guess you must know what you're doing and the risks your taking, that's your business. Thanks but no thanks, the only advice I can offer is you get out of that lot as quickly as you can."

There was a surprised gasp at the other end of the line as the import of my obviously unexpected refusal sank in. "I hope we can count upon your discretion" he said lamely.

"Ernie, what you do is your affair, as for me let's just say that last night never happened."

Why didn't I report this meeting to the Yard? To be honest, I preferred not to know and just as importantly, who could I safely report it to? To me at that time, the Dirty Book Squad was of absolutely no strategic importance.

Ever since policing began, there has always been an element of corruption in the implementation of laws especially those which do not enjoy public support, such as drinking after hours, street bookmaking and prostitution. Pornography fell into that category and it was only years later I fully comprehended how, once the canker set in it could affect other aspects of police work. My refusal to join the Obscene Publication Squad turned out to be the best decision I could have taken for several years later the whole squad were arrested, convicted of corruption and sentenced to a total of 100 years imprisonment. Somebody was obviously looking over my shoulder that day.

In my day two types of wrongdoing were acknowledged, 'bent for the job' sometimes referred to as noble cause corruption, or 'bent for self'.

As far back as I can remember, anybody who was 'bent for self' was on his own and when suspected or detected, he would be ruthlessly hunted down and either disciplined or sacked long before Sir Robert Mark turned it into a public spectacle.

The appointment of Mark needed to happen. Incidents like the porn squad racket, concern over Drugs Squad investigations and the 'Times enquiry' made it inevitable that a thorough independent overhaul of the Metropolitan CID was necessary.

There was just too much complacency within the higher echelons of the CID, a totally autonomous organisation responsible for its own internal enquiries into police malpractice. Perhaps my own attitude and experience with the approach to joining the Dirty Book Squad was indicative of the ambivalent attitude which existed at the time. I just didn't want to know. Whilst having no wish to participate, I had long regarded investigation of pornography as well down our list of priorities. This may be difficult for anyone from outside the job to comprehend, and it was much later in my career I realised the pervading effects this could have upon the spread of organised crime in other areas.

Mark's book *In the Office of Constable* (William Collins & Co 1978) described the Metropolitan CID as being the '*most routinely corrupt organisation in London*'. I thought that epithet could more appropriately be attributed to another influential bunch located on the other side of Parliament Square. I have always objected to this totally unjustified slur upon a body of men, the vast majority of whom were loyal, dedicated and honest. Indeed, this slur has been the prime motivation for my writing this book.

Please excuse my being dense, Sir Robert, but not even you can have it both ways. Perhaps he would have been better to reserve his comments for that small cabal of senior officers at the top of the tree who through sheer greed caused inestimable damage to the Department.

Sir Robert Mark was always a staunch supporter of the need to reform the criminal law and he was right, this was undoubtedly the cause of many corrupt practices in those days. Many of the more extreme defects in the system have since been addressed by changes in legislation which by itself confirms my contention. With advantages in technology, forensic science, recent and proposed changes in the criminal law no conscientious copper will be placed in the predicament so often faced by his predecessors.

Despite his caustic indictment of the probity of the whole department, he later corrected it in a quotation from his book. "*As an organisation, the CID was and is, professionally and technically highly competent and rightly proud of this. It cannot be over emphasised that notwithstanding its defects, it always contained a considerable number of thoroughly honest, dedicated and skilled detectives at every level*". Too late Sir Robert, by then the damage had already been done.

What cannot be denied is that until the advent of Mark, many CID officers were prepared to 'stretch' the rules of evidence when dealing with professional criminals. Many criminologists acknowledge the criminal law was so defective it was almost impossible to secure convictions in a court of law without a confession.

Some defence lawyers routinely set out to pervert the course of justice by a practice referred to as an Ambush defence whereby defendants exercised their right of silence. When the prosecution completed its case at jury trial, at the last minute, the so called ambush defence would be mounted. This might be by way of producing a false alibi it was impossible to check out or by suddenly springing a procedural defect that arose at either committal proceedings or upon arrest that could lead to acquittal of clearly guilty prisoners. Happily, with alterations to the wording of the caution upon arrest and also changes in law such practices have been largely curtailed.

The Official Encyclopaedia of Scotland Yard (Virgin Books 1999) by Martin Fido and Keith Skinner acknowledges the phenomenon described as 'noble cause corruption'. It concedes this was often done 'to make the system work' in the inevitable cut and thrust of combating street wise arrogant criminals fully aware of their legal rights. If any active thief taker in those days could place his hand upon his heart and claim never to have done any of the above than he is a far better man than I. It is no exaggeration to say that in many walks of life there is a world of difference between theory and practice.

Mark, in his memoirs wrote, "*I am one of those who believe that if the criminal law and the procedures relating to it were applied strictly according to the book, as a means of protecting society it would collapse in a few days. The quickest way to achieve long overdue reform would be for police to apply existing laws and procedures strictly according to the letter. The effect would be quickly disastrous. Only the weak, the spontaneous and the intellectually underprivileged would continue to be amenable to the law.*"

That's all very well Sir Robert, I fully agree and applaud your attempts to amend the law but in the meantime how could we protect the law abiding citizen?

Nobody can deny that Mark cleaned up the Met. Nobody can deny it was badly needed, but at what price? No reasonable person could deny there was a need for Mark to sort out the bad eggs that gave the job such a bad reputation but what nobody has ever calculated was the effect this one man crusade had upon public confidence. It merely accentuated the distrust of the public, destroyed police credibility and led to an escalation of jury acquittals. Defence counsels just delighted in reminding gullible juries of Mark's words when intimating their clients were the victim of crooked policemen who had 'fitted them up'.

Did corruption exist? Of course it did, in a society riddled from top to bottom with corrupt practices, what would have been even more extraordinary would be that it didn't; nor has it changed since.

I suspect that like the reports of Mark Twain's death, the stories of police corruption are greatly exaggerated. Of course we will never know, by its very nature many alleged cases are of necessity based upon anecdotal reports. What became very clear to me during my working life as a detective was the existence of a small cottage industry of people claiming to have access to Police, probation officers or even Judges, able to influence the outcome of investigations or trials by placing envelopes into the right palms or by speaking to the right people. Every working detective would have offers made; it was almost part and parcel of the job. There can be no other walk of life where temptation is so rife and bribery is so regularly offered.

As our first Prime Minister the manifestly corrupt Sir Robert Walpole used to say three hundred years ago, "Every man has his price". Was mine £200,000? I would like to think not but will honestly never know. This leads to another scenario which unfortunately muddies the water where deals are struck between crooks and arresting officers.

In his book *'Doing the Business'* by Dick Hobbs (Clarendon Press 1988) the author talks of the entrepreneurial spirit of the detective working in the East End of London and the social milieu in which he operates.

Hobbs applies this to the working of the CID which as he puts it, *'with its essentially deviant persona forged by an idiosyncratic and ambivalent relationship with the state differs from its more formal, uniform counterpart.'* He defines the business collaboration which takes place between accused and CID where the former *'may offer information, pliability, perjury, or a 'guilty' plea in exchange for the dilution or dropping of charges, future immunity from arrest or a sympathetic rendering of both evidence and previous convictions.'*

The inherent dangers in such practices do not need to be spelt out and the opportunities this inter relationship provides to the corrupt copper are obvious. This is where the definition 'bent for job' or 'bent for self' comes to the forefront. For all its failures and for the lamentable fact the occasional individual officer fell by the wayside and succumbed to temptation, much crime was not only solved but also prevented by these practices. Hobbs recognises that the appointment of Mark served to emphasise the structural, operational and ideological rifts between the detective and uniform branch which further exacerbated the already strained relations between the two.

Before Mark, most complaints against CID officers were investigated by officers from another Division whilst serious allegations were handled by Central Office. It was only when Bill Moody, the Chief Superintendent in Charge of Central Office was found to be on the payroll of pornographers that an independent branch, A.10 was established by Sir Robert and a uniform officer placed in overall control. Mark completed the task by a brilliant militaristic style coup, described in his book.

By this time, the rank and file of the CID were concerned with the ever rising number of complaints of criminal activity which were reaching totally unacceptable levels. Our credibility was being stretched to the limit and this was reflected in the numbers of acquittals chalked up by juries who no longer believed in the integrity of police. Fed on sensational stories in the press, the public became conditioned into accepting the most farfetched allegations of 'planting' and verballing' as being the norm.

Chapter Seventeen

You have enemies? Good, that means you have stood up for something, sometime in your life.
Winston Churchill, 1874–1965

I was promoted Detective Inspector in March 1970 and posted to Crime Intelligence Department, (C.11) New Scotland Yard. It took thirteen busy years to reach the rank but in those far off days before accelerated promotion that was considered pretty good going. Whilst C11 was definitely not my first choice, it was a plum posting and considered by some to be the gateway to early promotion. Our role was the collation, evaluation and dissemination of information relating to prominent criminals and organised crime.

C.11 was formed in 1960, one of its earliest officers being my old guv'nor and mentor Peter Vibart. Whilst not so pro-active, it was in some respects at least a direct descendant of the legendary Ghost Squad, disbanded some ten years earlier principally and officially at least due to staffing shortages. Somewhat unorthodox in their methods their success rate was prodigious and it was generally accepted, at least by the cognoscenti, their disbandment was a major strategic error. Generally accepted that is by all except certain senior officers, fearful for their pensions and also by the criminal fraternity who must have thought Christmas had come early when the decision was made to disband it. In the new post war era where it did not pay to rock the boat, think outside the box or use unorthodox methods of crime detection, the Ghost Squad was doomed to failure through its own success.

By the time of my appointment, C.11 Department was a mere shadow of its former more pro-active incarnation and the new buzz word of policing generally was 'don't rock the boat and keep your head down.' I was introduced to Norman Hoggins the Commander of C.11, a thorough gentleman who would have looked equally at home in an exclusive St James Club or a military senior officers' mess. He assigned me to Number One District, a quarter of the Metropolitan Police area that covered my old patch Chelsea, the West End, Hammersmith, Fulham and Shepherds Bush areas. There was one lesson he hammered home which I scrupulously followed although as later experience was to prove, it did not always serve either myself or the job well. As an intelligence gathering organisation, C.11 needed to gain the trust and confidence of Divisional officers, uniform and C.I.D.

Any suspicion the Department was involved or collaborated in any way with the recently formed A10 (Internal Police Complaints Department) would destroy any chance of our liaising successfully with Division and severely cripple our operational efficiency. Divisional CID, linked with its system of uniform collators at each nick, was a natural source of information to feed back into C.11 – the twenty five thousand plus front line officers policing the streets were our first line of intelligence, our eyes and ears. Cultivating that source of intelligence gathering was one of my directives and anything that threatened to disrupt these working relationships was totally counter – productive. I cannot stress this highly enough for that was my guiding principle during the next few years.

The Second in Command at C.11 was Detective Chief Superintendent David Dilley. Don't ask me why, but from the moment we first met I sensed a mutual degree of animus between us. Dilley, an experienced officer of the old school had served on the Flying Squad in South London and at West End Central. By the very nature of its ground, West End Central Police Station has always enjoyed a somewhat controversial if not chequered history. This is not surprising and is in no way a slur on the hundreds of honest Police officers who at some time in their service have served there.

Within its borders lies Soho, probably the most concentrated area of illegal gaming dens, nightclubs, casinos, prostitution, pornography and gangsters within the whole of the British Isles. Dealing with the dregs of society it is inevitable that allegations of drug dealing, corruption, bribery and misbehaviour would be levelled against officers and human nature being as it is, it was equally inevitable that a few would succumb to temptation.

Two of the leading crime bosses in the West End from the 1950s through to the 1970s were Bernie Silver and Frankie Mifsud who took over from the notorious Messina Brothers. During the latter part of this period Detective Sergeant David Clarence Dilley served at CD (West End Central) before he was promoted and posted to New Scotland Yard. Incidentally, for reasons that will become clearer much later in the narrative, Detective Inspector Wally Virgo, later to become a Commander at Central Office (C1), also served at CD at that time.

Subsequent events showed both these men became too matey with Bernie Silver who controlled most of the prostitution and pornography rackets in the West End.

My team at C11 consisted of four Detective Sergeants and a Photo-fit Officer. In addition of course I could call upon the services of the Department's motor cyclists who specialised in tailing suspects, photographers and the 'telephone intercept section'.

This was known to all and sundry as the 'secret squirrel squad'. We also had a range of nondescript vehicles for surveillance purposes and liaised closely with a range of little known Government Departments. I had only just begun to settle into my new role when in July, 1970 I found myself selected to attend the Inspector's course at Bramshill National Police College in the leafy glades of stockbroker Hampshire. This was an intensive six month residential course directed towards the Intermediate ranks of the Service who were destined for higher rank. It was intended to broaden our outlook and turn us into little gentlemen. Selection to Bramshill, particularly in Provincial forces, was an indication an officer was being groomed for accelerated promotion.

Well at least, that was the general idea, I'm afraid it didn't quite work that way for me. What it did was invaluable, but hardly what the powers-that-be intended. It showed me there was a wider, dare I say more interesting world outside the Metropolitan Police Force. It soon became clear to me the way to promotion within the Service was by refraining from being at the sharp end, involvement in the cut and thrust of practical thief taking. Oh dear no, much better by far to keep one's nose clean, head safely below the parapet and climb to the higher ranks through a structured career in administration and training establishments with the minimum of exposure to operational street duties.

In short, 'don't make waves' and conform to the new politically correct Police Service that was being constructed before my eyes. I say this without the slightest rancour; it is after all the way of the world and is certainly not confined to the Police Service as any aficionado of W.S. Gilbert operas will be aware like the Admiral who got to the top because he polished the brass door knob so well.

Despite any reservations I may have felt about my time at Bramshill it would be churlish not to acknowledge the benefits I derived from the experience which stood me in good stead long after I left the service, indeed it may have sub- consciously influenced my decision to do so.

The second half of the course devoted to police duties was largely irrelevant to my future career as a detective. I mean, what good did it do to me to practice parking and traffic arrangements for the West of England Show and the like?

I did manage to pursue one piece of original research while at Bramshill.

In 1968, Jacques Penry a photographer with a lifelong interest in facial topography presented a far more sophisticated version called Photo-fit to the Home Office in London. Photographs, rather than drawings, of individual features were used to construct an image of a suspect. The system was first used in relation to the murder of James Cameron in Islington in October 1970.

Having read about this development in the press, I realised the significance and potential benefit of substituting Identikit with Photo-fit in my more comprehensive suspect building profile 'Identicode'. I met with the inventor, Jacques Penry and discussed the possibilities with him. My final objective was to take photographs of the top two hundred criminals, particularly the active robbers in C.11 Main index, then reverse the procedure by reducing their photographs into the numerical Photo-fit formula. Witnesses could then build up a picture in the usual way, the numerical code would be fed into the computer together with all the other additional data and in theory this should produce only a handful of possible targets.

Months later, when back in C.11 Dept., I took The One District Photo-fit officer to the canteen for a cup of tea. "Tell me Bob, if I was to produce a photo of a villain from our robbery index, could you reduce his facial features into a photo-fit code?" Bob took a long sip of tea and leaned back in his chair, "Course I could guv. In fact some bright spark put up a paper suggesting we converted all Main Index men into a photo-fit formula just like you said."

"Really, and what was the result?"

"Well, all four photo-fit officers talked it over and we came to the conclusion it would take bloody months of hard work so we sent a report back and said it was unworkable and that killed the whole thing dead."

"Thanks for that Bob, I happened to be the bright spark that submitted that paper".

The combined effort of all four trained photo-fit sergeants was enough to kill my idea stone dead and I was wise enough to realise there was not a chance in hell of it ever being implemented.

My spell at Bramshill eventually came to an end and it was approaching time to leave the hallowed halls of academia and return to the cut and thrust of the real world. A few weeks later my final report reached the Yard- for what it was worth, much better than I had expected or deserved. "This man is suitable for immediate promotion." Some hopes, during my absence Commander Hoggins had retired and his place taken by his deputy, Dave Dilley. Life would never be the quite the same, at least, not for me.

There now comes one of those awkward moments when I had to think hard and long what I write about my nemesis, the wily Commander Dave Dilley aka The Kipper. There is an old Latin tag, 'de mortuis nil nisi bonum' which by convention is applied to the recent dead but recedes with the passage of time.

As the man died years ago it loses some of its relevance and I no longer have any compunction in naming him as he has already been outed by the National Press and also denounced in another book about C11.

Much of what unfolds in this narrative needs to be told; it's not necessary to like everybody you work with but one thing that did impress me was the Kipper's remarkable capacity for self preservation. Nothing that follows is written through malice or bitterness, on the contrary, although neither he nor I realised it at the time, he was actually doing me a favour.

Dilley had that awful habit I have seen in quite a few senior officers of surrounding himself with 'yes' men; a quality I have never possessed. I soon found I was not alone in this assessment and later learned well before I came upon the scene, his nickname outside his immediate circle of cronies was "the Kipper". Nicknames, like political cartoons can be very cruel and whoever bestowed that particular epithet considered it appropriate for as it was explained to me over a cup of tea in the canteen, kippers were two faced and had no backbone.

I managed to get the team I inherited replaced with younger, more active officers who were not averse to spending long periods of surveillance upon known robbers in draughty, uncomfortable observation vans.

Virtually without exception all my team, myself excluded, left C11 on promotion, one finished up as a Commander although much later on unhappily, he turned out to be something of a personal disappointment to me.

Much as I wanted to become more involved with Divisional CID officers – after all that had been my specific brief – as time went by experience soon showed the practical advantages of working with the Flying Squad, a highly mobile force of experienced, case-hardened detectives without the burden of heavy crime case loads. It could be slightly galling to do much of the donkey work, be in on the kill when robbers were apprehended, then fade back into obscurity.

There were some difficult areas of practical coppering as policy dictated we did not show out, make statements or give evidence unless it was absolutely vital. Some of the evidence given in court originated from telephone intercepts and initial surveillance work by my team but by one means or another it all worked out and generally speaking common sense prevailed.

For reasons I have never understood, contrary to practice in U.S.A. and other jurisdictions, evidence could never be given in

Court of taped telephone recordings. Take for example a simple illustration of where we monitor the phone of a known villain. We hear him plotting with his accomplices, discussing robbery venues, weapons, etc., and then with Squad officers we stake out the scene and catch them bang to rights.

How can the arresting officers legally introduce these facts into a Court of law? Well of course the answer was they did, by means of skilful interrogation, question and answer. The legal situation remains quite complex and to my simplistic mind somewhat ridiculous. As the law stands whilst not illegal to bug somebody's phone, it is forbidden to use the information obtained in a Court of law. When dealing with hardened criminals who deliberately put themselves outside the law, any analogy with cricket or level playing fields is inappropriate. This ain't a game, it's for real.

At long last the Force in general and the Flying Squad in particular succeeded in making armed robbery an exceedingly hazardous occupation and this pro-active approach together with the later so called 'super grasses' succeeded in quite dramatically reducing the incidence of armed robbery in the capital. I was in my element away from the long, arduous, paper ridden life of the Divisional detective where we were always chasing our tail. Even having to do round the clock surveillance work, sometimes crouched in the back of an ill equipped observation van with only an empty bottle to pee into was an acceptable price to pay.

The pay off was when a job came off, the adrenaline flowed and a team was caught bang to rights in the act of staging an armed hold up.

A well known criminal barrister once remarked that *'British Police were scrupulously fair in their preliminary enquiries into crime, but once they have made up their minds to charge, they are absolutely ruthless in their methods.'* Fair enough, I'll go along with that.

In his book *10 Rillington Place*, Ludovic Kennedy quoted an unnamed law Lord who whilst describing Police methods sagaciously remarked, *'There is a tacit understanding between the public and the Police that as long as convictions remain high, few questions will be asked as to the methods of obtaining them, for it as necessary to the public for its security as it is to the Police to justify their existence. This licence is the price the public have agreed to pay for the maintenance of law and order: they trust the Police not to abuse it and on the whole their trust is justified.'*

Sadly, over the past few decades, a series of scandals broke down this trust, public confidence was eroded and this destroyed the delicate balance that prevailed in previous generations. I fear it may never return. That is the unfortunate and heavy price the majority of honest cops and of course the general public have to pay for the occasional rotten apple.

One of the major difficulties facing working detectives has always been in the handling of informants. They are, or at least were, a necessary, tool in the fight against crime. Informants often have every reason to lie but without them, many prosecutions of those committing serious crimes would simply never take-off. The relationship between a police-handler and his informant is a delicate one and a constant test of an officer's integrity and honesty. Whether or not an officer's relationship with his informant is publicly perceived to be corrupt to some extent depends upon the publics' attitude to the Police at any given time which makes it imperative to regain their trust. David Rose, in his book "*In the Name of the Law – The collapse of Criminal Justice*", (Vintage 1996) castigates the concept of 'noble cause' corruption but fairly makes the point that wrongful acquittals and wrongful convictions are but two sides of the same coin. Accepting as he does, that crime is a real problem which damages real people's lives, Rose poses the question of whether institutionalised malpractice existed because the participants believed that without it, successful investigation and the proving of cases beyond reasonable doubt could simply not be achieved. That in turn begs the next question namely "if that was what practitioners instinctively felt, could they, in fact have been right?"

The late Lord Chancellor Hailsham of bell ringing fame once described "The gulf between logic and the law". He robustly attacked the 'so called right of silence'. He made the point that any innocent person accused of crime would wish to speak out and would not hide behind the right to remain silent. His view was that when an accused stood trial there should be logic and openness on both sides with all logical and probative facts presented to a reliable tribunal of fact with a reliable appeal procedure to guarantee a reliable result. He concluded '*There are more sacred cows in our law of criminal evidence and procedure than would fill Smithfield market in a decade.*'

In theory at least, the Home Secretary has to personally authorise every telephone intercept but in practice, bearing in mind there are over fifteen hundred authorisations each year, this is delegated to a Home Office Department that liaised closely with C.11 and the Security Services.

The intercept office for obvious reasons operated behind closed doors. The physical aspects were handled outside the Yard and a squad of typists were kept busy making transcripts of all 'dodgy' telephone calls. The first man to have access to the transcripts was The Kipper and it was rumoured with some justification the man knew all there was to know about the secrets, peccadilloes and affairs of every senior officer in the job. This made him a dangerous man to cross. It also made him all powerful within the hierarchy at the Yard for as time was soon to tell, there was plenty that certain top cops would wish to keep under wraps.

Chapter Eighteen

A nation can survive its fools and even the ambitious
But it cannot survive treason from within.
Cicero (106–43BC)

Shortly after his appointment, Mark lost no time setting about the mess he was detailed to clear up. He confronted the senior officers of the CID and let them know in no uncertain terms of his intentions to root out corruption. The following year Mark appointed Deputy Commissioner Gilbert Kelland to investigate corruption at the Yard and Commander Ron Steventon was deputed to co-ordinate police action against corruption and the pornographic empire being run by Bernie Silver and Frankie Mifsud. By this time at the instigation of Commander Virgo, a certain Jimmy Humphries had been introduced to Bill Moody the corrupt chief of the Obscene Publication Squad and soon became a major player. Humphries was moving in elevated circles and in 1970 was invited by Commander Ken Drury to a Flying Squad Annual dinner.

In August, 1971, a brave officer, Police Superintendent Gerald Richardson, from Blackpool was shot and killed by Freddy Sewell, a London robber during a botched up jewellery heist. Shortly before the shooting, Sewell and others were under surveillance in London by C.11 officers working with a team from the Flying Squad. Dark rumours even circulated that Sewell was a grass for a high ranking Squad officer, a close associate of The Kipper. Questions were quite properly being asked about how Sewell managed to pull a job in Blackpool whilst allegedly under twenty four hour surveillance in London and the Yard was a hive of rumour and activity.

The Kipper called in a few of his trusty's and a wall of silence fell over the whole enquiry. One of the villains turned over and arrested in a flurry of Police activity was Joey Pyle, the South London gang leader who master minded the Mitcham Casino blagging mentioned earlier. Pyle was arrested for possession of a firearm that he alleged was planted upon him and he was eventually acquitted at the Old Bailey. This in turn led to Pyle denouncing Ken Drury, Commander of The Flying Squad for holidaying in Cyprus with Jimmy Humphries, the Soho pornographer and that sparked the high level enquiry that terminated in Drury's imprisonment for corruption in July 1977.

In the light of troubling rumours regarding Sewell's alleged involvement in certain Police circles in London, a separate team of officers from Blackpool was posted to Tintagel House, well away from the Yard to investigate independently of the Met. Newspapers were full of allegations of Police corruption and morale was at its lowest, suddenly everybody was suspect and there was a feeling of uncertainty, nobody knew who could be trusted any more.

In his hard hitting book *'Undaunted'*, written after leaving the Force, C.11 Police photographer Jimmy Smith relates how prior to the shooting of Superintendent Richardson, he was instructed by a officer from C11 to keep observation in Hatton Garden where a well known robber was meeting up with some mates 'to discuss a bit of business'. Jim took a series of photographs which included some of Frederick Sewell. A few days later he was told by the same officer the 'Hatton Garden team' were going to do a job 'up country'. One of the C11 officers was disgusted they were not being allowed to follow them up and hit them at the scene but the guv'nor (Dilley) vetoed this saying they should be allowed to do the job and hit them when they came back with the gear (crime proceeds). Jimmy prophetically added, "Someone, some day is going to get badly hurt."

On the day of the Blackpool killing, Jim Smith saw Dilley closeted all morning in his office with two chums, Commander Ken Drury, head of Flying Squad and Commander Wally Virgo head of C1 (Central Office). Both these men were later sentenced to long periods of imprisonment for corrupt practices unconnected with this particular case. There is an old and apt truism, 'You will be known and be judged by the company you keep.' Much later I was to become painfully aware of the close relationship between Dilley and Virgo.

When the Blackpool officers arrived in London they came to C11 in an effort to identify the team that had murdered their guv'nor. Dilley buttonholed Jim Smith, told him to show photos of the usual subjects but to 'keep the Hatton Garden photos out of the way at this time'. Now why on earth would he give such an order? Needless to say, when a Blackpool officer went to see Jimmy, the former 'inadvertently' turned over a photograph and as he did so emotionally exclaimed, "Shit, that big bastard is wearing the same jacket as he was when he killed the boss". Both men returned to the C.11 main office where there were various senior Squad officers closeted with Dilley in his office. In Jim Smith's own words, when Sewell's photograph was produced, "If looks could kill I would have been dead at that point as Dilley stared at me."

Standing next to Dilley was one of his close associates Alec West, a senior officer whom many officers would not work with as he was considered 'dodgy'. Much later West was arrested upon a separate unconnected corruption case but was later acquitted.

Jim could not have been too surprised when shortly afterwards, following a heated exchange with The Kipper, he found himself returned to uniform duties upon the feeble excuse given that his cover had been blown over the publicity following a hostage taking and shooting incident at India House in which he was involved and decorated for bravery.

These are not the sort of things that get bandied about the office and from my perspective; at the time of these matters I was totally unaware of the swirling undercurrents. It would not be putting things too strongly to say that had I known the full facts that emerged later from Jim's book, my subsequent actions would have been somewhat different but then, as we all know it is easy to be wise after the event. It was in this atmosphere of distrust and suspicion bordering on paranoia that Robert Mark was appointed Commissioner.

Around that time I received a telephone call from an old friend, a solicitor with offices in Shaftesbury Avenue. "David, can we meet? I have some rather explosive information you should know."

Jeff was the solicitor who handled the defence of Archie Duffield, the man I arrested in Chelsea for attempted murder. I like to think we had mutual respect for each other and was intrigued to learn the reason for his call. I booked out my car, call sign 'Central 36' and drove to Shaftesbury Avenue to meet with Jeff. His opening gambit was, "Do you know a Commander Virgo?"

I had never worked for or with him, our paths never crossed and I knew nothing of his reputation, good, bad or otherwise. Jeff seemed reassured by this but appeared hesitant, "I think you should know, Virgo is taking bribes from pornographers, the Press have got hold of it and it will be in the papers this weekend, I only hope you are not involved."

"No way Jeff, but what do you expect me to do about it?"

"Dave, I'm pleased this doesn't affect you, but you should take this straight to the top, somebody will have egg on their face if the news breaks first."

I returned to the Yard, wondering what I should do with this rather incomplete but damaging allegation, clearly it was not something I should keep to myself, frankly I would rather not have known. I found myself rather reluctantly knocking on the Kipper's door. "Guvnor, I think there is something you should know". I recounted the story to Dilley who seemed more than interested. For once, he appeared to be matey. "Who is your source Dave? Does he have any more details?"

After telling him, the Kipper bounded from his desk, "Follow me Dave" he commanded. Dilley led me straight downstairs to Central Office and to my surprise I found myself ushered straight into Commander Virgo's office. This was the first time I had formally met the man. "Wally, there is something you should hear".

I just couldn't believe what was happening, it left me totally flabbergasted and completely unprepared for what followed. The very last thing I expected was to find myself repeating the conversation to Virgo's face. Here was a man that was about to be exposed in the National Press for corruption and Commander Dilley was deliberately marking his card. To my mind he should have been reporting these facts at Deputy Commissioner level so the job could have taken steps to put its own house in order before exposure in the press. At the very least, had the man been suspended before the story broke it would have mitigated any embarrassment and harm to the Met's reputation. "Who else knows about this?" demanded Kipper.

"Only you guv".

"Good, well let's just keep it like that shall we Mr Woodland? There are very good reasons for all this that certainly don't concern you "

You bet there were! Our friendly little honeymoon was quite clearly over and I was dismissed. As I left the office The Kipper was huddled in earnest conversation with Virgo. That strange incident certainly set off warning bells but even then these were tempered with caution. I did what I thought was right, the matter was now firmly outside my hands.

Rumours about the activities of the Obscene Publications or so called Dirty Book Squad had been circulating for some time and perhaps Virgo's name had been deliberately put into the frame to create a smokescreen and allay suspicion of the real targets; who knows? Well I guess the answer to that is I certainly do now, many years later! Nobody, but nobody could be trusted any longer, confusion reigned. Before long the 'very good reasons' were soon to become apparent but not in the way I had anticipated.

Shortly after my meeting with Jeff, the story broke in the National Press. Dawn raids were carried out upon the whole of the Obscene Publication Squad personnel and amongst those arrested were none other than Wally Virgo himself, Detective Chief Superintendent Bill Moody, Superintendent George Fenwick, and my old chum Ernie Carver.

Subsequent enquiries revealed that Virgo had been the prime mover behind the whole mucky business. He was instrumental at the outset by introducing Moody and other bent officers to the notorious Bernie Silver who, with Frankie Mifsud, controlled the majority of night clubs, clip joints, dirty book shops and prostitute flats in Soho.

Silver also had a reputation as being a corrupter of Police and boasted of the officers he figuratively had in his pocket. Whilst researching this book many years later, I found Silver had been photographed at a C.11 social function, a stag night held at the Surrey Oval cricket ground. He was invited as a personal guest of none other than the Kipper. This association had clearly lasted since Dilley's days at West End Central. Dilley actually referred to Silver as 'my man' to one particular C.11 officer who quite understandably does not wish to be identified.

After retiring from the job, Jim Smith the ex C11 photographer revealed in his book '*Undaunted*' that in 1972 whilst working at the Department, he and a colleague, DC John French photographed Bernie Silver and Frankie Mifsud in Soho and upon return to the office found that for some strange reason there were no official C11 photos of the former. When Dilley saw the prints he wanted to know who had commissioned them and ordered them to be destroyed as in his words, "He (Silver) is history".

That's as maybe, but in September 1974, Silver was targeted by Commander Bert Wickstead, aka 'The Old Grey Fox', the incorruptible boss of the Yard's Serious Crime Squad. The previous year, tipped off by a bent copper, Silver fled the country. Notwithstanding, Wickstead bided his time – let it be known the man was no longer of interest. Then, having been lured back into the country, Silver was arrested.

In December 1974 he was sentenced to six years imprisonment for living off immoral earnings. Newspapers reported no less than three senior Police Officers gave evidence for the defence. I wonder who?

The following year Wickstead arrested Silver again for the murder of Tommy Smithson, a notorious hard man and 'minder' in the West End. He was convicted of the murder in 1975 but this was quashed upon appeal the following year. Not bad for a 'has been'. It is totally beyond credibility or belief that Commander David Dilley, boss of Crime Intelligence, New Scotland Yard, was unaware of Silver's activities. With his previous service in the West End and the resources at his disposal, he would have had to be either a deaf and dumb mute or a total imbecile not to and believe me, David Clarence Dilley was neither.

Returning to the Virgo story, when investigations started, it transpired that Virgo had personally recommended to the Home

Secretary that he disregard the findings of Lord Longford's Commission on Pornography. How convenient to have friends in high places as it was dangerous to make enemies at the top.

Meanwhile, my old boss Fred Lambert was getting too close to the truth for comfort upon the *Times* enquiry into 'a firm within a firm'. He stumbled upon a line of enquiry leading directly to the activities of the Dirty Book Squad and was immediately removed from the enquiry by Virgo. When Fred asked the reason why, Virgo replied to the effect that Lambert had 'backed the wrong horse.' Fred persisted in his enquiries and Virgo transferred him to another 'nothing job' at Interpol Office. Poor Fred became yet another example of 'collateral damage' when sickened by the deceit and lies, he left the job. What a waste of an honest, dedicated cop.

Virgo was later sentenced to fourteen years while altogether eighteen members of the Porn Squad were sentenced to a total of more than 100 years imprisonment. It now began to stack up and make some sort of twisted logic. Dilley's forewarning to Virgo placed a wholly different perspective upon his involvement with the Dirty Book Squad. What better man to have in your corner, watching your back than a man in Dilley's privileged position? Yet again, armed with the benefit of that wonderful commodity called hindsight, only one possible conclusion could be drawn namely that Dilley was also on the Dirty Book Squad payroll. As they say in the East End, "There ain't any taste in nuffing".

Several years after my retirement, I went to the British Newspaper Library, Colindale, determined to discover more of this story and the unwelcome spin off effect it was to have upon me. An article in *News of the World* dated June, 1977 entitled "I find Godfather [Judah Binstock] on the run" and continuing "Top Yard men quizzed over rich friends" had photographs of Dilley and Mike Franklin, together with Judah Binstock, and a report upon their activities. The timing was such as to confirm without any doubt, at least in my mind, that Ron Steventon, A.10 Department was more concerned with a damage limitation exercise than uncovering the true facts about Dilley. Although my revelation of the information received from my informant about Judah Binstock was but a small part of the jig-saw, any investigator worth his salt and seeking to establish the truth would have jumped at the opportunity I presented to explore this avenue of enquiry. I don't blame Ron Steventon in the slightest; he was only doing his level best to preserve what little still remained of the job's image.

Chapter Nineteen

'Who'll come a waltzing Matilda with me?'
Attr. to Banjo Paterson, 1895.

Let us get away for a moment at least from office politics and skulduggery and back down to real Police work. Shortly after my return to C.11 (Crime Intelligence Branch) from Bramshill Police College I received a phone call from Len Mountford, ex Flying Squad Detective Inspector, who in his retirement headed the American Express security team in the Haymarket. Len came straight to the point.

"When the hell are you blokes going to do something about the Aussies?" he asked, "They're tearing the West End apart, there isn't a Bank they haven't hit over the past six months and nobody at West End Central seems remotely interested."

After a beer and sandwich, I studied the thick dossier Len had prepared. By a series of ruses, a team of Australians were robbing Banks using diversionary tactics and making off with thousands of pounds of travellers' cheques and foreign currency.

Within days or even hours these cheques were being cashed with forged passports and identity documents all over England and the Continent. Their method simple but effective, was diversion fraud. One of the team would go to the Foreign Exchange desk in the Bank and ask for a series of dollar travellers' cheques or currency in various denominations. The Exchange Clerk would take bundles of cheques out of his drawer to make up the order. At the same time, other members of the team would enter the Bank and create a diversion. Sometimes one would pretend to be drunk and vomit on the floor, on other occasions a man would rush into the Bank, clutching his face which had a convincing looking facial wound pouring make believe blood, another would urinate in the corner of the banking hall or two men would start fighting. A female member of the gang would do an impromptu striptease which was sure to distract everybody in the Bank. Whatever ruse was used, everybody's attention would be fixed upon the incident at which stage the 'customer' would lean over the cashier's till, slip an extended telescopic car aerial with a bent up ferrule under the rubber bands holding the bundles of notes then very quietly and unhurriedly leave. His confederates would follow immediately after and it would be some time before the cashier realised he had been robbed.

Very neat, no violence and correspondingly there was little co-ordinated police activity. As far as the various Central London Police Stations were concerned, this was just another walk in theft, often below ten thousand pounds. It was not the sort of job that would be reported to C.11. Branch by an overworked Divisional detective – it would be just another undetected entry in the Crime Book.

Len Mountford had done his homework well, some of the thieves had been captured on camera and this was a good starting point. "Dave, we have been hit for over a hundred and fifty thousand pounds and Visa and Access have also been badly hit this team must be making fortunes."

Now one hundred and fifty thousand pounds in these days is pretty small beer, but in those seemingly far off days, with the accumulation of similar scams committed against the banks and other major credit card companies it was worthy of serious attention.

"Len, you know the trouble as well as I, the Aussies are careful never to use violence and we tend to regard them as glorified shop lifters, nobody seems to have the time or resources to go after them especially while they keep such a low profile."

Len nodded, "Sure, everybody's up to their necks in paper work and they tend to concentrate on the jobs where there is a chance of a quick collar".

It seemed to me the other man was holding something back.

"Come on, Len, we all know there are more paper hangers to the square mile on this patch than anywhere else, let's have it all."

Mountford chuckled, "O.K. if you want it spelled out when it comes to the Aussies they are well minded, nobody wants to know. When I was on the Squad, they always used the pubs and clubs around Bayswater, told a bloody good yarn, pushed the occasional drink across to Old Bill who never paid them much attention. You know the score, one thing leads to another, there's a few well placed officers that have the occasional drink or even more..."

Len looked at me quizzically; this innocuous understatement was a simple test to judge my reaction.

"Len, leave it with me and by the way, keep it to ourselves, I know there are a few blokes on the Squad and Division who socialise with them and have the odd beer, and nothing wrong in that but that's how leaks could happen so we'll play this one close to the chest."

Len was a shrewd operator and his response gave me room for thought, without expanding further he merely said, "Well, watch your back, the leaks may come just a little closer to home than you may think, if you take this job on you may end up wishing you hadn't".

After a few discreet chats with local collators and long sessions in Criminal Record Office we began to build up a picture of some of the team involved. My squad started to hang around the Bayswater pubs and clubs the Aussies frequented. Eventually, with the help of Jimmy Smith the C.11. photographer, we updated the 'Australian Index' a data base and scrap book of photos, many of whom were not previously known to Police. I didn't have any snouts or contacts in the Aussie community. To break into their closely knit fraternity and identify the many faces that were coming to light in both the bank photographs and through our own surveillance reconnaissance, we needed to put names to faces, establish their associates, the places they frequented and the fullest possible pattern of their daily lives. In this way we could hopefully put ourselves one jump ahead and with a pro-active approach hope to catch them literally on the job. This intelligence driven response was beginning to show results with armed robberies, why not adopt it in other areas? There was nothing new about such a methodical approach. Initial research indicated two of the foremost and most active members of the Aussie team were the Lloyd Brothers, identical twins, some of whose exploits I have already described in

Chapter Ten. Both had considerable form both in England and Sydney, New South Wales, from where they originated. Police Forces from all over the Continents of Europe and Australasia had experienced their predations but they were very rarely convicted. There was a hard core of some ten to twenty men and when suspicion fell upon any one member, he would return to Sydney and be replaced by one or more operators which didn't make our task any easier. Clearly it would be a great advantage to tap the telephones of my main suspects to see what leads developed.

I had a certain degree of autonomy in deciding how any intercepts unofficially allocated to me would be deployed and I had a quick chat with Wilf Pickles, the DI in charge of C11 Intercept Section. Each morning would find me in one of the 'reading booths' supervising typed transcripts of my suspects' conversations which initially, promised to be quite productive. However, within a few days Wilf called me into his office and showed me the latest transcript from Wee Jimmy Lloyd to his brother Cecil. The import was clear; I felt a sense of anger and frustration as I read through the transcript. "Watch out for your 'dog and bone', I'm being tinkered, meet me at the usual place".

The implication was obvious and very worrying. Within a few days Jimmy Lloyd had been tipped off his phone was being monitored and that information could only have come from a highly placed police source or possibly a crooked telephone engineer. If it was the former I had great difficulties, it must have been from within my own Department. Len Mountford's warning came back to me with a vengeance.

Wilf broke the silence, "Sorry Dave, but you've been blown out, we may as well take these intercepts off, the guv'nor wasn't that happy when he first heard about it, told me you were wasting your time"

I bet he wasn't; I wasn't particularly overjoyed myself, I needed to think long and hard of my best strategy. At least this indicated I was on the right track and it also warned me of the possibility of internal sabotage and from what quarter I could now hazard a pretty reasonable guess.

"No, Wilf, do me a favour, let it run for a few weeks and let's see what develops."

"Be it on your own head, but don't say I didn't warn you".

Although to all outward appearances the lines appeared unproductive, we nevertheless built up much useful intelligence. Good old fashioned physical surveillance techniques, mostly in the back of draughty, uncomfortable observation vans, soon cracked the methods they were using to conceal their movements and deter my surveillance team, all of whom were handpicked and totally trustworthy. Every phone call made and received, however innocuous the content, allowed us to build up names and addresses of the suspects and their associates. Being aware of the potential 'enemy within' I was obliged to resort to concocting spurious diary entries, in themselves disciplinary offences, to cover the amount of time and effort being put into this operation. My small team from No 1 District Squad spent many laborious days clocking the activities of the Aussies, none more so than Jim Smith the photographer who performed sterling work in his observation van. It was time to brief the team upon developments to date and warn them of the possibility of interference from within, even possibly from somebody high up within our own Department.

"Jimmy, keep up the obo on the "Dennis" Club but book these assignments out to me. If anybody asks what you are doing show them the pictures of that blagging team we were plotting last month, that should keep them happy."

"OK guv, what shall I do if any police officers turn up there?"

"Let me know but keep the prints and negatives out of sight, there's enough backstabbers in the job without giving ourselves a bad name, as long as we know who we are dealing with they should be no threat to us."

Jim Smith was one of several Police Officers called to a hostage incident at the Indian Embassy where two armed suspects threatened the officers with a gun and were shot dead for their trouble. It all went rather pear shaped when it turned out the weapons used by the suspects were in fact replica guns and not the real thing. Still, if you are looking down the barrel of a firearm the last thing on your mind is considering whether or not it is a replica.

Although the officers acted quite properly and with great courage, it caused a minor diplomatic incident and questions were asked as to how to deal with the officers involved. Happily, in this instance sanity prevailed and Jimmy was awarded the British Empire Medal for meritorious service.

Whilst maintaining surveillance upon the Aussies, another telling incident happened when Jimmy, crouched in the back of a small mini-van only recently acquired by the Department, waited for Jimmy Lloyd to emerge from a flat in St John's Wood. There was no doubt Lloyd had been tipped off he was under surveillance and nothing demonstrated this more than the steps he took to ensure he was not being followed. This confirmed my earlier suspicions as to the source of the leak.

Without the slightest hesitation, Lloyd marched directly up to the newly acquired observation van and tried unsuccessfully to gaze through the windscreen into the darkened interior. He circled the van, trying all the door handles with the same degree of success and finally resorted to banging loudly upon the metallic roof causing the magnified noise to reverberate through the confined rear section where Jim Smith lay uncomfortably awaiting the next assault. This took the shape of verbal abuse directed against the hapless undercover detective whose presence and identity had so obviously been blown.

"Come out you spying little bastard" Lloyd demanded imperiously "and I'll punch your bleeding head in".

Jim Smith, cramp creeping up his legs, felt his temper rising and had to resist the urge to break cover and confront his tormentor which he realised, was precisely what the Aussie was trying to make him do. By now a curious group of onlookers had gathered around the rather unusual spectacle of a man addressing himself to a seemingly empty van. Lloyd, obviously prepared for the confrontation, was equipped for this eventuality. He squirted shaving foam from an aerosol methodically across the windscreen and windows of the van reducing Smith's visibility to nil but more importantly, psychologically rendering him more vulnerable to the predations of his unseen foe. As the level of vituperation grew, the situation developed into a classical candid camera situation. "What's the bother mate?" queried a cloth capped bystander.

"What's the bother?" mimicked Lloyd indignantly, "I'll tell you what the effing bother is. There's a dirty little private eye in the back of that van trying to dig up some evidence for the old woman who's after a divorce".

The gathering bystanders murmured sympathetically as Lloyd, working himself into a sense of simulated indignation ripped off the car aerial.

Fortunately, before he did so, Jimmy Smith managed to transmit a muffled call for assistance over the Department's radio channel.

As Lloyd directed his attention to the van's side mirrors, divine providence in the shape of a patrolling panda car turned the corner. A young P.C., his attention drawn to the ever growing knot of onlookers, parked his car and walked towards the Australian who, intent upon wrenching a spring loaded wing mirror from its base failed to register his approach. "What's going on here then?" asked the officer. The time honoured, hackneyed phrase produced a ripple of laughter from the gathering crowd, clearly delighted at this latest development. Lloyd span around to face his new adversary. "What does it look like you daft bastard?" he replied with feeling.

"Did you break off that aerial?" the officer asked, pointing with his foot to the twisted object lying in the gutter and to the jagged stump on the front of the offside wing, damning testimony to the destructive rage that appeared to have blinded the little Australian. His anger spent, Lloyd turned to his accuser, "No you daft sod, that was caused by the high winds."

The PC bundled Lloyd into the back of the Panda car and the crowd, disappointed by the official intervention that ruined an otherwise interesting afternoons sport, gradually dispersed.

Back at St John's Wood nick, the young PC sought out the Station Officer. "Here skip something funny here, I've done a computer check on that damaged van and it's owned by the Receiver of the Metropolitan Police".

The Sergeant, fearing the dreaded Al0 (Internal Investigations Branch) was operating on his patch instructed the youngster to check with Transport Department to find which Department was allocated the van.

Jimmy Smith was raging; it took a pint of Tartan bitter in the nearest hostelry to calm the raging Scot. "He obviously knew about that new van guv, my cover was definitely blown by some bastard in the job."

"If you show out now Jimmy, that will blow the whole operation and that', the last thing we want at this stage" I counselled.

At St John's Wood nick, I revealed my identity to the Station Officer, relieved to find this was not a rubber heel operation on his patch. "I shall need a statement from the driver, Sir."

"Sorry skip" I replied, "no can do, there must be some confusion, no damage was caused."The skipper was flabbergasted and looked at me suspiciously, "What do you mean not charge him? That is Jimmy Lloyd, a notorious Aussie villain and my PC caught him bang to rights damaging the police van."

Whilst I patiently explained the score to the understandably confused Station Sgt over a cup of canteen tea, Jimmy slipped Lloyd's house door key from the prisoner's property bag and sped round to Lloyd's flat.

He spent an industrious and productive (albeit technically illegal) ten minutes photographing entries in telephone and address books, diaries and some interesting group photos of some of the Aussies at boxing dinners and sporting functions surrounded by their usual hangers on and it has to be said, a handful of CID officers including one familiar face that Jim recognised. I speculated as to who had blown our cover and later events confirmed my belief as to the man's identity.

Several weeks later, I was called into Commander Dilley's office. He wasn't a happy chappy. "I've been through the transcripts of those intercepts on the Aussies, you're wasting your time, they're quite unproductive, take them off". That hardly came as a surprise to me; I had been expecting this for some time. Dilley was quite adamant, the intercepts were to come off and I didn't try to dissuade him. Despite what was clearly wilful disobedience of a direct order, I coaxed a further two weeks grace out of Wilf Pickles and gathered whatever material I had accumulated. Fortunately, the Kipper had taken two weeks annual leave.

Then miraculously and totally unexpectedly, out of the blue it happened just before the intercept was due to be taken off. Jimmy Lloyd phoned his brother. "It's off, this is the big one,

I'm going to see my uncle in Manchester, we're on the 8.15am out of Euston tomorrow."

I read the transcript over slowly, and then read it again; sure it was ambiguous and could be perfectly harmless, on the other hand...... Just to add to my uncertainty the following day was the Grand National at Aintree, could this be 'the big one?' If so, why Manchester, why not Liverpool?

Was this yet just another coded meet? If it was harmless then why bother to cover the venue? On the other hand, Wee Jimmy's surname was Lloyd; could the target be Lloyds Bank in Manchester?

I couldn't afford to allow my initial uncertainty to last for too long, the whole purpose of my role in life at that time was to collate, assess and evaluate information about organised crime. This was decidedly not the time to speculate but to act. I knew that if I squandered this tenuous break, my last chance to nail the Aussies, I would be letting myself, my team and the job down and would never forgive myself.

I called in my team and briefed them; the rest of the day was spent in feverish activity. Happily as it turned out, the gods smiled down upon me, the Kipper was still on leave. It was now down to me to see that all Jim Smith's and my teams' efforts paid dividends. Jim prepared sets of photographs, descriptions and other information gleaned over the course of the enquiry. Meanwhile I telephoned Manchester Regional Crime Squad, told them I was coming up on a job and would like the services of a surveillance team for an unspecified assignment.

The Metropolitan Police, like so many other large organisations, is hide-bound by regulation. In these circumstances I should have submitted a report to my Commander to justify my departure from the MPD (Met. Police District) and any expenses incurred. Frankly, I didn't have much confidence in Dave Frew; Dilley's second in command that was too close to his boss for comfort. I was pretty sure by now that could prove counter – productive so I kept things to myself and made an early start next morning. My whole team was in place at Euston and sure enough, some of the familiar faces we had plotted all those weeks congregated on the platform. Without seeking prior authority

I made a few more phone calls, bought a plane ticket then flew to Manchester.

Shortly after 9am, an unmarked Police car was waiting for me and we drove to a Briefing room at City Headquarters where I was amazed to see over one hundred plain clothes officers awaiting my briefing. The co-operation couldn't have been better, these guys were really good and within an hour everybody was well briefed, supplied with photos and posted. Now it was out of my hands. I needn't have worried. Not only Lloyds Bank but every Bank in Manchester Piccadilly and the centre was covered. A team covered every vantage point at the Railway Station where I sat with the RCS Detective Superintendent having the first of several cups of hot sweet coffee.

I don't mind confessing I was on tenter-hooks; this was an awful lot of manpower deployed upon what was really not much more than a hunch on my part. I think the expression 'a sixpence and half crown job' will convey my feelings, at least to older readers. What on earth would they think if this turned out to be a scrubber? If the operation failed, not only would there be egg on my face but more to the point it would give the Kipper the much needed excuse to bring into question my judgement and have me moved.

I needn't have worried; it was a text book operation. The London train rolled into the Station, the Aussies alighted followed closely by my team from the Yard. As they cleared the platform, each suspect was followed by members of the Crime Squad surveillance teams. I sat in the operations room as the reports came flooding in. Two men were nicked at Barclays Bank with a load of travellers cheques. Two more at the Automobile Association offices in possession of blank International drivers' licences. One by one they drifted in, all caught well and truly in the act. Before they were nicked the arresting officers watched as they posted their goodies off back to London. These were eventually recovered from the General Post Office. There was only one disappointment, the wily, elusive Jimmy Lloyd had managed to evade the dragnet and had it on his toes.

Needless to say the Manchester cops were delighted as well they might be. As for me, I had accomplished something I could never have done in London, not merely through out and out villainy but the vague, nebulous links that exist in the sometimes murky waters of crime detection. It also gave me a feeling of satisfaction that if I had been sabotaged from above as I suspected, I had cocked a snook at the perpetrator or should that read traitor?

All the Aussie team were charged with conspiracy to steal from Banks and eventually in February, 1973 appeared before the local Crown Court and went down for three years apiece. An attempt was made before the trial to bribe Jim Smith but that backfired with devastating effect. A certain Flying Squad officer approached him, offering him three thousand pounds to concur in Court that he could have been mistaken in his identification. Sure enough, at the trial, defence Counsel pulled out a photo which he showed to Jim and asked whether he could identify it as being William Lloyd (wee Jimmy) the prisoner in the Dock.

Jim pointed out that William had an identical twin and it was impossible to tell from a photograph which was which. Counsel instructed Jim to turn the photograph over and leaned forward smugly, "Read what it says on the back officer".

"This is a true likeness of William Lloyd."

Defence Counsel positively glowed, "Read the date and the solicitor's name" which of course Jim did.

"So you see officer, as my client was in Australia thousands of miles away having his passport photo taken the day before you say you saw him on the train to Manchester that would be impossible would you not agree?"

Only then did Jimmy drop his bombshell, "William Lloyd has the top of his index finger missing, his twin brother does not, that is how I was able to identify him". Hey, this wasn't meant to happen, that wasn't in the carefully concocted defence script; at long last the crafty Aussies had been outsmarted. A perplexed Lloyd was ordered by the Judge to hold up his hands for the jury to see his fingers and lo and behold, as Jim Smith said later in the Tank with a grin, "All nine and a half". Game, set and match! Further details of this amusing encounter can be found in Jim's book *Undaunted*.

Following the initial arrests I had one further job to do back in London. My next move had been carefully planned in advance. Armed with the information obtained from telephone intercepts and physical surveillance, I applied for search warrants to tidy up the London end of the Aussie operation. Every known associate of the arrested suspects was targeted, thirty in all.

Under the strictest secrecy, I arranged a briefing at the Yard with officers from the Flying Squad, Regional Crime Squad, C11 and Divisional officers.

They were divided into thirty teams of four, each accompanied by a C11 officer and one from each of the various units. That cut down the possibility of any collusion or leaks.

Being so close to home I couldn't keep this operation quiet. My cover story was that we would be raiding an active bank robbery team. Each team was given a sealed envelope containing a search warrant and address to be searched then directed to a map co-ordinate close to their designated target.

All telephone calls were forbidden. At 0900 hours the teams reported to me they were at their respective co-ordinates. They were instructed to open their sealed envelopes and effect their search warrant. This all sounded terribly melodramatic and I was taking an awful lot upon my shoulders, but conscious of the possibility of sabotage from within I wished to ensure every possible step was taken to avoid any leakage of information, intentional or otherwise.

The strategy worked and more than a dozen arrests were made of people with stolen and forged passports, travellers' cheques, false drivers' licences and other incriminating evidence. The operation planned and executed by myself had been a total success and fully vindicated the work my team had put into combating the vaunted Aussie gang.

The next evening I was amused and irritated in equal measure to read in the *London Evening Standard* how a team of detectives led by Detective Superintendent David Frew, assisted by Detective Inspector David Woodland of C.11 Department had broken up the notorious Aussie team in London. Oh well, so much for the Secret Squirrel Department, obviously in some quarters self-aggrandisement was considered more important than keeping a low profile. As for my Commander, not as much as a word was uttered from that particular quarter when he returned from leave, I didn't bother or need to ask the reason why.

Wee Jimmy Lloyd was arrested in Brussels, Belgium and C1 Passport office requested that I travel to Brussels with a Detective Constable from that Branch to look into other potential passport offences that had been committed by the gang. This is always a difficult assignment as protocol at that time ruled that foreign police officers have no jurisdiction outside their own territory. Sometimes this can be side stepped but without being deliberately obstructive the Belgian Police were sticking to accepted practice and it was made clear we could not interview him but they had no objection to our being in attendance while he was interrogated by their own officers. That interview was a farce, I would have loved to tape it but of course that was impossible. The senior investigating officer did his best to play the hard cop and tried to impress upon Jimmy Lloyd the severe consequences if he failed to co-operate. Jimmy Lloyd had been through this procedure a thousand times in a dozen different countries and I knew from the outset the man was wasting his time. Jimmy listened as the man harangued him non- stop for over five minutes then eventually responded. "You daft bastard, just who do you think you are, Inspector Clouseau?" I couldn't conceal my grin as Jimmy turned to me, "Here mate, get this twat off me back, he's getting effing boring."

Extradition proceedings were instigated and eventually Jimmy was returned to face the music in Manchester. The D.C. from Central Office and I returned to the Yard the day after Jimmy's interview, obviously being unable to question him ourselves we were wasting our time. Never mind, it was a good evening out in Brussels where we both had an enjoyable meal of moules frites washed down with several jugs of excellent Belgian beer.

Many years later in 2010, through the ex CID Officers Association, I met up with Adam Shand, an Australian writer and gangland journalist who wrote a book and published a film *'The Kangaroo Gang – Thieves by appointment'*. I played a small part outlining my role in their downfall and the film was shown in Australia and also by BBC channels in UK.

I spent a few pleasant days filming in London being re-united with Jim Smith and also, to my amusement, members of the team that Jim and I had spent so much time pursuing back in the 1970s. We all enjoyed a pleasant dinner with a few drinks while reminiscing over those times and true professionals that they were, there was no bitterness or ill feeling, we had just all been a bunch of guys on different sides of the track doing what we had to do. Anybody interested in the Kangaroo gang can view their exploits and download videos free on the Internet. The story, a Full Box production was narrated by no less than Barry Humphries, a.k.a. Dame Edna Everage.

There was one further incident which contributed to my disenchantment with Dilley and undoubtedly hastened my eventual departure from C.11. During the highly unpopular Vietnam War, Dilley who quite properly liaised closely with his counterparts in FBI and CIA instructed me and other C11 officers to meet up with FBI agents based in the US Embassy.

The CIA is probably the most powerful intelligence agency in the world and was accused by the respectable *New York Times* of, amongst other things, performing 'wet jobs' or assassinations of foreign leaders and other illegal acts. This included at that time surveillance of over seven thousand US citizens in the US and elsewhere involved in the anti war movement in the aptly named 'Operation Chaos'. Our orders were to assist FBI in tracing US Nationals and pressurizing so called 'draft dodgers' of which incidentally ex President Bill Clinton was one, into returning to US to enlist for Vietnam War. Under no stretch of the imagination could the use of British Police officers to harass US citizens who had committed no crime either in this country or indeed their own be justified. In short this was not only distasteful but both illegal and improper. After one such operation I was so incensed by the heavy handed conduct of the FBI agents I confronted Dilley in his office and told him of my feelings in no uncertain fashion.

No explanation, no justification, the man's face hardened, he looked up at me through gimlet eyes and after several moments silence responded. "Close the door after you, Inspector Woodland."

I make no judgement whatever of the FBI officers involved, they were obeying instructions from their Government in what was at that time a highly charged and tense atmosphere.

After his retirement, the Kipper was offered a post at Selfridges, part of the Sears Holdings Empire which allegedly was infiltrated with CIA agents who regularly used large US commercial concerns worldwide to plant their operatives. Dilley secured his post through a personal recommendation given by Sir Eric Miller, of whom we shall hear later, to the late Sir Charles Clore who owned Sears Holdings.

One thing is for sure, retired Police Commanders do not come cheap and he certainly was not being paid to keep would be shoplifters from Selfridges and their connected enterprises. However, with his impeccable connections and access to sensitive and highly secret information he would be considered a valuable asset for any organisation such as the CIA.

Chapter Twenty

"We are all in the gutter,
but some of us are looking at the stars"
Oscar Wilde 1854–1900

Since the formation of the Metropolitan Police in 1829, there have been periodic incidents of corrupt practices, the most notable of which occurred within the plain clothes or detective departments. Unfortunate but not surprising, bearing in mind the opportunities and degree of temptation to which officers may be exposed. What causes these periodical outbreaks of criminality amongst the very people entrusted with upholding the law? Naturally, there is not one simple answer but having passed through the process of disillusionment with the workings of the criminal justice system I can understand at least some of the causes. I have known good, honest coppers, who feel they owe a duty to protect the public being totally disgusted with perverse jury acquittals and feeble sentences, vowing that in future, where necessary they would take whatever steps they could to ensure that villains received their just desserts.

Others took a contrary view and kept their heads down knowing the less contact they had with the criminal fraternity the less likely they would be to have complaints made against them.

Whilst not condoning such practices, I can sympathise when many an otherwise conscientious copper, keen to see justice, resorts to 'gilding the lily' – I am referring to what is generally referred to as 'noble cause corruption'. I subscribe to the school of thought that contends 'noble cause corruption' was the product of a seriously flawed system. Like the pious perjury of old, like the collusive evidence accepted with a nod and a wink in the divorce courts, it was convenient to allow it to happen. Such things had little to do with law but more to do with common sense and justice. Make no mistake, everyone from the Home Office down involved in the administration of the law, whilst not actively encouraging it, deliberately chose to ignore it. Did a generation of judges genuinely believe that hardened villains aware of the consequences would consistently make incriminating admissions that would ensure their conviction and imprisonment? I think not, although of course many would, even if only to seek a lower sentence. The politically correct, liberal do gooders will no doubt recoil in righteous horror and indignation excoriating the views I express in this book. How dare I suggest that Police officers should have the right to act as judge and jury or to frame 'innocent people' by attributing false statements to secure convictions? The simple answer is that I do not.

The initial euphoria felt by the silent majority when efforts were made to 'clean out the Augean stables' by Mark's reforms was soon undermined by the manner in which certain members of the newly formed A 10 Department chose to investigate their colleagues. It was clear they were expected to show results and some of their methods soon produced a backlash that overwhelmed any initial goodwill felt towards them. Some were fired by personal ambition whilst a few resorted to the type of sharp practices they were supposedly combating. As a result, the whole of A10 Branch became despised by hard working coppers.

The job has always had its own way of dealing with deviants within the ranks but when accounts of the duplicity and devious tricks used by certain A10 officers were exposed, the ranks instinctively closed against them. I have clearly expressed my concerns earlier that I was not prepared to allow my role as District Intelligence Officer at C11 to be compromised upon Division by allowing or undertaking any actions which could be construed as 'rubber heeling'.

There will always be an element of corruption within the Police, just as there is in any sphere of activity. With the vast sums of money being made from drugs the temptations are now much higher, more officers are tempted and some will undoubtedly fall.

One final brush with A10 was to leave a nasty taste in my mouth and led to my being accused of misguided loyalty with possibly some element of justification. From time to time, Andre Bertrand an active informant provided me with high grade information. One day he phoned me at the Yard and gave me information about Nixon, a major criminal involved in a counterfeit dollar scam and that a job was coming off shortly where an East German Banker would be buying a large quantity of forged dollars. My first port of call was C.ll main index indicated that recently enquiries had been made by Detective Inspector Don Baker, (C.6) Company Fraud Squad, a man whom I knew and had served with at Chelsea and had no cause whatever to distrust. I phoned the Fraud Squad and arranged to meet Baker who was definitely interested. "Nixon, I've been after him for ages, what have you got on him?" Without a second's hesitation I told him what I had gleaned from my snout. "Can I meet with him?" he asked. This was clearly out of order. "Sorry Don but he's very twitchy, won't deal with anyone but me".

"Fair enough, but could you ask if anything is going down next Saturday, that might tie in with something I'm working on currently" As I dialled Bertrand's telephone I noticed Baker was obviously trying to clock the number and automatically turned my back on him. Three days later I received a phone call from a very agitated Bertrand. "You've blown me out" he accused. Bearing in mind the nature of the beast and the tightrope upon which informants operate, it is not unusual for them to get paranoiac on occasions, it goes with the territory. "Don't be so bloody silly, "I counselled, "Pull yourself together".

"Where did you telephone from the other day?" he demanded. Now this is a rather strange role reversal, I should be the one asking the questions, but he was clearly in a panic and I indulged him.

"Don't worry, it's perfectly safe, he's an old pal on the Fraud Squad and doesn't know who you are." Bertrand was nearly hysterical; I almost sensed the fear oozing through the line. "Whoever you were with is working for Nixon, he's just confronted me. Your 'old pal' noted the telephone exchange you were dialling and I'm the only man that Nixon knows living in the Putney area".

I went cold with anger, my initial thought was to return to the Fraud Squad and confront Baker. A moment's sober reflection told me that was just about the worse thing to do, only serving to confirm what at this stage could only be strong suspicion as to Bertrand's identity. Not wanting my informant to be worked over or even worse, I decided in Bertrand's interest to bide my time.

A few days later I was with the other DI's from C11 on the usual Friday night 'conference' the polite sounding name for a 'piss up' called by Dave Frew, the Detective Superintendent. One of Frew's party pieces was to play 'rugger' by tossing a full bottle of scotch from one to another across the room of his office. That's really all I wish to say about him. Frew received a phone call from Tug Wilson, a Detective Superintendent at Central Office, working on counterfeit currency. It was clear from the conversation that both men were discussing Nixon. I had a clear duty of care to warn Frew of the Baker incident over which I was still fuming. "Guvnor, I think you should know Nixon has a close contact in the Fraud Squad." I acquainted Frew with the telephone incident and felt it right and proper he should know of Baker's connection with the suspect, Nixon. It was unthinkable to have an operation sabotaged by a bent copper. Frew thanked me profusely. Several days later I received a telephone call to report to Detective Chief Superintendent Jones, A10 Department. "Ah Dave, I've heard from David Frew that bastard Baker sold out your snout, this is the break through I've been waiting for, now we can nail him properly, here, just sign this." Jones handed me a statement, ready typed up in advance, just waiting for my signature. I read it through in mounting disbelief. Whilst it bore some relation to the facts related to Frew, it had been added to in such a manner as to amount to a complete stitch up of Baker. Furthermore I realised that if the enquiry ran its natural course, it would involve interviewing Bertrand and blowing his cover. Baker was hardly my favourite policeman at that precise moment but I wasn't prepared to sign a false statement and give perjured evidence that would send a police officer to gaol, not even a bent copper like Baker. "I'm sorry guv but I can't sign this, it's just not a truthful record." Jones glared across at me, all pretence of cordiality gone. He positively snarled, "Never mind that, just sign the bloody thing" I felt myself bristle, instead of co-operating I suddenly felt a strong case of amnesia settling over me.

"I don't even remember who I spoke to in the Fraud Squad office and I'm certainly not stitching up a Police Officer just to please A10." I strode from the interview room fuming with anger, just who did these people think they were? To my mind they were every bit as bad as Baker. Two days later I was summoned back to A10 but this time there was no pretence at civility. Jones threw a Message Book across the table towards me. "Read the entry on September 9th", he ordered. There it was, in black and white in the telephone message book, 'DI Baker, speak to DI Woodland, C.11. re info'.

"Do you still maintain you didn't speak to Baker?" he demanded, "now perhaps you will sign that effing statement".

"I will write my own statement thank you" I replied, which I did to the effect that after all that time I could not recall who I spoke to. That little interlude certainly earned me no brownie points.

In a similar incident a good friend of mine on the Flying Squad refused to give perjured evidence against Ken Drury, his Commander who was charged with corruption. For this refusal my pal was suspended from duty for nearly two years, finished up in the dock at the Old Bailey and charged with conspiracy to pervert the course of justice before he was rightly acquitted.

Despite my lack of co-operation, Baker was finally charged. I was later called to give evidence at the committal proceedings and virtually treated as a hostile witness against Baker who quite properly received three years imprisonment for corrupt practices. God help any copper who finished up in prison, they were liable to receive worse treatment than sex offenders or child molesters.

Following the Baker incident, not surprisingly I heard little from my man Bertrand for nearly two months and had given him up as a lost cause when suddenly out of the blue he telephoned me at the Yard asking for a meeting. We met in Green Park and I was staggered by the story he related. It could have been a thriller script for a Freddy Forsyth novel. The gist of it was as follows: Judah Binstock, an International financier and notorious lawbreaker (alleged) was mounting a massive scam in Rwanda. The story was that ore samples had been substituted from an active copper mine in nearby Rhodesia and attributed by a crooked assayer from Johnson Matthey, a reputable London exploration and assay company, to a worked out non productive mine in Rwanda. Binstock had purportedly acquired private companies that effectively controlled a publicly quoted Company on the London Stock Exchange.

The objective now was to leak the false assay report in the right circles, wait for the stock to rise on the market and make a killing. Despite still officially wanted for questioning in respect to this and other criminal activities in England and Spain, Binstock has miraculously always managed to escape prosecution although being well known as a perpetrator of 'white collar crime'. There is no doubt whatever in my mind he is still being protected by powerful interests. A legal associate once described him as 'probably the most bent person the world has ever known.'

According to Bertrand, who supplied a wealth of detail, the scheme was close to fruition and would net hundreds of thousands of pounds from duped investors. I realised this was not the usual run of the mill job and was certainly not within my particular sphere of activity. After the Baker fiasco, I felt unable to trust anybody at Company Fraud Squad with this information; once bitten, twice shy, I contacted Commander Dilley by radio and outlined the facts and he sent his deputy Frew to meet up with us. As we slowly drove around the park perimeter, Bertrand repeated the story to Frew. Afterwards I left a full report with Commander Dilley.

Within two weeks of that meeting, my informant was arrested by officers from a little known crime squad operating out of Tintagel House, south of the Thames. After searching his address, taking away much personal documentation and holding him for several hours, a most aggrieved Bertrand was released without charge. He telephoned me a second time talking of betrayal.

I was called to A10 for another confrontation with Detective Superintendent Jones. Let's just say the meeting was far from friendly, the main purpose of the interview being to serve me with a Discipline Form 163, alleging I had an improper relationship with a known criminal. Jones questioned me as to how Bertrand, a convicted criminal was in possession of my home phone number and also my telephone number at the Yard. This was sheer bollocks and Jones must have known it. Bertrand had one previous conviction for selling a car subject to an HP agreement some ten years earlier and the cultivation of informants was an important part of my brief. It was clearly 'get even' time. Balanced against that was a long record of successful, well documented cases that Bertrand supplied, all with the knowledge of Dilley who had authorised previous payments to him from the 'Informants Fund'.

I made a three or four page statement setting out in great detail the full extent of my connection with Bertrand, all of which, I added, could be corroborated by Commander Dilley. I left that interview room literally fuming, quite convinced this was deliberate harassment due to the earlier incident involving the crooked D.I. Baker. It only reinforced my already low opinion of the rubber heel squad and their dubious methods. Subsequent events and the effect upon my career showed these feelings were wholly justified.

Chapter Twenty-One

Behind every great fortune lies
A great crime.
Honore de Balzac 1799–1850

The one thing I enjoyed about the CID and C.11 in particular was you never knew from one day to the next just what was in store and life was one long roller coaster adventure.

In September, 1971, came the incident which I like to refer to as the robbery that never was. Robert Rowlands, amateur radio enthusiast, was sitting in his Marylebone flat when randomly he turned his radio dial and picked up a two way conversation between what was obviously a look-out and a member of a gang breaking into an underground bank vault. At one point the lookout man was heard to say, "I'm off home now, I'm cold and hungry" to which one of the gang replied, "You can't go now, we're almost there". The lookout man responded, "Money may be your God but it's not mine, I'm fucking off".

It later transpired the equivalent of over five million pounds was stolen. The radio ham was asked by Police to tape the conversation as at that stage the bank could not be identified. The robbers communicated with a lookout on a nearby roof via walkie-talkie while they tunnelled for 40ft from beneath a nearby handbag store into the vault of Lloyds Bank, Baker Street, central London, cutting through the reinforced concrete floor with a thermic lance. They gained entry through a 15in hole, prompting speculation that a woman or child had entered the vault.

After first believing it to be hoax, the police eventually identified which bank was being robbed.The initial response was one to be expected at the scene of any major crime scene. The Bank, vault and all surrounding areas were soon swarming with photographers, scenes of crime officers, fingerprint experts followed closely by Flying Squad and C.11 officers of whom I was one. Scrawled inside the safe were the words: "Let Sherlock Holmes try to solve this."

Officer in charge of the investigation was Detective Superintendent Bob Chalk at Paddington Green Police Station. One of the senior investigators was DCI Alec West who has variously been described as "one of the best informed Police officers in London" and perhaps less favourably as "the most corrupt detective in London".

I met him for the first time upon this enquiry but his reputation preceded him. A former colleague once admiringly spoke of West's ability to turn criminals into informants. It was said he would take £200 from one criminal for bail or assistance then give it to another in return for information. This was not too different from the methods used by early thief-takers, two hundred years earlier.

There were suspicions of another, uglier side to West's activities. A notorious criminal by the name of Reg Dudley, who allegedly acted as a go between for criminals and corrupt police officers, named West as his contact within the law. If Dudley was to be believed, over the course of a long friendship with West, he channelled hundreds of thousands of pounds his way. According to Dudley this was not a one way traffic as West would trade with him stolen jewellery and the proceeds of safe deposits from bank raids, in one instance receiving sixty thousand pounds.

Whether or not there was any connection between this and what became known as the Baker Street Bank job will never be known. One thing was certain, many of the contents of safe deposit boxes came from dubious sources and a major difficulty facing investigating officers was in finding losers prepared to come forward and report their losses. To all intents and purposes these became practically victimless crimes.

For unrelated matters, Alec West was eventually arrested but later acquitted in the police corruption trials of the seventies and retired to a public house he owned at Newmarket where he died of a heart attack. It is not for me or anybody else for that matter to critically judge him especially on the uncorroborated word of a villain who obviously had his own agenda.

His crime arrest record was outstanding and whilst his methods were unorthodox and unacceptable in this day and age, different standards applied then.

There were one or two strange circumstances regarding the Baker Street job, one being that Police released copies of the suspects' taped voices over the radio and asked for suggestions as to their identity. This could have been routine police work but on the other hand it could be a way of concealing the fact they already had inside knowledge from an informant as within a short period one suspect's identity was known and a telephone intercept put on his line. It transpired from one tape he was due to meet an Asian money changer at Cumberland Hotel, Marble Arch where he was to hand over seventy thousand pounds in a hold-all.

The Hotel and surrounding streets were alive with Police, including myself and Detective Inspector Roy Davies from Paddington Green who accompanied me in my designated C11 vehicle, call sign 'Central 36.'

The Asian turned up, collected the holdall and disappeared in a taxi literally under the noses of the surveillance teams. What a monumental cock up.

Acting purely upon instinct, I headed in Central 36 at high speed down Constitution Hill into the Mall. Just before reaching Admiralty Arch I spotted and overtook the taxi containing our prey and forced it to a halt. Pulling the rear cab door open, I hauled out the astounded passenger, complete with holdall and threw him into the back of our vehicle. The cab driver, a true old Londoner who had probably seen it all before, didn't turn a hair and stoically accepted he had lost his fare now safely in the hands of Old Bill.

I glanced inside the holdall and gasped as I saw it crammed full of bank notes. Now seventy thousand pounds was about eight years pay and in those days could have bought a row of houses. Roy Davies and I looked at each other. Nothing was said but I'm sure the same thought must have passed through both our minds as I am sure it would others. There was one frightened prisoner, obviously facing the possibility of a long prison sentence and the last thing he wanted was to see the inside of a nick or indeed the contents of that bag again.

Anybody faced with that situation would have been tempted but there is a world of difference between being tempted and succumbing to temptation.

Without a second thought upon either of our parts, Davis and I set off to Paddington nick where the prisoner and holdall, contents intact, were handed over to the investigating officers. Of course, the Kipper had read the transcript and several days later sent for me. He did his best, a very poor best incidentally, to appear jovial and friendly.

"Hello Dave, just had an update on the Baker Street job, nice little tickle, anything you want to tell me?"

"Don't think so guv, just a routine job."

The friendly look disappeared, "What do you mean routine? According to Paddington Green there was only sixty eight grand recovered, what happened to the other two?"

"Guvnor, I was just as much aware as you are of how much was in that bag at least according to the intercept, but it was handed over untouched to Paddington Green. If there ever was a missing two grand I suggest you speak to them." Dilley's eyes narrowed as he glared at me, no trace of bonhomie left in his voice, he took a draw upon his cigar, leaned right back in his chair and glared long and hard at me, "Shut the door behind you when you leave Mr Woodland".

Several days later, at Bob Chalk's request, myself and D.C. Boocock C.11, kept surveillance upon a bungalow in Kent. We followed a car containing one man until it crossed the boundary into the Met. area, pulled it over and deposited the driver at Bromley Police Station where I contacted Paddington Green. In the prisoner's coat was three thousand pounds, presumably part proceeds of the Bank raid and potentially vital and incriminating evidence. This was taken to Paddington Green and deposited with a senior officer.

Although the national press was full of the raid at the onset, within a very short time all press coverage ceased and it allegedly turned out that MI5 had placed a Government gagging order or 'D- notice' upon all the Press effectively banning any further reporting 'in the interests of national security'. This in itself was a most unusual happening.

Everything went quiet thereafter, I did learn that eventually four people was charged and convicted of offences arising from the enquiry although some press reports still maintain no property were ever recovered. Not a particularly good result for a full squad of detectives working upon a lengthy enquiry when I had personally felt two collars and recovered over seventy thousand pounds.

That would have been the end of the matter until at the Cannes Film Festival in 2007 a film was released purporting to tell the true story behind the bank raid. '*The Bank Job*' written by Dick Clement and Ian Le Frenais allegedly based upon fact, claimed the robbery was staged by MI5 as a means to recover compromising photographs of a Royal Princess.

Nobody was left in very much doubt as to just who that was. Of course this was seized upon by Fleet Street and various newspapers vied with each other to print the most lurid details supposedly supporting this theory.

Princess Margaret's friendship with a London villain Johnny Bindon, was well covered. He was seen by some to be a colourful character, but by others as a notorious gangster, acquitted of a contract murder in 1971. Bindon openly boasted of his friendship with the princess and claimed to have taken drugs and had sex with her in Mustique. His main claim to fame was reportedly his private parts, upon which, according to legend, he could balance five half pint beer mugs.

Whatever the truth regarding that particular legend, or indeed to an MI5 connection to the robbery, will I suppose, never be known. Like anybody else I am entitled to my own opinion and although there were certainly some strange aspects to the job, I prefer to keep these to myself.

One thing I will share however; the character 'Lew Vogel' in the film, portrayed as the porn king of Soho, corrupter of Police who received eight years imprisonment bore a striking resemblance to dear old Bernie Silver. In the film version, Vogel purportedly kept a record of bent coppers in one of the safe deposit boxes. I'm sure it is purely coincidental that again in real life, soon after the robbery, Scotland Yard underwent a major purge of corrupt Police Officers and it is rumoured that certain senior Government officials also resigned following revelations in the film about activities at one particular high class brothel. Rumour, of course is one thing, facts another and as all Government files on the incident remain classified in the British National Archives the truth, or at least a sanitised version of the truth will not be made available until 1st January, 2045 by which time I shall certainly be pushing up daisies.

By this time I had been in C11 for three years and time was fast approaching for a selection board which I had high hopes and good cause to believe would lead to promotion to Detective Chief Inspector. Some chance! My work record had been extremely good and securing the conviction of the notorious Aussie team had received good reports – at least in some quarters. With the Bramshill course under my belt I had every reason to feel confident.

Dilley went on leave and it was often laughingly commented upon that whenever trouble was brewing he was away from the office. One bright morning, full of the joys of Spring, I walked into the office and was told Detective Superintendent Frew was asking for me.

"You wanted to see me guvnor?" "Yes Dave, Ernie Bond (Deputy Assistant Commissioner Crime) wants to have a word with you."

"Oh, what about guv?"

"Dunno, he didn't say but I think it may be a promotion board" – What a snake!

I was ushered into Mr Bond's office and he looked up from a docket in front of him. "I have a report here into a complaint that you have an improper relationship with a known criminal." This was clearly a reference to a matter I felt had been long done and dusted. In fact since my interview with A.10 where I gave a full statement concerning the matter, I hadn't given it a further thought, it was so inconsequential.

"Hardly a known criminal guv, one previous conviction over ten years ago for selling a motor car subject to an HP agreement, he's been a good informant for years."

Bond looked up and said sharply, "There's no mention of that here, when his address was searched, the officers found a diary with your office and home telephone numbers."

"But I've made a full four page statement outlining all my dealings with this man, giving details of rewards he has received from the Informant's fund, you can check it out, he is known personally to Commander Dilley."

Ernie Bond leaned back in his chair and said icily, "You are an experienced Detective Inspector, you should know better in this day and age to get so close to an informant, you will be returned to uniform immediately and think yourself lucky you are not on a discipline board."

I just couldn't believe what I was hearing; this was outrageous, what on earth was going on? There was clearly more in this than met the eye, what could Dilley have put into that report to justify such drastic steps? I knew that all my dealings with Bertrand had been quite open and above board. "Lucky not to be going on a board?" I heard myself saying as if in a trance, "why don't you give me one, at least I would have a fair hearing that's better than the Mickey Mouse justice you are handing out to me here".

Ernie Bond ignored my outburst, "You will report to the uniform Commander, "M" Division at 10am next Monday, you are in Police Orders tonight". Just like that!

I turned and walked out of the office literally in a daze. The whole thing had obviously been orchestrated, decided and sentence passed before I had even been given an opportunity to explain or defend myself. In short, I had been well stitched up by the Kipper, Commander Dilley. It was to be three full years more before I found the true reason.

I spent three happy years at C11, was good at my job and well respected, at least by the majority of the lads who were as shocked as me at the news. Within a couple of hours they organised a farewell do, somebody rushed out and I was presented with an engraved tankard, a lasting memory of the past three years. Well bollocks, I wasn't going out with my tail between my legs, we had a bloody good night, much drink was consumed and finally, deprived of my official car, I was driven home by one of my team. The following morning I took stock of my situation. That this was a stitch up was perfectly obvious and it was pretty clear who had arranged it.

Several months later I had a chance meeting at a social event with Peter Walton, the DC I encountered on my first day's duty at Tottenham Court Road many years ago. We met socially on occasions and Peter was now a Deputy Assistant Commissioner at the Yard. Peter obviously knew precisely what had happened to me and had no hesitation in marking my card. As regrettably he has since passed away, I now feel at liberty to repeat what he said to me which was quite simply, "Dave Dilley stuck the knife into you".

I realised there was nothing I could do. I had been well and truly 'kippered'. I had not been disciplined or demoted but moved over the course of a weekend to uniform duties as an Inspector patrolling the Elephant and Castle area of London.

It came as no surprise when shortly after my transfer I received a visit from Jim Smith the photographer informing me he had also been returned to uniform under the spurious pretext his cover had been blown following the publicity surrounding the India House hostage shootings.

Well done Kipper, at a time when storm clouds were looming heavily over the Yard, that was two potential dangers conveniently dealt with and out of the way before the balloon went up. The net was slowly closing upon the festering carbuncle of corruption surrounding Bernie Silver and top men at the Yard.

The last time I saw Ernie Bond was about a year later in Golders Green at Peter Vibart's funeral. He made a point of coming over and shaking my hand but obviously that was neither the time nor the place to try to get to the bottom of things. Of one thing I am certain, Ernie Bond a highly respected officer, would never have taken the trouble to come over and shake the hand of a crooked copper. By the time of the funeral Mr Bond would most certainly have known more than he did at our previous disastrous encounter.

What happened to The Kipper? It was several years before the National Press caught up with him and he was exposed on the front pages of the *News of the World*.

Not that anything came of that, despite the fact other crooked senior officers including his second in command were arrested and sentenced to long periods of imprisonment for various corrupt practices. The Kipper miraculously survived the purge and retired in August 1976 having been awarded the Queen's Police medal for meritorious service. Well deserved – some might say.

From what I gleaned afterwards, it wouldn't have surprised me in the least if he had been knighted in the 'Lavender List', Harold Wilson's notorious 1976 Resignation Honours. Knowing the devious way the job worked and the need to limit fallout from the damage, it is certainly not beyond the realms of speculation that in return for his silence a deal was struck which combined his resignation with the medal.

Chapter Twenty-Two

Forgive your enemies,
but never forget their names

John F Kennedy

I had a weekend to come to terms with the unpalatable truth that my career as a detective was over and quite frankly it was not easy. The galling part was that I had no legitimate redress, the new Commissioner had expressed his intention of introducing interchange between the CID and uniform branches and transfer from one branch to another was not considered a demotion – game set and match.

"He who steals my purse steals trash, tis nothing, but he who filches my good name robs me of that which does not enrich him but leaves me poor indeed." How true those words are. Not content with ending my career as a detective I was later informed that Dilley had vainly attempted to discredit my reputation.

Two Detective Chief Inspectors from Central Office were deputed to review my old cases, visit prisons and interview villains I had put away to find out if any wished to make formal complaints against me. This vendetta, for that is precisely what it was, did not end even after I had left the job, however that is another story.

10 am Monday, 2nd July, 1973, I presented myself to Commander Bodycombe at Southwark Police Station, just down the road from the Elephant and Castle. I was ushered into his office and was immediately given the pariah treatment.

"I won't beat about the bush, you have come to this Division under a cloud, in future when you report to me you will see to it you are properly dressed." I looked down at my trousers, were my flies undone? Then of course it sunk in, I was being admonished for not wearing a uniform I did not even possess or ever thought I would ever wear again. What the hell was the point of all this? I turned on my heel and walked towards the door. Bodycombe looked up in astonishment,

"Just one moment, where do you think you are going?"

"I'm leaving, this interview is concluded."

"Concluded, concluded? Just who do you think you are talking to? I'll decide when this interview is concluded".

I turned at the door facing him, "I have been in your office for five minutes, for the first three you deliberately ignored me, you have reprimanded me for not wearing a uniform you know full well I don't possess and you have said I have come here under a cloud. I am no defaulter; I have never even been disciplined and will not be treated by you or anybody else as a defaulter".

Mr Bodycombe sat there, a look of astonishment on his face as I turned back towards the door. Nobody spoke to the great man in such insubordinate tones and it clearly rattled him. "One minute, one minute Mr Woodland," I stopped; knowing full well that if I went out of that door my whole career was finished. "Come back inside, take a seat."

"Thank you sir, I prefer to stand".

The Commander changed tack completely. This time he opened a drawer and took out what was clearly my personal file. After several minutes reading, he looked up. "Well Mr Woodland, reading this it appears to me you are a professional, competent Police Officer, I have no idea of the reason you have been transferred to me but I see no reason why, provided you settle down well, you should not return to the Department in twelve months time." Now there was a strange thing, returned to uniform with no explanation upon my record? Curiouser and curiouser.

"Mr Bodycombe, I am as puzzled as you appear to be as to the reason I am here, but I have no intention of considering myself placed upon probation to return to a Department I should never have left in the first place. However, now I am here I shall make a career for myself within the uniform branch." The man looked up, a positive beam upon his face.

"Well done, well done, that's the spirit; you will work here at Southwark until I decide where you should be posted to."

For three years I served in the uniform branch at Southwark, Rotherhithe and Peckham Police Stations. One night, while patrolling the dingy back streets around the Elephant and Castle with my Section sergeant I was called to what at first sight appeared to be just another routine domestic dispute. In a first floor tenement apartment in a pool of rapidly congealing blood laid a Jamaican woman moaning and obviously in extreme pain. Her wrist had been practically severed and fortunately night duty CID soon arrived applied a tourniquet and called for an ambulance. I'm about as useless as a jam sandwich when it comes to first aid but I knelt by her and gently stroked her forehead. "Hang on dear, the ambulance is on its way, hang on now." When the ambulance crew eventually arrived I saw for the first time the whole of the back of her skull had been sliced open, her brains exposed and throbbing. Needless to say the poor soul didn't even make it as far as Guys Hospital and with a shudder, died in my arms.

Later in the early hours we picked up her boyfriend, still covered in blood. He eventually appeared at the Old Bailey and his defence to the charge was ludicrous. He claimed she was a witch doctor and had cast a black magic spell upon him. After anointing herself with goat's fat she invoked a curse which rendered him impotent. The only way to release the spell was to kill her so of course that made it alright to chop her about with a machete. What should have been a straightforward conviction for murder was reduced to manslaughter and he was sentenced to three years imprisonment. I don't know, just call me old fashioned but in my book this was quite straightforward, murder is murder, forget all this different culture and mores crap.

I met a great bunch of guys in the uniform branch but there were others who really took the biscuit. In February, 1975, whilst going to the assistance of other officers, Stephen Tibble a young unarmed off duty police constable was shot dead in the Hammersmith area by a member of the Provisional I.R.A. An official appeal was raised. Knowing the time such things can take, with my relief at Southwark I arranged a darts match with a local publican and through the generosity of the locals, we raised £150. By common consent, to ensure this money went as soon as possible to the young man's widow, I and one of my sergeants went to Hammersmith Police Station to meet with the Chief Inspector charged with co-ordinating the fund raising appeal. Having explained our intentions, I handed the money to the Chief Inspector who looked up from behind his desk. "Where's the receipt?"

"Receipt, what receipt, this is a collection raised at a local pub?"

"How do I know you only raised £150, for all I know you raised much more and have pocketed the rest?"

Fortunately my sergeant placed a restraining hand upon my arm.

"That might be the sort of thing that you might do" I growled, "but where we come from we don't steal from dead colleagues."

No doubt that worthy rose to achieve high rank in the Police. It left me wondering how such a narrow minded man could achieve high rank but unfortunately there were plenty more like him.

Young Stephen Tibble was posthumously awarded the Queen's Police Medal for gallantry and a memorial erected on the spot he was killed in Barons Court. That year we all, both uniform and CID had our work cut out dealing with a wave of Irish terrorism that culminated in the siege of Balcombe Street. There were over forty terrorist incidents in the capital and the citizens of London lived under a sustained attack not experienced since the blitz some forty years previously. Around a dozen people were killed and many injured. I cursed my inability to be playing a more important role.

One of our roles within the uniform branch was keeping the wheels of commerce turning by dealing with large numbers of suspected letter bombs reported by a vigilant, but justifiably nervous public. We would casually place the suspect letters and parcels into the boot of the police car then drive them to the nick where they were placed in a hastily devised sandbag emplacement in the Station yard to be sorted out by Bomb disposal officers later. If the letters and parcels had passed through the tender hands of the G.P.O. without exploding, they were unlikely to do so until the letter flaps or parcels had been opened thus breaking the circuit. It was not so easy for the brave bomb disposal officers who had to deal with the real thing and every day placed their lives at risk from I.R.A. devices. Captain

Roger Goad GC BEM was tragically killed whilst dealing with an I.R.A. bomb in Kensington. After a busy day of call outs, Capt. Goad volunteered to deal with one further incident before going off duty. He raised his protective visor temporarily and paid the ultimate price.

Although this will be little comfort to his widow, some good arose from the tragic and pointless killing of P.C. Stephen Tibble, a brave young officer. At the scene of his shooting, a young detective leaped upon PC Tibble's motor cycle and gave chase which in turn led to the discovery of an IRA bomb making factory. Police followed a stolen car carrying four members of an IRA active Service Unit to a flat in Balcombe Street where they seized two hostages. There was a six day standoff before they were arrested, found guilty at The Old Bailey and sentenced to no less than twelve life sentences. In 1999, under the terms of the 'Good Friday Agreement', Liam Quinn, Tibbles's murderer, together with the rest of the Balcombe Street gang were released.

Then came my last serious brush with the vagaries of the jury system which I think is worth recounting in some detail. Lord Devlin once wrote *'Trial by jury is the lamp that shows that freedom lives*". Pretty rhetorical stuff and I am sure he is right in the majority of cases but there have been occasions when the light emanating from there was more like a Toc H lamp glimmer than a shining beam of justice.

An informant working in Soho area was keeping company with some Maltese thieves from the West End. They decided to go big time and sought to recruit my informant to drive a 'switch vehicle' after they had robbed a bank somewhere in the Elephant and Castle area. Guidelines about the use of informants in the commission of crime are quite specific. If an informant is co-operating fully with Police, if he is not involved in the plotting of the crime and if his participation is minor, it is, or at least was, considered acceptable.

We mounted separate surveillances upon four possible banks. A car pulled up outside Barclay's Bank in Southwark Street. A check upon the registration mark showed it had been stolen from North London a week previously.

I hastened to Borough High Street and saw two men entering the Bank while the third, remained behind the wheel of the stolen car, engine running. Inside the Bank one of the men, revolver in pocket, handed a petrified cashier a note across the counter "Fill up the bag or I will shoot". Forensic laboratory subsequently proved it had been hand written by him. So there we had it, three armed Maltese villains in a stolen car, caught bang to rights in the act of attempting to rob a Bank. Nice and easy wouldn't you say? Not a bit of it, the men appeared before the Central Criminal Court charged with possession of a stolen car, attempted robbery and possession of a firearm. Their defence was a classic. They had never seen the stolen car before; it had been planted by Police as of course was the firearm. What other possible explanation could there be? Defence counsel conceded the demand note had been written by one of the defendants some weeks earlier when they had been 'playing around'. He didn't realise he still had it in his pocket and passed it across the counter by accident.

Would you believe it? The jury bless them did. They couldn't agree and a re-trial was scheduled for Snaresbrook Crown Court that adopted some of the more dubious (non) convicting tactics of the old and non lamented West Ham Quarter Sessions.

At the re-trial a new tactic was adopted by the defence who suggested to gullible jurors the informant had colluded with Police to set up his poor, innocent clients. The final straw was when asked whether I had originally been a Detective Inspector and was now a uniform Inspector. With knowing glances at the jury, defence counsel brought up the recent CID scandals, the clear inference being I was painted with the same brush. Nice one Sir Robert!

Do I need to spell out the result? As happened in so many prosecutions before and since, the case collapsed when defence lawyers demanded the names of informants. This was just one other example of how the law, as it then stood, was used to protect the guilty. The law has since changed and 'public interest immunity' certificates may now be granted to protect an informant's identity.

One of the most effective ruses used by defence lawyers when their clients are caught bang to rights is to steer juries' thoughts away from the real issue and to concentrate upon some irrelevant side issue, in short a big fat, juicy red herring. The jury fell for this story hook line and sinker and acquitted all three men. Reluctantly, after a gruelling session in the witness box at the hands of the defence I was forced to the conclusion the whole criminal justice system had turned into a farce and Police really were wasting their time.

When I first joined the job, jury nobbling was rife. Persons acting on behalf of a defendant approached jurors or their families and either by outright bribery or threats of recrimination against family members, persuaded the juror it would be in his best interests or his continuing good health, to return a 'not guilty' verdict. Much of this mischief was prevented by the introduction of majority verdicts in 1967, however, at the turn of this century, attempted jury nobbling still occurred in up to one hundred trials each year in England and Wales.

The mid-1970s saw a time of political unrest with growing antagonism between Greece and Turkey fuelled largely by the invasion and division of Cyprus. This was to some degree reflected in the prejudices and actions of the two different factions living and working in London.

I never broadcast my change of role and one day received a call from an old informant who believed I was still working in Crime Intelligence Department. A drinking acquaintance of his was approached by the Greek Military attaché in London, keen to gather information about prominent Turkish Cypriots in the community.

After meeting the attaché I drove straight to the Yard and insisted to a rather bored night duty Detective Sgt from Special Branch that he record full details of this encounter in the official SB log book.

A close surveillance operation was mounted and two weeks later both men arrested. The Military Attaché claimed diplomatic immunity, was declared 'persona non grata' and returned to Athens where I certainly hope nothing too draconian happened to him. After all, like me, he was only doing his duty. The Greek Cypriot acquaintance appeared at the Old Bailey indicted upon two counts of attempted bribery and an offence under the Official

Secrets Act. He received eighteen months imprisonment for his pains and I received my final Commissioner's Commendation, a first I believe for this type of offence awarded to a uniformed officer.

One night duty, driving round the Elephant and Castle with my duty Sgt. we heard an armed robbery had taken place in a house in Shooters Hill.

Robbers armed with shot guns forced their way into a house and threatened to kill the wife and daughter unless the owner, a bookmaker opened his safe in a first floor bedroom. The owner opened his bedroom wardrobe which contained not only the safe but also a loaded shot gun.

He shot one of the robbers in the leg causing the rest to flee, empty handed taking their wounded mate with them. I called Casualty Department at Guys Hospital and asked that if anybody came to Casualty, for whatever reason with gunshot wounds to the legs I was to be notified immediately.

Half an hour later the Porter's Lodge phoned to say a car had pulled up outside the Hospital and a man with gunshot wounds dumped on the pavement as the car sped away. The man was bleeding profusely from a leg wound and told me he had been ejected from a night club in Tottenham Court Road and shot by a bouncer. Likely story – I put him in a wheelchair to wheel him to Casualty. Unfortunately, I lost my way in the maze of corridors and there was some delay before we arrived at Casualty during which time he freely volunteered he was shot during the attempted robbery in Shooters Hill. It struck me that if I was to give evidence of the circumstances of the admission in a Court of law, some clever defence lawyer would have a field day alleging Police deliberately withheld treatment and any statement of admission would undoubtedly be thrown out. I called the Night Duty CID officer who properly cautioned the man who conveniently made a full statement of admission under caution.

After my recent experience at Snaresbrook Court I didn't want another genuine case thrown out through jury manipulation. So, with a little reluctance, that was the end of my involvement but

I understand the other gunmen, confronted with the admission, were also arrested and dealt with.

By now I had held the rank of Inspector in both CID and uniform branches for eight years and despite a promising start it was pretty clear, at least to me, my career was going nowhere fast. I knew the system well enough to know that once your cards are marked they stay marked; nothing short of a miracle could restore my fortunes. By this time I felt totally disillusioned with the job and already felt it was time to make a fresh start elsewhere not only for myself and family but also the job.

Chapter Twenty-Three

The only true wisdom is knowing you know nothing
Socrates 469–399BC

There came a time, despite my mixed feelings of disillusion and downright despair, when for one glorious moment I thought I would be vindicated and restored to my former position. Dilley had retired and early one Sunday morning in June, 1977, I saw in the early edition of a Sunday newspaper he had hit the front page headlines along with John Groves, a Detective Chief Superintendent from Crime Intelligence and Mike Franklin, a retired Detective Inspector at Company Fraud Squad. The latter, prior to his promotion, worked closely with The Kipper at C11 Department as a Detective sergeant specialising in Casinos, with special responsibility for monitoring attempts by the American Mafia to infiltrate the London gaming scene. One such casino was the Victoria Sporting Club jointly owned by Judah Binstock and George Wynberg, the latter an American, both strongly suspected of involvement in Police corruption and with links into organised crime.

Eyebrows were raised when only years before he was due to retire on full pension; Franklin put in his papers and went to work for Binstock. Yes, that is right dear reader, the very same Judah Binstock that, prior to my sudden fall from grace, I received the information I passed to Dilley. On the front page were photographs of all four men, Dilley, Groves, Franklin and Binstock. Under the heading 'the Guilty Men', were details of Binstock's alleged criminal activities and the clear allegation he was being minded by Dilley and other high ranking officers. It was the answer to the question I had asked myself a thousand times – why?

I felt a surge of fresh optimism- at last the vindication I had longed for these last three years. Then and only then I felt at liberty to speak out. The following week I telephoned A10 Department and spoke to Ron Steventon, my old Detective Superintendent at Chelsea, now a Commander in A 10 charged with rooting out corruption in the job. Things were getting better and better, the man knew me and my record, I would not just be another unknown name to him. I was on a high as, buzzing with excitement and optimism; I made my way to the Yard and was ushered into Steventon's office. He was pretty formal and I handed him a copy of *News of the World* which regrettably I left with him.

Steventon must have seen the article already but I put over the facts in a clear and succinct manner. I left nothing out including my information regarding Binstock and that surreal meeting with Dilley and Virgo when Dilley advised him of the forthcoming press exposure.

Steventon listened in total silence, finger tips to his forehead, his brow wrinkled in concentration. I wasn't exactly expecting thanks but was wholly unprepared for his response.

"Where's your evidence, Mr Woodland?"

I was dumbstruck pointing at the headlines in the newspaper, "My evidence, my evidence?" pointing to the newspaper in front of him,

"There's my evidence what more do you need?"

"I'm not interested in that rag, I wouldn't investigate a senior officer without something more concrete, you'll have to come back with something more positive than that."

My mind raced, this was a response I just hadn't contemplated; it was totally bizarre. Could it be that Steventon was also involved? Could he be part of the crooked set up? The unpalatable truth struck home in stark clarity. Of course he was not involved, Steventon was an honourable man, as straight as a die. He represented the Establishment, an establishment still reeling from the scandals that had rocked Scotland Yard to its foundations. The Yard needed a new scandal like a hole in the head. Now, to his mind, an embittered Police Inspector with a bee in his bonnet was demanding an enquiry into no less a person than Kipper Dilley, ex Commander, Crime Intelligence

Branch. Dilley, the man with total access to every single telephone intercept, knew more secrets about the working and private lives of every dodgy politician, every senior policeman than anybody else, very often even their wives. Dilley knew them all – that was his job, all secretly recorded and safely archived, if canteen gossip was to be believed. To investigate him would be pure dynamite, it would open up a veritable bag of worms, enough to completely destroy the Yard's already shattered reputation and lead to the public enquiry being demanded from various influential quarters.

How Ron Steventon must have loved me. His refusal to investigate what may have been a relatively small but still significant piece of evidence was a classic cover-up, as later events will show.

I couldn't leave without at least one last token effort. "You asked me for evidence Mr Steventon, don't ask me, ask the libel lawyers of the *News of the World*, they wouldn't have dared to print that story unless they had one hundred and twenty percent verifiable evidence of the truth." That was an indisputable fact, I knew it, Ron Steventon knew it but it was the end of the road, I could not or would not take it any further outside of the job.

After leaving Steventon's office, I reflected over the past three years and the feeling of injustice I experienced when returned to uniform duties for no apparent reason, more importantly the damage it caused to my health.

One way or other it seemed clear that without satisfaction, like Fred Lambert before me, there was no alternative but to leave the job I loved, the job that had been the major purpose in my life for so many years.

Why then am I resurrecting this matter over forty years later? It will do me no good whatever to open this particular bag of worms but this is a story that needs to be told. Quite simply nothing I say or do now will tarnish the reputation of Scotland Yard whose days are numbered under the new regime. The world has moved on and nothing could harm Dilley, this is all now nothing more than a historic footnote.

The start made by Sir Robert Mark has now come full circle with the proposed closure and sale of New Scotland Yard. As I write this, plans are being put in place to axe many of the Yard's specialist teams including drug squads, burglary and car crime squads and to put eight hundred detectives back to Division in uniform.

Simon Byrne, Assistant Commissioner in the new squeaky clean Police Service described such men as "Constables in T-shirts and jeans. The word detective is bandied about but the distinction doesn't really exist, – we don't want to put labels on things, these are labels of the past."

With the insipid advance of political correctness into every aspect of everyday life, I am now fully convinced the lunatics have taken over the asylum. The successors to the Krays, Richardsons and other organised professional gangsters and criminals will be laughing all the way to the Bank and as usual it is the poor honest hard working citizen that will suffer in the long run.

Let's be honest, given the option, most people were not too worried if the old style detective felt obliged to deal ruthlessly with career criminals provided the streets were kept safe to walk in, their lives and property protected. We lived in the real world where, unlike the new socially conscious breed of senior officers, we couldn't afford the luxury of shedding a tear for the poor misunderstood and persecuted victims of a system that drove them to crime.

Back at Peckham nick I penned an application to see the Commissioner of Police. That is the right of every officer; can be exercised without giving any reason and is set out quite clearly in Force General Orders. I was bounced through various senior officers, all applying pressure and all anxious to know my reasons but I dug in my heels and got my way except by the time I reached the top there wasn't a Commissioner. Sir Robert Mark had retired and was busy carving out a fresh name for himself selling Michelin tyres and the new Commissioner in waiting had yet to be formally appointed.

Finally, I was ushered into the office of Deputy Commissioner John Gerrard a uniform copper of the old school for whom I felt an immediate affinity. Now I had not the slightest doubt by now Mr Gerrard knew exactly the reason I wished to see the

Commissioner nor have I any doubt it was his role to placate me and keep me on side.

He sat there resplendent in his uniform and I sat in my rather less splendid uniform in front of him. "Now what can I do for you Mr Woodland?"

"Well sir, are we speaking Deputy Commissioner to Inspector or are we speaking man to man?"

"Man to man, if that's what you want Mr Woodland."

"Good, in that case you won't mind if I take my uniform jacket off."

This was quite deliberately insubordinate and confrontational but to his credit Mr Gerrard followed my example and we both sat there in our shirt sleeves. My story tumbled out, starting from the meeting with the informant, the allegations over Binstock and Dilley's involvement. I told him of my informant's improper arrest and turnover, my return to uniform upon a trumped up discipline issue, the subsequent disclosures by the *News of the World* and finally my dismissal by Commander Steventon.

John Gerrard listened intently, irrespective of his role I sensed he sympathised with me but naturally his potential courses of action were fairly limited. After all, how do you compensate a man for three years loss of seniority and the destruction of his career?

"What exactly would you like me to do, Mr Woodland?"

"What I would like sir is to go back to what I am good at, nicking villains. You have seen my record; I was one of the better informed, detectives at the Yard. Now I'm wasting my time and any talent I may possess is put to work avoiding treading in dog shit around the Elephant and Castle at two in the morning."

Mr Gerrard sat there silently for a moment, studying me intently. "Let me put it this way Mr Woodland, you have a fine record and I do not dispute you may have had a rough deal, but you are asking me for the one thing I just cannot give you."

"Cannot or will not sir?"

"Cannot, you are a sixties detective, times have changed and we are now in the seventies, neither you nor I can put the clock back whether we wish to or not."

He paused to let the bitter truth sink in then tried to soften the import of his words. "Look, you have just over three years to go for your pension; you have done your fair share. There are plenty of easy jobs for Inspectors at the Yard in one of the Administration Branches; you have my word that you will be given priority consideration for any job you see published in Police Orders."

I stood up and replaced my uniform jacket, "Mr Gerrard, thank you for your time but I think with respect you have missed the point. I didn't come here looking for a soft number, I came looking for justice but I realise you are not in a position to give it."

We shook hands solemnly and I made my way back to Peckham deep in thought. Within a few weeks I was due on a selection board for uniform Chief Inspector. With eight years service in the rank this was my last chance of a board. From being one of the youngest Detective Inspectors in the Met, I had no intention of finishing up as the oldest uniform Inspector. More to the point I knew enough about the system to be aware these things are not decided merely by one's performance in front of a selection board. Mr Gerrard would have known of the forthcoming board and could easily have suggested I wait for the outcome. He didn't, and could do no more than prepare me for eventual rejection by offering me a sinecure posting at the Yard to while away my time until eventual retirement.

Came the day of my Promotion Board, I felt perfectly calm knowing I had little or nothing to lose. I sat among a group of younger uniform Inspectors, all looking nervous, some actually bragging of their exploits nicking errant motorists or licensees for drinking after hours. I would willingly have bet a week's pay few would even know their way to the Old Bailey let alone give evidence there.

The Board Chairman was Deputy Assistant Commissioner (DAC) Gilbert Kelland a respected uniform officer who led the investigation into the allegations of corruption in the Soho porn enquiry.

Commander John Morrison from Central Office, another experienced senior detective, was the CID representative. He would be well aware of my departmental reputation. My spirits soared until I saw the third individual, DAC David Powis, an ex

Portsmouth naval dockyard policeman later destined by the new interchange policy to be promoted from the uniform branch to the post of CID Assistant Commissioner.

He swiftly earned the nickname TCP and the opprobrium of practically every working CID officer who came into contact with him and even those who didn't. Powis had many bees in his bonnet. He suspected rewards from the informants' fund were not necessarily finding their way to their rightful recipients and issued an instruction he was to be present when any award over one thousand pounds was to be made. A Detective Sgt from the Squad one day confided to me, "Do you know Dave; I've never been so embarrassed in all my life. We drove down East with two grand (two thousand pounds) to pay over to my snout and TCP sat in the back of the Squad car. He introduced himself as 'the Chief of all London detectives' handed over the two grand and said to the snout, "Here my man, take this, go and tell all your mates in that pub over there, there's plenty more where that came from." The informant turned to my colleague and said, "Keep that wanker away from me he's effing mad, if anybody knew I'd grassed, my throat would be cut from ear to ear."

Powis was known to one and all in the Department as 'Crazy Horse' or by an even ruder nickname, 'T.C.P.' which modesty precludes me from elaborating upon. He wrote a book *'The Signs of Crime'*, which was greeted by utter disbelief and derision by the rank and file of working CID officers.

It contained such literary gems such as '*How to identify a drug taker; usually an unkempt or haggard young person possibly with patchy face or acne taking inordinately large helpings of sugar in his coffee which may indicate he is an addict. Scratching their upper arms or sides of chest and frequent yawning are also signs. If combined with red eyes and a runny nose you are almost certainly looking at a drug addict and by natural inference, a thief*'.

Dear God, please save the thousands of innocent hay fever sufferers that came under TCP's eagle eye. In the same book Powis recommends the following advice upon how to search derelict buildings. *"Give commands to an imaginary dog handler implying the dog is particularly savage, if necessary bark like a dog"* Perhaps the masterpiece was his observation that *"of all the really skilled, inside sneak thief, ponces I have known, everyone was homosexual.*"

You don't believe me and think I'm making all this up? Well, go to the public library and read and judge his book for yourself.

The Board started in the usual, routine fashion with the Chairman running through my career to date. All the time TCP sat there glaring at me as if I was something the cat had dragged in.

John Morrison kicked off and was clearly trying to give me a leg up, "Let's see Mr Woodland, you have recently received a Commissioner's commendation for a job under the Official Secrets Act, that's quite unusual for a uniform Inspector, would you like to tell the board about it?"

Powis interrupted, "Let me remind you this is a uniform selection board, I'm not interested in your CID antics, when did you last do a licensee for drinking after hours?"

I looked around the room. What on earth was I doing here? Did I really want to be a uniform Chief Inspector raiding pubs and the like for the next three years? I hadn't any pre-conceived game plan; in fact I knew there was even a remote outside chance I could pass this Board even if just to keep me onside. All those thoughts vanished, this was it, the moment of truth, I just didn't feel inclined to participate any longer in this ludicrous charade.

At a time the Provisional I.R.A. were running amok in London, when armed gangs were terrorising Banks and Building Societies, robbing armoured cars, this bigot wanted to know how many licensees I had done for drinking after hours. It wasn't really a difficult decision for me to make, I had no wish to remain a 'has been', going through the motions, whiling my time away until retirement like so many other disillusioned guys I knew.

"Gentlemen, I have been in this job for twenty one years, an Inspector for the last eight, I have never done a licensee for drinking after hours nor will I ever do so, in this day and age there are far more important things we should be targeting, I am wasting your time and you are wasting mine, I bid you good day."

That was hardly what they wanted to hear, I knew this was the death knell to my career. The trouble was the job had changed; political correctness was quite incompatible with the concept of policing I was brought up with. No complaints, that's just the way it was. I walked out of that Interview room and a fresh faced young uniform Inspector doubtless straight from an accelerated promotion board at Bramshill, clutching his clipboard waylaid me. "How did you get on?" he asked solicitously.

I smiled, "Well, I don't think I got through the Board but they may have booked me for the next Christmas pantomime."

By the time I returned to sunny Peckham, news of my irreverent and deviant behaviour had already reached the nick. An Inspector guided me into the canteen where over a cup of tea he warned me that plans were afoot to find some pretext, any excuse to discipline me for my insubordinate conduct. That made sense, its how the job worked with non conformists, I hadn't envisaged anything different.

In a humorous moment I envisaged TCP gathering his subordinates around him and commanding, "Who will rid me of this turbulent man?"

I can reflect and joke about it now, but can't deny that stress had taken its toll. For the first time in my career I went sick with dangerously high blood pressure brought on without a shadow of a doubt through the accumulated stress of those past three years of uncertainty. Trouble is you are not even aware it is happening until suddenly it hits you.

It was time to turn the page. I never went back. Despite belated, last minute attempts to persuade me to change my mind, I retired with a reduced ill health pension. Mr Gerrard signed my Retirement Certificate and immediately above his signature were inserted the words, "His service record was exemplary". Thank you for that Mr Gerrard, that last kindness was much appreciated. At a time when newspapers were full of reports that up to five hundred police officers had either retired, been suspended or convicted as a result of Mark's purge of the CID, those remarks from somebody who knew the truth, at least put my retirement into some form of perspective and made the pill easier to swallow.

This couldn't put an end to some of the rather lurid stories that circulated amongst the canteen cowboys when my resignation eventually appeared in Police Orders.

According to the rumour factory that was working overtime, there just had to be a good cause why an up and coming D.I.

was suddenly returned to uniform. After all, why let the truth get in the way of a good story?

An independent Doctor diagnosed my stress was brought on through the job and reported back, "I repeat I recommend his retirement from this specific career, there is no reason why he should not recover completely in any other chosen occupation".

I couldn't have put it better myself as during my period of enforced sick leave I was head hunted by a respected firm of International Loss Adjusters at Lloyds of London who recruited me as a fraud investigator. The very same day my service officially terminated, I flew to Hong Kong, Singapore and Thailand to embark upon my new career; I like to think with some success. Once again, I was a trained investigator but without the backup and support available in my old job. I travelled all over the world, Florida, Panama City, Columbia, the Far East, investigating major shipping frauds before finally settling upon a more sedate career until my final retirement.

As for the Kipper, the final time I bumped into him was at a CID Reunion dinner at the Connaught Rooms, London when we found ourselves at the same long table where he was holding court, surrounded as usual by a group of his acolytes. He button holed John Legge, an old pal of mine and queried, "Here matey, what's that Woodland doing nowadays?"

John, knowing the history of our dealings played his part to perfection. "Oh he's really fallen on his feet since leaving the job; he lives in a large detached house in Banstead, drives a new Mercedes and earns over a hundred grand a year".

Not quite true I must admit, but it certainly did the trick. I walked down the table and slapped Dilley playfully, maybe even a little too playfully, across the shoulders to the consternation of his fellow diners who weren't quite sure how this confrontation would end. The Kipper went the colour of puce and looked up, a sickly apology for a smile on his face. "Oh, hello matey, how are you going?"

I beamed delightedly and dropped into my passable Harry Challenor impersonation.

"Bloody marvellous, me old darling and to think I owe it all to you!"

Chapter Twenty-Four

Corruption is nature's way of restoring our faith in democracy.
Peter Ustinov (1921–2004)

The Police and Press have always enjoyed a somewhat fragile relationship, each to some degree being dependent upon the other. Never underestimate the power of the fourth estate. The public owe a great debt to investigating journalists who often at peril to themselves, place their careers at risk to expose corruption in high places. It was the *Times* enquiry that originally exposed the crooked 'firm within a firm'.

In June, 1977, under two headlines, '*Top Yard Men in Quiz over rich friends*' and '*Champagne caviar and baked potato*', *News of the World* reporter Trevor Kempson revealed an investigation had been launched by A.10 into links between ex members of C11, Crime Intelligence Department and '*several top English and international financiers.*' That expression of course in some circles is politically correct non libellous, litigation proof jargon for 'crooks' and I make no excuse for adopting it.

The first of the two articles establishes the relationship between Sir Eric Miller, deposed boss of the 'crashed' Peachey property empire, Judah Binstock, known as 'Mr Big' of international currency deals and Mike Franklin innocuously described as "one of Binstock's closest associates who was in C11 for a considerable time and resigned in 1969."

Franklin was, and remains something of a mystery character. He served as a Detective Sgt. at C11 with special responsibility for monitoring Casinos. A progeny of Dilley, upon his promotion to Detective Inspector he transferred to C.6. Company Fraud Squad. Doubtless before his promotion he knew of Judah Binstock who with his dubious connections was being investigated by the Gaming Board as to his suitability to remain a Director of Victoria Sporting Club. Eyebrows were raised within the job when close to retirement Franklin left the Police and went to work for Binstock.

Franklin was of good character and left the Force of his own accord, right into the welcoming arms of Judah Binstock and by doing so relinquished a potentially lucrative Police pension.

The article also mentioned "a serving policeman, Detective Superintendent John Groves and a third man who will be helping the enquiry, ex Commander David Dilley, head of C11 for six years."

It was a well informed article and reported that Dilley made the following statement to A10. "In no way do Police enquiries affect me, as far as I am aware I've never met Judah Binstock in my life but I do know of him". Too bloody right he did!

In the second article Kempson listed other note worthies who had been entertained by Sir Eric Miller. Groves and his boss Dilley were clearly moving in high circles. These included P.M. Harold Wilson, Lady Falkender, and Home Secretary Sir Reginald Maudlin, advisor to Peachey Property Corporation, who was referred to by Miller as 'the caviar kid' because of his liking for the delicacy served with baked potato.

Miller, knighted by Harold Wilson in his final controversial Honours List, was terrified of Judah Binstock, who was reputed to carry a gun in a shoulder holster. When he came close to being arrested for fraud, Miller is reported as having blown out his own brains ironically on the Jewish day of Atonement. Playing for such high stakes, perhaps I was fortunate to escape with nothing more than a spoiled career. One thing however is certain, although by very different means, both Miller and I were effectively silenced in quite different ways as of course was Jim Smith who resigned from the Force and is now a successful private investigator. His book *Undaunted* touches upon this sorry chapter in the Met's history in more detail.

Ron Steventon's blanket rejection of the salient facts I tried to lay before him, makes me even more certain there was no desire at the Yard to probe too deeply into these allegations about Dilley. 'Let sleeping dogs lie' as the venal first Prime Minister Sir Robert Walpole said centuries earlier.

Detective Superintendent John Groves was appointed Dilley's second in command at C.11 after I left the Department. When had he been corrupted? Trevor Kempson revealed, "*Groves was a frequent 'recipient of hospitality' by Sir Eric Miller, as had other top Yard men including ex Commander David Dilley, now security chief at Sir Charles Clore Group. Groves was interviewed by Commander Ron Steventon, A10 Branch and resigned from the Yard shortly after we contacted him to discuss his relationship with Sir Eric*".

Ron Steventon was a high flyer, a charming guy being groomed for the higher echelons of the job, having been seconded for training at the FBI HQ in Washington. However, judging from my limited knowledge of the man, based upon a joint investigation we once conducted at Chelsea, he was not the greatest investigator – at least in my book.

John Groves was charged and committed for trial upon offences under the Prevention of Corruption Act and the Official Secrets Act for passing a secret dossier upon Judah Binstock to Miller. He was later sentenced to a long period of imprisonment.

The one hundred and fifty four page secret dossier referred to in the Press article was a copy of the C.11 report upon Binstock and his activities. When Binstock was tipped off and left England he was seen by Customs Officers at Dover to tear up some papers and put them in a rubbish bin.

An astute Customs Officer retrieved these papers which were assembled to reveal the C.ll. docket that in turn was passed to Ron Steventon at A.10. Upon the evidence of the Customs Officer alone there appeared to be a prima facie case to charge Binstock with conspiracy or at least with receiving stolen documents and possible offences under Official Secrets Act. Somebody obviously didn't want that to happen. I am sure at least some of that dossier contained the damning information I supplied all those years earlier to Dilley about Binstock's alleged criminal activities that directly led to my fall from grace and removal from C.11.

It certainly doesn't need spelling out that removal of Binstock's details from C11 files would command a very high price. I'm not quite sure what the going rate would be to remove a pushy, well informed Detective Inspector.

It seemed the Kipper's deputies suffered a high fallout rate, anybody being promoted to that position should have been advised to wear a Government health warning around their neck.

John Grove's predecessor at C.11, Detective Chief Superintendent Peter Shemming, a man who regularly socialised with Dilley, also came under investigation for alleged dodgy dealings. When suspicion fell upon Shemming, Dilley not only ditched him like a hot potato but submitted a damning report condemning his old drinking pal as being unfit to hold office.

Shemming, whose large detached house in the leafy suburbs of Essex was named "The Coppings", left the job before disciplinary proceedings were taken against him. He was later arrested, stood trial with D.I. Alec West upon alleged corruption charges but was acquitted. A clear pattern arises where Dilley always manages to be one step removed from the guy who ultimately takes the rap- but then isn't that what pals are for? My one regret was that in the end, The Kipper remained 'the one that got away'.

It is for this reason I have no compunction whatever in denouncing Dilley even though he is not here to defend himself. As Voltaire said over two hundred and fifty years ago. *"To the living we owe respect but to the dead we owe only the truth."*

What happened to The Kipper? He miraculously survived the purge at the Yard that claimed so many of his close associates and retired having been awarded the Queen's Police medal for meritorious service. Well deserved – some might say.

Oh but how the job changed, the emphasis is now firmly upon community policing and political correctness. To change the old culture every Police Office had to display a 'Statement of Common Practice and Values'. But nowhere did this include nicking villains.

Too many senior officers appear motivated by self serving political zealotry and think crime can be contained by the imposition of meaningless targets. I can only admire present day coppers forced to work under the new regime.

My years as a Police officer stood me in good stead, I learned much about life and looking back wouldn't have missed a moment of it. I had an exciting career, took a few risks, perhaps even pulled a few strokes here and there but retained my personal integrity. One thing is for sure, in these days of political correctness our old style of policing would not be considered acceptable. If it all went wrong at the end well, what is it they say? 'He who lives by the sword…'

The Police Service is now obsessed with meeting totally meaningless Government imposed targets deliberately being used to mislead the public into the belief that crime is being contained within acceptable levels.

In January, 2013, Chris Greenwood, *Daily Mail* Crime reporter exposed this deception by showing the deliberate distortion in figures by improper use of the caution. One serial crook was given a Police caution despite admitting over one hundred burglaries and car break-ins. Greenwood revealed one in four violent criminals is cheating justice by escaping with a caution, tens of thousands of crooks, including sex offenders and burglars are wrongly let off with a 'slap on the wrist' by police. Cautions were originally aimed at first-time offenders caught committing relatively low level offences. In 2012, more than two hundred thousand cautions were handed out to criminals in England and Wales. Recently, Bernard Jenkin, Chairman of a Parliamentary Select Committee described the series of techniques used to massage the crime figures as institutional corruption. He revealed "There was a system of incentives given to Police that has become inherently corrupt."

A young Police Officer recently appeared before the Select Committee and revealed that Police were routinely manipulating crime figures in order to meet targets. This brave young whistleblower was placed under investigation for 'bringing the Force into disrepute'. Perhaps that is a charge that more appropriately should be laid against his senior officers.

Please don't be hoodwinked by the specious propaganda being spoon feed to us that crime is being reduced; it aint!

What has changed and what lessons are to be learned? Defence lawyers must now disclose their case pre trial which means an "ambush" defence can no longer be mounted by producing a witness or alibi at the trial at the last moment that it was impossible to closely scrutinise.

Other measures include a relaxing of the rules whereby evidence of the defendant's bad character may be admitted especially when it shows a propensity to commit a certain type of crime. Perhaps my two nurses would have seen justice in the rape case mentioned earlier had this been in effect. Justice and laws need to be re-aligned so the object should be to seek the truth and we should shed at least some aspects of the current ludicrous adversarial system where all too often the verbal dexterity and skills of the lawyer and the depth of a villain's purse determines the outcome of a case.

More emphasis must be placed upon the rights of decent citizens and less upon the so called rights of the hardened career criminals who prey upon them. Nobody ever asks to be the victim of crime; at least the villain has a choice.

One of the outstanding detectives in the post Mark era was my old pal Dick Kirby, a tough, no nonsense Flying Squad officer who joined the job in 1967. After his retirement, Dick became a successful author and wrote several books telling it just the way it was at the sharp end of crime busting.

His book '*The Real Sweeney*' (Constable and Robinson, London, 2005) pulls no punches and is a must read for anybody interested in the workings of the Flying Squad.

If anybody is still in denial regarding my criticisms of the jury system, Dick graphically explains 'The Dalston Defence'. By various delaying tactics, defendants manage to finish up at Snaresbrook Crown Court as happened to me on the Elephant and Castle Bank robbery trial. In his inimitable and colourful style, Dick describes jurors at Snaresbrook as *'a dozen prime examples of local pond life'*. He concludes that any police officer disassociating himself from these sentiments has never *'taken a copper-bottomed and watertight case to Snaresbrook Crown Court, as I have on many occasions, only to see it chucked out with the bath water.'*

In my earlier days at C.11, I proposed we formed a unit to liaise with Tax Authorities to concentrate upon established mobsters and gangsters to determine the origin of their wealth, such as Bank accounts, lavish houses, yachts and expensive cars but this sensible measure was pooh-poohed.

I pointed out that in USA, Mafia Crime bosses were targeted in this way and Al Capone was only convicted and imprisoned for tax evasion. Dilley ridiculed this suggestion. Years later, my view was vindicated by the crime writer Martin Short who castigated C.11. Dept for 'failing to perceive changed patterns in crime and proved stubbornly oblivious to the fact that international organised crime was infiltrating the United Kingdom.' Sorry to put the knife in Kipper, but this was all on your watch.

In 1970, the U.S. enacted RICO the (Racketeer Influenced and Corrupt Organisation Act) which permitted the forfeiture of all ill gotten gains or interests in businesses gained through criminal activity. Initially aimed at the Mafia, this now covers any form of criminal activity. Hopefully, with new legislation, the newly formed Serious Organised Crime Agency merged with a larger National Crime Agency will deter organised professional criminals motivated by financial considerations. If forfeiture of a criminal's assets is conducted ruthlessly, if robbers, drug dealers, fraudsters are aware that upon conviction the proceeds will be robustly confiscated, most of the incentive to commit crime will be lost.

It certainly wasn't for individual police officers to stick out their necks and seek to balance the scales; in this at least I can agree with Sir Robert Mark, a stout advocate for the need to change the law.

In many ways the law has changed. Majority verdicts make jury nobbling more difficult and dangerous to achieve. Despite grave misgivings about much of the Act, tape recording of prisoner's statements and other safeguards introduced by Police and Criminal Evidence Act, 1984, (PACE) has reduced the opportunity for prisoners to allege they had been 'verballed' and hopefully allows the jury to place more credence in Police evidence.

So what did Sir Robert Mark's reforms produce? He did what everybody accepted needed to be done, he rooted out the corrupt, venal core that permeated through to the upper ranks of the CID and filtered back downwards. He ensured control of policing in the capital was vested firmly in the hands of the uniform branch as a result of which we now have an eviscerated, weakened Police service incapable of stemming the tide of crime that now floods our streets. We need more experienced detectives and specialists, Assistant Commissioner Byrne's cheap jibe about 'labels' (Chapter 23) should be exposed for the fallacy it is.

More and more powers granted to Police threaten the very liberties that generations of Englishmen have cherished and held dear. The new draconian powers given to counter- terrorism measures are in danger of turning this once great nation into a totalitarian regime. People defending themselves or their property against the predations of the criminal find themselves being denounced and arrested.

England now holds the dubious distinction of having more CCTV cameras spying upon our citizens than any other country in the world. We are the most routinely supervised and scrutinised people in the civilised world. Despite a Conservative party policy commitment to '*Reversing the role of the Surveillance State*', no action appears to have been taken in this direction. We can no longer freely express our beliefs or feelings without standing in danger of being arrested by the thought police. Can we no longer voice an honestly held, even if erroneous belief?

Voltaire once said "I do not agree with what you say but I will defend to the death your right to say it."

People defending themselves or their property against the predations of the criminal find themselves being denounced and arrested. In his book '*The Retreat of Reason*' Anthony Browne warns the growth of political correctness is one of the most disturbing features of modern life. Its advocates defend the socially disadvantaged and poorer criminal who in their view needs to be supported against the more privileged and richer victims of crime. This ludicrous belief unhappily is held by many senior officers. Browne warns that political correctness is not some ludicrous absurdity to be dismissed but a totalitarian device to subvert the whole of our moral, political and social order. Police now find it safer to target so called hate crimes than to tackle the real menace on our streets.

The eminently sensible, albeit controversial journalist, Peter Hitchens in his book '*A Brief History of Crime*' similarly warns that *political correctness has created a liberal elite class where the newly 'reformed' police serve the demands of their political masters rather than the law of the land.* To paraphrase Edmund Burke, 'all it requires to go further along this dangerous road is for good men to do nothing.'

Hitchens puts forward strong and logical arguments for a return to preventive policing in the form of the beat bobby, for the proper punishment of crime and a revival of public morality and responsibility.

He supports the views I express in this book more succinctly. "*Let us not deceive ourselves, the Police in former times repressed crime and criminals without much gentleness or finesse. We know if we were honest that we were guarded by men who kept the rough world away from us by rough methods. Now the Police are all but powerless because of regulations imposed by unrealistic utopians that do not have to live with the consequences of their reforms. Millions of others do and long for help. Can anyone say that what has followed is better that what went before, for anybody except the wicked?*"

We should all be concerned with the legacy we are leaving for our children and their children. Perhaps it is now time for me to conclude and I leave you with the words of Ed Murrow, that great American broadcaster and champion of liberty. *"Cassius was right, the fault dear Brutus is not in our stars, but in ourselves. Good night and good luck."*

Bibliography

Brown, Anthony, *The Retreat of Reason* (Civitas, Institute for the study of Civil Society 2006)

Campbell, Duncan, *The Underworld* (BBC Books 1994)

Cox, Barry; Shirley, John; Short, Martin, *The fall of ScotlandYard* (Penguin Books 1977)

Fido, Martin and Skinner, Keith, *The Official Encyclopedia of ScotlandYard* (Virgin Publishing 1999)

Hitchens, Peter, *A brief history of crime* (Atlantic Books 2003)

Hobbs, Dick, *Doing the business* (Clarendon Press 1988)

Kennedy, Ludovic, *10 Rillington Place* (Grafton Books 1971)

Kirby, Dick, *Villains* (Constable & Robinson 2008)

Kirby, Dick, *Rough Justice – Memoirs of a Flying Squad Detective* (Merlin Unwin Books 2001)

Kirby, Dick, *The Real Sweeney* (Constable & Robinson 2005)

Kirby, Dick, *Your Nicked* (Constable & Robinson 2007)

Kirby, Dick *Death on the Beat* (Pen and Sword Books 2013)

Kirby, Dick, *Scotland Yard's Ghost Squad* (Pen & Sword Books 2011)

Mark, Sir Robert, *In The Office of Constable* (William Collins & Co 1978)

McBride, Alex, *Defending the guilty* (Penguin Books 2011)

McLagan, Graeme, *Bent Coppers* (Orion 2004)

Morton, James, *Gangland* (Little Brown & Co 1992)

Morton, James, *Bent Coppers* (Little Brown & Co 1993)

Powis, David, *The Signs of Crime* (McGraw Hill 1977)

Rhodes, Linda, Shelden Lee, *'The Dagenham Murder' – The London Borough of Barking and Dagenham*

Rose, David, *In the name of the Law* (Jonathan Cape 1996)

Seabrook, David, *Jack of Jumps* (Granta Books 2006)

Shand, Adam, *King of Thieves* (Allen & Unwin 2010)

Woodland, David, *Wild's Law* (Etica Press 2006)

Index